W9-AHO-536

Evaluation Techniques for Classroom Teachers

McGraw-Hill Series in Education

HAROLD BENJAMIN, *Consulting Editor*

AYARS · Administering the People's Schools
BARON AND BERNARD · Evaluation Techniques for Classroom Teachers
BEAUMONT AND MACOMBER · Psychological Factors in Education
BOGUE · The Community College
BROOM, DUNCAN, EMIG, AND STEUBER · Effective Reading Instruction
BROWNELL, GANS, AND MAROON · Public Relations in Education
BRUBACHER · A History of the Problems of Education
BRUBACHER · Modern Philosophies of Education
BUTTERWORTH AND DAWSON · The Modern Rural School
BUTTS · A Cultural History of Western Education
CARTER AND MCGINNIS · Learning to Read
COOK AND COOK · Intergroup Education
COOK AND COOK · School Problems in Human Relations
CROW AND CROW · Mental Hygiene
CROXTON · Science in the Elementary School
DE BOER, KAULFERS, AND MILLER · Teaching Secondary English
FERNALD · Remedial Techniques in Basic Subjects
FOREST · Early Years at School
FRANSDEN · How Children Learn
GRUBER AND BEATTY · Secondary School Activities
HAGMAN · The Administration of American Public Schools
HAGMAN · Administration of Elementary Schools
HAMMOCK AND OWINGS · Supervising Instruction in Secondary Schools
HAMMONDS · Teaching Agriculture
HECK · The Education of Exceptional Children
JORDAN · Measurement in Education
KEMPFER · Adult Education
MCNERNEY · The Curriculum
MCNERNEY · Educational Supervision
MACOMBER · Teaching in the Modern Secondary School

Mays · Essentials of Industrial Education
Mays · Principles and Practices of Vocational Education
Melvin · General Methods of Teaching
Meyer · An Educational History of the American People
Micheels and Karnes · Measuring Educational Achievement
Mickelson and Hansen · Elementary School Administration
Millard and Huggett · An Introduction to Elementary Education
Mort and Ross · Principles of School Administration
Mort and Vincent · Introduction to American Education
Mort and Vincent · Modern Educational Practice
Moustakas · The Teacher and the Child
Mursell · Developmental Teaching
Mursell · Successful Teaching
Myers · Principles and Techniques of Vocational Guidance
Pittenger · Local Public School Administration
Prescott · The Child in the Educative Process
Remmlein · The Law of Local Public School Administration
Remmlein · School Law
Samford and Cottle · Social Studies in the Secondary School
Schorling and Batchelder · Student Teaching in Secondary Schools
Sears · The Nature of the Administrative Process
Sorenson · Psychology in Education
Thut and Gerberich · Foundations of Method for Secondary Schools
Weber · Personnel Problems of School Administrators
Wells · Elementary Science Education
Wilson, Stone, and Dalrymple · Teaching the New Arithmetic
Winslow · The Integrated School Art Program
Yoakam · Basal Reading Instruction

Evaluation Techniques for Classroom Teachers

DENIS BARON, Ph.D.
Oregon State College

HAROLD W. BERNARD, Ph.D.
General Extension Division
and
University of Oregon

McGRAW-HILL BOOK COMPANY

1958 New York London Toronto

EVALUATION TECHNIQUES FOR CLASSROOM TEACHERS

 Library of Congress Catalog Card Number 57-10903

9-MP-9 71

03798

Preface

Tests and measurements—their techniques and devices—are valuable aids to the kind of pupil evaluation that encourages optimum growth. However, there are teachers who either have blind faith in the efficacy of tests or are unreasonably skeptical concerning their use. Our aim is to help teachers use tests appropriately and constructively.

This book is an outgrowth of the authors' experiences in conducting various courses in "tests and measurements." In these courses we have found it advisable to cover less material with more illustrative examples in order to achieve good communication. Even experienced teachers, whom both authors have met in extension classes, are frequently apprehensive of the statistics and technicalities involved. Students preparing to be teachers also frequently doubt their ability to comprehend test usage. We have dared to presume that teachers and teacher candidates in other states are much like those encountered in Oregon: (1) They need to have the subject of testing presented with a minimum of statistics. (2) They need to know the limitations of tests. (3) They need to perceive the substantial aid that appropriately used tests can give. (4) They should have these "needs" met in an effective manner. Our aim, then, is to present the basic features of tests and testing in terms understandable to classroom teachers.

Brevity has been one of our guideposts, for the sheer bulk of some books on measurement intimidates the teachers who enroll in our classes. The desire to make our treatment brief has sometimes caused us trouble in the writing of this book—we should have liked to go into more detail in explaining contributing and conditioning factors in various situations. In the first draft the chapters were longer and more cautiously detailed, but one or the other author pared and whittled until both agreed that the minimum for effective communication had been reached. We hope that users of the book who might have written it differently will bear in mind the desirability of brevity and simplicity in the presentation of basic material.

Another of our guideposts has been the intent to direct the material to classroom applications. The question, "Is this section (or paragraph) pertinent to the kinds of work teachers do?" was asked repeatedly while the chapters were being written and in each author's evaluation of the other's chapters. We feel that we have come close to fulfilling our criterion of classroom pertinence.

Some readers will not be able to share wholeheartedly our criticism of grades and personality tests. The senior author has prevented the expression of skepticism regarding these techniques from being even more emphatic. Our hope is that the presentation will stimulate thinking—as did the preparation of the material. Instructors who encourage their students to discuss the points of view presented will find that students' evaluations will elicit many of the concepts of evaluation and bring forth a recognition of the merits and shortcomings of testing devices.

Our third guidepost was to keep the book in such form as to provide for flexible use. Brevity makes it possible for instructors to develop their own points of emphasis. For those who plan further study, we have selected and annotated readings and provided study and discussion items.

We wish to express our gratitude to the publishers of books and tests who have given us permission to use copyrighted materials. We also thank Mrs. Alta Diment, who typed and edited the manuscript from what was in many instances very rough copy.

Denis Baron
Harold W. Bernard

Contents

CHAPTER ONE

Sampling Pupil Behavior

In earlier times costly tunnels were driven into mountains to find out whether quartz outcroppings indicated the presence of ore beneath the surface. Often the effort was fruitless—discouraging, time-consuming, and financially ruinous. Today it is possible to save time and money by using diamond drills, which, driven from various locations and at different angles, bring up *cores,* or *samples,* of the mountain's interior. The extent of the ore body can be determined fairly accurately from these cores. Promising cores are sent to assayers, who determine by tests the amounts of lead, silver, and copper contained in the samples. The results of these tests—the cores and the assayer's chemical analysis of them—make it possible to estimate the value of the ore that will be obtained if the expensive tunnel or shaft is driven.

There are tools available to teachers today which, like the diamond drill, save time, energy, and frustration in working with pupils. These tools are tests—samples of the behavior and traits of individual pupils that indicate quickly and with reasonable accuracy their status at a particular time and their potential. Tests provide samples of intelligence, knowledge, social orientation, and special aptitudes. They enable the teacher to get a clearer view of the "inner workings" of his pupils.

The miner takes a chance when he drives a tunnel; the presence of ore does not ensure his success. Faulty earth may cause cave-ins, underground water may be expensive to combat, a slump in the stock market may create a poor sales field, and technological advances may reduce the demand for his ore. So, too, although the samples that the teacher obtains through tests may promise well, serious illness, a broken home, a shift in values (as during a war), or a quarrel with a cherished friend may threaten the realization of what is indicated by the tests.

Tests, in short, are not panaceas; they do not solve all the problems of education and classroom management. They are useful devices in "sizing up" pupils in a better than trial-and-error fashion. We would prefer a physician who felt our pulse, took our temperature, and made a urinalysis and a blood count to one who merely glanced at us and prescribed his stock "pink pills." Similarly, the pupil, if he had the background for fuller understanding, would prefer an educational program fitted to his particular needs to an automatically prescribed program. The analysis the teacher makes on the basis of observation of the pupil certainly has its place; when it is supplemented by analytically interpreted test data, the child's school life is more rewarding. We should, in short, obtain samples of the pupil's intelligence, interests, social adjustment, knowledges, skills, potentialities, sensory acuity, and physical health if we are to work with him as efficiently as possible.

WHAT TESTS DO

The tests made by the miner and the physician do not yield answers or make analyses. The person who knows the tests and what they do must make the diagnoses. *Tests provide only data upon which to base a diagnosis.* Educational and psychological tests do not make analyses or suggest what should be done; they give indications which may serve to sharpen and clarify the judgments teachers make on the basis of their experience, training, and understanding.

Attitudes toward Tests

As samples of behavior which yield indications, tests depend for their usefulness upon the attitude and knowledge of teachers. This entire book is directed toward the development of this essential background. Before we proceed, however, let us examine some characteristic attitudes toward tests.

1. Some persons have blind confidence in tests. They appear to feel that all one has to do to solve an educational problem is to give a test, record results, and file the data. This attitude toward test results is, of course, absurd, because there are no simple answers in relation to complicated personalities. Too many teachers give tests in order to discover that Johnny has an IQ of 90, is up to age-grade standards in most of his schoolwork, and is "average" in terms of personal and social adjustment. The results are recorded in his cumulative folder, and classwork goes on in the same perfunctory manner as before.

2. Tests are often regarded with an element of fear. Undue emphasis may have been placed on test results in the teacher's school experiences, and he may fear that tests will produce similar anxiety in pupils. This attitude is unfortunate. It is not the tests which should be feared but the misuse of test data. If one is to be failed because of his test score, he has reason to be apprehensive. However, if tests are used to promote understanding and diagnosis, they will be welcomed. Actually, most of us like to take tests—if the results are not to be used against us. Many people enjoy the tests in *Time,*

Look, and the *Reader's Digest* because nothing but self-evaluation is based on the results. It is entirely possible that children could learn to enjoy educational tests if the element of threat were removed and if the results were useful to pupils and teachers in their efforts to achieve better understanding.

3. Tests are regarded by some with tentative confidence. This attitude approaches the sound and realistic view expressed by the person who says, "I'll take the tests for what they are worth and permit myself to be guided by the results." If, however, the hesitating confidence is expressed as "I'll use the results as long as they agree with views I already hold," the test results can serve little constructive purpose.

4. An attitude that seems sound is to accept test data as rather accurate *supplementary evidence*. The teacher who accepts this view uses tests to get a more complete picture of the individual. He realizes that tests are not entirely accurate, but he uses them with due regard for present limitations as he and others work to develop better ones.

This fourth view would be more readily adopted if teachers generally had a better understanding of what tests are and do. It will, for instance, be helpful to realize that tests *are not direct and absolute measures*. They are means to evaluation. One can learn how tall a youngster is by using a yardstick. His weight can be determined by using a scale. His pulse can be counted. His blood pressure can be measured by a sphygmomanometer. Intelligence, personality, knowledge, and interest, however, cannot be measured directly but must be *inferred* from indirect measures. Specifically, intelligence may be inferred from the subject's answers to a limited (and selected) number of questions, albeit the questions are designed to sample various areas of his total knowledge. Personality adjustment is evaluated by means of responses to questions designed to sample areas of social, academic, and personal adjustment. Similarly, knowledge and interest are inferred from representative questions which survey only part of the total area of knowledge and interest.

Measurement and Evaluation

Words often make understanding possible, but they sometimes cloud the issue. Unless the specific connotation of a word has been learned, prior interpretations may get in the way of understanding. Thus, *measurement* in education has a slightly but significantly different meaning from the same word applied to carpentry, a purchase of sugar, or a bank account. These types of measurement can be accurate—repeated measurements would yield identical results—but measurement in education cannot be repeated with identical outcomes. It might clarify our thinking if the word *evaluation* were substituted for *measurement*. But since the word *measurement* appears in educational literature and in discussions, it is advisable to indicate its specific connotation. Measurement by testing may be considered as a means by which evaluation is achieved. Evaluations are often made without the basic data supplied by measurement, but sound evaluation is based upon the results of measurement.

Considerable measurement is involved in purchasing a home. The amount of floor space; the cost of brickwork, lumber, and wiring; and the size of the lot are among the measurements to be considered. The judgments based on these measurements are an evaluation. Further, some intangible items would enter the picture: the style of the house, convenience of room arrangement in terms of family needs, and community environs would be taken into account although they are beyond the limits of precise measurement.

Similarly, some significant educational factors are beyond the limits of measurement by tests. For example, tests do not measure drive or motivation to use the knowledge or intelligence indicated by tests, nor do they measure the view that the pupil takes of learning or the appeal or effectiveness of teaching. Such data as anecdotal records, the teacher's evaluation of his pupils, health data, and recorded observations of play and social behavior should be used to supplement and validate test data. Both teachers and pupils must realize that, as in buying a home, measurement is at best a basis for evaluation. By means of it one can arrive at a more accurate evaluation than could be achieved by trial and error or by personal opinion.

By providing the measurements upon which we can base evaluations, educational tests can do much to help improve the effectiveness of instruction and guidance. (1) Tests can help to estimate the *present* potential of the pupil to learn. (2) They can give fairly accurate information regarding the pupil's academic knowledge. (3) They can show about how much a pupil has grown in a given period of time and thus help to evaluate the efficiency of methods of teaching. (4) Tests can help to locate specific areas of difficulty (though they do not tell what should be done about the difficulty). (5) Properly used, tests can be a factor in the motivation of pupils. (6) Test results can give guidance in the more equitable grouping of pupils for the purpose of economy in instruction. (7) Tests can provide clues to intelligent guidance of pupils in their academic choices and their personal adjustment. (8) Tests can provide supplementary data leading to a more objective evaluation of pupil status and progress.

It should be noted, however, that tests do not *completely* accomplish any of these things. They only help by providing clues and corroborative data.

TYPES OF TESTS AND MEASUREMENTS

Tests differ widely with regard to their nature and the purposes they are designed to serve. According to the way they are designed and used, tests may be classed as verbal or nonverbal, performance or pencil-and-paper, and group or individual. A verbal test is one in which language plays a major part. The ability of the pupil to speak, read, and write determines in a major degree his effectiveness on this kind of test. His ability to repeat statements and his ability to follow written or spoken directions are sampled by verbal tests. Nonverbal tests indicate the pupil's ability to see the similarity or dissimilarity between pictorial materials or geometric figures, follow mazes, or put parts of a puzzle together. Speed of manipulation, accuracy of movement, and sharpness of perception are sampled by this type of test, and the use of language is minimized but not eliminated. In a performance test, the subject may be asked to maneuver blocks into a pictured design, place the parts of a picture-board puzzle together, or repeat a series of digits given to him orally. In a pencil-and-paper test, the subject records his own answers. He checks the answers he selects, draws his way through a maze, or computes the answer to an arithmetic problem. Quite often, although not always, performance tests are nonverbal and pencil-and-paper tests are largely verbal. A group test is simply a test which a number of pupils take simultaneously. An individual test is one which requires one examiner for each examinee.

Tests may also be classified as to their purposes. Some are designed to sample aptitudes, others achievement, and still others specific difficulties. The most common aptitude test is the intelligence test, which is designed to indicate the pupil's capacity to learn. Musical-ability tests and reading-readiness tests are other commonly used aptitude tests. Achievement tests indicate the pupil's level of performance in specific academic areas such as reading, spelling, arithmetic, language usage, and comprehension of vocabulary. Tests designed to indicate specific areas of difficulty are called diagnostic tests. A diagnostic test in arithmetic may serve to indicate whether the pupil's specific difficulty is in multiplying, adding, or dividing or whether there is some particular number combination that he has learned incorrectly and uses consistently, e.g., 6×9 is 52.

Scales and Inventories

Many of the instruments that are helpful for more objective pupil evaluation are called by other names than "tests." The quality of a sixth grader's handwriting is difficult to evaluate, but a handwriting scale on which there are graded examples of writing may serve to objectify the judgment. Spelling scales group together words that have a similar degree of difficulty and familiarity and arrange them in order of increasing difficulty. There are rating scales which are used to record interpersonal evaluations. (See Chapter 11.) For example, a three-point or five-point scale may list under a heading such as dependability the following degrees of possession of the quality: "(1) Always dependable (2) Usually dependable (3) Unpredictable (4) Often undependable (5) Quite undependable." Clearly such a scale depends largely upon the rater's interpretation of the terminology used. Interests are sometimes studied through a preference scale. For example, interest in the study of biology may be scored, "Highly interested, somewhat interested, indifferent, uninterested, or strongly dislike." Used with due regard for their subjective limitations, scales provide supplementary data of value in pupil evaluation and guidance.

As a result of the difficulty involved in "measuring" personality the term *inventory* has come to be widely used in evaluating social and personal adjustment. The inventory is made up of questions, to which there are no "right" or "wrong" answers, concerning how the individual feels he would act in the situation described. No one question is regarded as crucial, but the *trend* of all the answers is taken as a clue to the person's total adjustment in home life, school life, interests, and views regarding what is correct and incorrect in daily behavior.

The questionnaire technique is often used to study attitudes and interests. The subject is asked to indicate whether or not he agrees with a number of statements regarding certain situations—for example, the activities and requirements of school. Again, no one question is regarded as giving an incontestable clue to the respondent's orientation, but the total score is regarded as indicative of trends in values and attitudes.

Projective Techniques

Projective techniques are coming to be regarded as valuable clues to personality. The projective technique permits the subject to "add structure to an unstructured situation"; that is, the individual injects his own meaning—theoretically, his own personality—into the situation. Specifically, a child may be given a set of dolls and doll furniture and told to do anything he wants to with them. What he does and how he treats the playthings is considered to be a reflection of his own personality. A picture with ambiguous content may be shown to the subject. What he describes as the content of the picture is, in part at least, a product of his own imagination. He may be told part of a story and asked to finish it; the ending he provides is considered a reflection of his inner feelings, past experiences, and wishes.

Obviously, it is hazardous to interpret these "projections" of the pupil's personality too precisely. But if used cautiously and interpreted in the light of more objective supplementary data, including interviews and observations, projective techniques may provide valuable clues in understanding children. Projective techniques illustrate the fact that a distinction must be made between measurement and evaluation. Results from these devices *must be* interpreted or evaluated; hence it is necessary that the teacher know something of the nature and dynamics of personality. Projective techniques include such activities as interpreting pictures, completing partially told stories or incomplete sentences, playing with toys, describing what one sees in ink blots or pictured cloud formations, painting, drawing, modeling clay, and writing stories and poems.

STANDARDIZATION

It is important that teachers understand the significance of the standardization of tests. Most of the published tests with which teachers work are carefully standardized; that is, norms or averages for each test have been established. For example, an achievement test in arithmetic is given on an experimental basis to a number of pupils in various localities. Questions that prove to be ambiguous are eliminated, and questions that seem to have little or no power to differentiate between high-scoring and low-scoring pupils are removed. The reconstructed test is then given to several hundred pupils, and the norms are established. Medians are perhaps most commonly used for this purpose, since scores typical of pupils at various grade levels are determined. This typical score for each grade is taken to be the norm or standard for that grade, and the test is said to be standardized. (Standardization will be dealt with in greater detail in Chapter 4.) A standardized test has the advantage of adding objectivity to the interpretation of the score. But it would be a mistake to think that the norm represents a standard in the sense that it is a goal to be achieved by individual students or a level of accomplishment with which to be satisfied in the case of others. Nor should the attractiveness of a standardized test lead the teacher to repudiate teacher-made tests, which have a place in a balanced program of evaluation. Teacher-made tests can be made to fit the local situation better; they can more pointedly refer to what has been taking place in a particular classroom; and they are economical devices for practice and drill.

SUMMARY

Tests are instruments for "sizing up" pupils. They yield clues, or "measures," based on sampling techniques, which can be used (when properly interpreted) to evaluate the motivation, ability, and growth of individual pupils. As yet there is no single test which provides enough clues to evaluate the "whole child." Hence, a balanced program for sizing up pupils will include a variety of tests which differ in mode of construction and in purpose. Used as a means to better evaluation, tests can save the time and energy of teachers and pupils, just as samples taken by diamond drills save the time and energy of the miner.

STUDY AND DISCUSSION EXERCISES

1. How does the growth principle which states that "growth is a product of the interaction of the organism with its environment" bear upon the measurement concept in education?
2. What could the classroom teacher do to make test taking a less emotionally upsetting experience?
3. In your own words, distinguish between evaluation, or appraisal, and measurement.
4. List a number of things that tests do not do.
5. How do you think a classroom teacher might most advantageously use a personality inventory?
6. In what ways might a projective technique be superior to a personality inventory?

SUGGESTED ADDITIONAL READINGS

Cook, Walter W.: "Achievement Tests," in Walter S. Monroe (ed.), *Encyclopedia of Educational Research,* rev. ed., New York: The Macmillan Company, 1950, pp. 1461–1478.

An excellent presentation of the uses and limitations of achievement tests, concepts used in evaluation, and problems involved in test construction. The extensive bibliography is especially commendable.

Durost, Walter N.: "Tests and the Junior High School Guidance Counselor," Test Service Notebook, no. 2, Yonkers, N.Y.: World Book Company, Division of Test Research and Service.

This and other pamphlets may be obtained on request. This one deals with intelligence tests, aptitude tests, and interest inventories and their uses in guidance. The author observes that with changed environmental circumstances there is a chance that the IQ will change.

Educational Test Bulletin, no. 1, "How Tests Can Improve Your School," Hollywood, Calif.: California Test Bureau.

This bulletin may be obtained free by teachers who submit their titles and grade assignment. Starting with a brief statement of the purposes of education, the authors show how tests can facilitate the achievement of those purposes. The use and cost of tests is briefly indicated.

Ross, C. C.: *Measurement in Today's Schools,* 3d ed. (revised by J. C. Stanley), Englewood Cliffs, N.J.: Prentice-Hall, Inc., 1954, pp. 3–59.

In these two chapters the authors discuss the place of measurement in the modern school and in the modern world, give a brief background of the testing movement, and describe some of the difficulties that have been encountered in making testing scientific.

Rummel, J. Francis: *Know Your Pupils,* Salem, Ore.: Oregon State Department of Education (no date), 37 pp.

This booklet deals with the meaning of evaluation and the instruments and methods for facilitating evaluation. Some valuable suggestions for interpretation of data, together with precautions, are given.

Wrightstone, J. Wayne, Josiah Justman, and Irving Robbins:

Evaluation in Modern Education, New York: American Book Company, 1956, pp. 3–59.

The meaning of evaluation and measurement, the historical background of evaluation, recent trends, steps in evaluation, types of evaluative devices, and characteristics of good test instruments are discussed.

CHAPTER TWO

How to Identify a "Good" Test

As we have seen, tests are used to evaluate certain personality characteristics or increments of growth. Some provide better bases for evaluations than others; hence tests themselves have to be evaluated. Since our purpose in testing is to see the pupil more clearly, we must use those instruments that facilitate clear vision. A camera or microscope with a scratched, clouded, or imperfect lens gives a distorted picture. So, too, a faulty, poorly constructed test provides a distorted picture of the individual whom we wish to understand better. This chapter is designed to help the teacher understand what characteristics of tests he should consider in selecting the instruments which are to promote improved pupil behavior.

The Criterion of Objectivity

One of the reasons for giving tests is to reduce the subjective element in judgment to a minimum. Teachers want to be sure that they are seeing Johnny's mental or musical ability or status in arithmetic for what it really is rather than being misled by his ready smile, willingness to take orders, or personal cleanliness. As a result of the "halo effect," or the tendency to believe that a child who is cheerful, clean, and cooperative is also bright, teachers are often surprised when a quiet or sullen lad achieves a high score on a test or when a blond, curly-headed little girl in a starched pinafore makes a low score. The element of subjectivity often leads to mistaken evaluations.

If a test is to increase objectivity, however, it must itself be objective; in it, the exercise of the teacher's judgment must be reduced to a minimum. The answers to questions must be easy to interpret as either right or wrong and must leave little or no occasion for the teacher to say, "I'm sure he had the right idea in mind; I'll give him credit." Objectivity is increased by the use of short-answer test questions such as simple-recall (in which one word will correctly answer the question), true–false, multiple-choice, and matching questions. If the material of these short-answer questions were dealt with in a hundred-word composition, the possibility of objectivity in scoring would be decreased; that is, different scorers would assign different values to the answer. However, even in the essay answer it has been found that objectivity is increased through the use of pre-formed model answers. Some intelligence tests provide such model answers, assigning varying weights, or values, to correct but differing answers. For example, some items on individual intelligence tests may be answered in several ways, but the sample answers provided in the manual give the test scorer some basis for scoring responses. By and large, the classroom teacher achieves objectivity by using the scoring key provided with the tests and by carefully adhering to printed directions for administration, scoring, and interpretation.

The Criterion of Validity

Since tests are designed to give an accurate picture of some aspect of the personality of the pupil, it is important that they actually measure what they are designed to measure. This characteristic of tests is called *validity.* A test is valid when the results it obtains correspond closely with those obtained by means of other criteria evaluating the same trait.

The meaning of validity may be made clear by describing an invalid "arithmetic" test which consisted of twenty items, each accompanied by a lengthy discussion intended to clarify the problem. Many of the pupils did ten of the twenty problems accurately but failed to finish the entire test in the time allotted. Study of the results indicated that the pupils' arithmetic scores corresponded very closely to their scores on reading tests. It was suspected that the test actually tested reading as much as arithmetic. When the test was redesigned and the reading material substantially reduced, the subsequent scores on arithmetic were much less similar to the pupil's reading scores, and the results of the second test corresponded more closely with the pupils' work in arithmetic classes. Thus the second test was considered to have greater validity. (Standing in arithmetic class was the criterion by which the validity of the test was judged.)

The concept of validity is further illustrated by the fact that intelligence tests are considered to be valid when their results correspond to scores on other recognized intelligence tests, to the pooled judgment of a panel of experts who know the examinees, to an estimate of the subject's intelligence as inferred from measures of his adjustment in various situations, or to the subject's achievement in school. The approach to validity from the standpoint of adjustment to life and success in school achievement is illustrated by L. M. Terman's follow-up studies of gifted children.[1] Subjects tested and studied in about 1921 were restudied after approximately twenty-five years. They were found, rather uniformly, to have been suc-

[1] Lewis M. Terman and Melita H. Oden, *The Gifted Child Grows Up, Genetic Studies of Genius,* 4, Stanford, Calif.: Stanford University Press, 1947.

cessful in schoolwork, to have achieved enviable occupational status, earned superior incomes, established stable marriages, developed a variety of constructive avocational interests, and in many ways to be well on the road to eminence as participating citizens and personally effective individuals. Hence the tests are considered to be valid from the standpoint of the "test of living."

It is advisable at this point to explain the concept of the *coefficient of correlation,* which makes it easier to comprehend some of the characteristics of a good test. A coefficient of correlation (or of validity, or reliability) is a number which indicates the dependability of the predictions that are made in terms of that number. Wind direction can always be inferred from the direction of the smoke drift; the correlation between the two is 1.00, or perfect. The volume of a gas is inversely proportional to the pressure exerted upon it, temperature remaining constant; the coefficient of correlation is —1.00. Relationships among human traits lie somewhere between these two extremes. The correlation between two valid and reliable measures of intelligence would probably be about .90. The correlation between intelligence and reading would be somewhere in the vicinity of .50 or .60 (read this "point five zero" or "point six zero"). The correlation between size and intelligence would be positive but so low as to make predictions for individuals extremely dubious—about .10 to .20. *These figures are not percentages.* They are figures which indicate how much credence can be placed in predictions based on that particular coefficient.

Table 1 should be read somewhat as follows: A coefficient of correlation of .90 increases forecasting efficiency by 56 per cent over pure guess and provides 78 chances out of 100 of predicting correctly from one measure the approximate level of performance on another measure. There are 22 chances out of 100 that the prediction will be incorrect. Even a coefficient

TABLE 1*

Correlation coefficient	Percentage increase in predictive efficiency	Chances in 100 of predicting at-or-above, and below average in future behavior
0.00	0.0	50–50
0.10	0.5	50.25–49.75
0.20	2.0	51–49
0.30	5.0	52.5–47.5
0.40	8.0	54–46
0.50	13.0	56.5–43.5
0.60	20.0	60–40
0.70	29.0	64.5–35.5
0.80	40.0	70–30
0.90	56.0	78–22
0.95	69.0	84.5–15.5
0.98	80.0	90–10

* Clifford P. Froehlich and John G. Darley, *Studying Students—Guidance Methods of Individual Analysis,* Chicago: Science Research Associates, Inc., 1952, p. 54.

of correlation of .99 is only 95 per cent better than chance. (The chances in 100 of predicting future behavior are computed by adding the per-cent increase of predicting efficiency to 100 and dividing by two.) Thus the user of a test must be aware of a noticeable margin of error in the predictive value of measures involving the concept of correlation. Generally speaking, coefficients of correlation may be viewed as follows:[2]

> .00 to .20 denotes indifferent or negligible relationship;
> .20 to .40 denotes low, slight correlation;

[2] Henry E. Garrett, *Statistics in Psychology and Education,* New York: Longmans, Green & Co., Inc., 1947, p. 333.

.40 to .70 denotes substantial or marked relationship;
.70 to 1.00 denotes high to very high relationship.

The coefficient of correlation may be used to give a numerical indication of the validity of a test. If the test were perfectly valid, the coefficient of validity would be expressed by the number 1.00. Each pupil would have the same rank in schoolwork as on the test, if rank in schoolwork were the criterion by which the validity of the test was judged. In other words, with perfect validity (1.00), an individual's rank would be the same on the test as in a ranking by experts or by school marks. Actually, this does not happen in practice, but the amount of shift in relative position is relatively small in a highly valid test. This is illustrated in the following tabulations:

Subject	Rank on test	Rank in schoolwork
A	1	1
B	2	3
C	3	2
D	4	5
E	5	4

According to some methods of computing correlations, the coefficient in the above illustration (between the test and the criterion of rank in schoolwork) is .80, a fairly typical coefficient for mental tests. If the rank in schoolwork of pupils B and C and of pupils D and E were reversed, there would be perfect correlation between test results and rank in schoolwork. The closer the coefficient of validity is to plus 1.00, i.e., the closer the test is to the criterion, the better it measures what it purports to measure. In selecting tests the teacher should consult published reviews and catalogues of the test to learn the basis on which the validity of the test was established (the criterion of success) as well as the validity coefficient claimed for the test. Typically, validity coefficients are lower than reliability coefficients, so differences between the two need not make the selector of tests apprehensive. Although the coefficient of validity should be as high as possible, it need not be as high as .70 or .80. Lee J. Cronbach has cited tests used in making military classifications which had coefficients as low as .45 but which were useful in predicting performance in specified military activities.[3]

The Criterion of Reliability

In addition to being valid, a good test must also be dependable for consistent measurements. The rubber rule that fishermen are reputed to use is an unreliable measure. The platinum measuring stick at the U.S. Bureau of Standards, protected from the air and maintained at a uniform temperature, can be depended upon to yield the same measurement year after year. The consistency with which a test measures whatever it does measure is called *reliability*. Even a very good test is less reliable than the platinum standard; but if similar scores result from administering a given test twice to the same individual with an interval of two or three days between, the test is considered to be reliable. In practice, the same test is not usually repeated, since practice affects scores. Hence reliability may be determined by the consistency with which equivalent forms of a test give comparable results. For example, an intelligence test is reliable if the subjects make a score within five points of their other scores on equivalent forms. If, however, the scores of half the students vary more than fifteen points from their first score, the measure would be considered unreliable.

Reliability, like validity, is numerically indicated by a coefficient. Equivalent forms of the test are administered, and coefficients of correlation are worked out for the two forms.

[3] Lee J. Cronbach, *Essentials of Psychological Testing*, New York: Harper & Brothers, 1949, pp. 252–253.

The coefficient in this case is called the *coefficient of reliability*. For a given test, this index number will be found in the manual and in published reviews. If the publisher of the test does not indicate the coefficient of reliability, it is probably so low that advertising it would do little good. Hence, teachers would do well to use tests for which the indicated reliability is somewhere between .80 and 1.00, remembering, of course, that it will never actually be 1.00.[4]

Each of two or three different tests of intelligence may be reliable although their results do not concur. Thus, three tests with reliabilities of .82 or better were given to one subject with the following results: test A—IQ 92, test B—IQ 115, test C—IQ 123. However, on equivalent forms of each of the three tests, the scores of the same individual varied no more than seven IQ points. This observation is made to impress upon teachers that it is important to indicate *what test is being referred to* when an IQ is reported. It is also important to know that scores on a test in which there is a large nonverbal factor (test C above) will often vary markedly from scores on a test in which language facility is an important factor. In short, a test that is reliable in itself may seem unreliable when it is compared with another type of test.

The Criterion of Comparability

Another desirable characteristic of tests is comparability. If the teacher is to gain anything more from the test than a knowledge of the status of a pupil at the time he took the test, which is helpful but limited information, he must use tests which are comparable. This will make it possible to see how much the pupil has grown in a given period of time.

[4] Leona E. Tyler cites a table which shows how specified percentile scores may be interpreted in terms of given coefficients or reliability. See Leona E. Tyler, *The Work of the Counselor,* New York: Appleton-Century-Crofts, Inc., 1953, p. 117.

That is, a test is given at the beginning of a unit of work or a semester and a comparable (equivalent) test is administered at the end of the period. The difference between the scores indicates how much the pupil has grown during the period. If the tests are not comparable, they present a distorted view of the pupil. For example, a reading test with supposedly comparable forms was administered by two teachers. One gave form A first and the other gave form B first, and each gave the alternate form at the end of an intensive reading-instruction program. The average gain in pupil scores by the teacher giving form A first was 30 percentile points, whereas the average change in pupil scores by the teacher giving form B first was a loss of five percentile points. The order in which the tests were given by each teacher was reversed in another trial on different groups of pupils, and this time the pupils of the second teacher made remarkable gains and those of the teacher who had been so successful on the first trial showed a slight loss in average percentile standing. Obviously forms A and B were of different degrees of difficulty—the tests were not comparable.

Comparability is usually achieved by the use of what are known as equivalent forms of a test. Most tests have two equivalent forms, and some tests have three or four forms. The teacher who wishes to know what progress his pupils are making will want a test with at least two equivalent forms. Two forms of the same test may be prepared by what is known as the *split-half* method. A long test is given, and an item analysis is made; the test is then split into two parts, each part containing the number of questions that were missed by, say, 25, 30, or 35 pupils. For each question missed by a certain number of pupils on the trial run of the test, a parallel item is included, worded differently. A carefully designed test with equivalent forms would yield like results on successive days, when administered to the same pupils, if it were not for "practice effect." Some test manuals instruct the teacher to subtract a given number of points from the second test to correct for practice effect and hence obtain comparable results. Regardless of whether form D, C, B, or A is given first, practice effect should probably be considered in interpreting the score on the second test.

The Criterion of "Sampling" Adequacy

If a test is to reveal how much a pupil knows, it must sample adequately; that is, it must contain enough questions to be truly representative. Let us assume that two pupils are being tested in geography. One of them knows one of the ten items of information on the test and the other knows nine of the ten. A test of two items is given. If it includes the one item the first pupil knows, he will get a score of 50 per cent; and if it happens to include the one item the second pupil does not know, he, too, will get 50 per cent. Yet one knows nine times as much as the other. Warped views of test subjects can be avoided by adequate sampling, i.e., by including enough items so that the gambling chance is minimized. Adequacy of sampling is achieved by including enough items so that additional items no longer seem to influence the score of the individual. At the same time, tests usually include only enough items to minimize the chance factor, for additional items do not seem to add to the accuracy of the test. Some tests, however, have a limited usefulness in spite of inadequate sampling. One intelligence test, for example, consists of fifteen items. In the hands of a clinical psychologist it possesses the advantages of a rough but rapid screening device. But persons who do not fully appreciate the handicap of limited sampling might easily form an erroneous opinion of the test subject on the basis of this test.

Some standardized tests have what are known as long and short forms. The longer form is used when there is plenty of time for administration. However, experimental administrations have indicated that the short form samples widely enough so that there is little difference in its reliability as compared with the longer form. Using fewer questions than are provided in the short form leads to such variability in results that further reduction in the number of items is considered to be inadvisable. Using more items than the long form includes does not give more consistent results; rather, the additional items are subject to the law of diminishing returns.

The Cost Factor

The use of tests in obtaining a clearer view of the abilities of pupils is sometimes limited by cost factors. School-board members and administrators often feel that the cost of tests is prohibitive. It is therefore desirable to get the least expensive tests available *for the advantages derived.* Fortunately, the most costly tests are not always the most dependable from the point of view of adequacy, reliability, or validity. Many tests that are relatively inexpensive on a per-pupil basis give quite valuable clues to understanding pupils. Expense is further reduced by the provision of scoring sheets. Thus, the same test booklet can be used over and over by inserting new answer sheets. This makes it possible to reduce the financial outlay to a penny or two per pupil once the booklets have been purchased.

It is hard to generalize about monetary costs. As the teacher examines tests, he should study the various test catalogues to see how much a package of twenty-five tests will cost, whether the manual of directions is included in the price, and whether or not there are separate answer sheets available. The price tag is not a highly dependable criterion, because one must consider that the objective is to get the best test for the price paid.

Nor is the question of economy limited to a consideration of financial outlay alone. Good tests should be economical of the teacher's time—that is, the results should be easily scorable. Preferably, the teacher should be able to score a test simply by counting the correct or incorrect responses. Little computation should be required, for computation not only takes time but provides a chance for error to creep in and thus reduces the reliability of the test. Economy of time should also be considered in giving the test. Specifically, the directions should be easy to understand and easy to explain clearly to the pupils. Examination of the manuals of directions of two different tests of the same knowledge or ability will indicate that they differ widely with regard to the ease with which they can be understood and administered.

The Test Manual

In order to be of maximum usefulness to the teacher, the test should include a manual of directions. This manual should do the following specific things: (1) It should explain the specific advantages, features, and purposes of the test. (2) It should explain the process of its standardization so that the teacher will know how much confidence can be placed in the results obtained. (3) It should give clear and concise directions for administering the test. The total time to be allowed and the time allotment for individual parts should be clearly indicated. (4) Even if the scoring procedures seem perfectly obvious, they should be described in detail. (5) Considerable space should be devoted to an interpretation of the scores. The meaning of specific scores in terms of average grade placement, quality of work, or comparative standing in a group should be indicated. (6) Suggestions should be made for the intelligent use of the results in pupil guidance.

SUMMARY

Tests differ widely in the care with which they are constructed, and they are not of equal value in achieving an objective view of the pupils. The relative worth of tests can be judged in terms of their objectivity, validity, and reliability. The better tests are economical of time, effort, and money; they sample widely; and the manuals that accompany them are sufficiently detailed to indicate exactly how the test should be viewed, administered, scored, and interpreted. Tests that meet these criteria will be of real help to the teacher in establishing realistic but growth-inducing goals for pupils.

STUDY AND DISCUSSION EXERCISES

1. Does the desirability of objectivity imply that the teacher's judgments have no place in evaluation and appraisal? Explain your answer.
2. Evaluate this statement: A test may be reliable without being valid.
3. Can a test be valid without being reliable?
4. What kind of predictions can be made on the basis of a coefficient of .20 (e.g., the coefficient of correlation between size and intelligence)?
5. Are there test situations in which the factor of comparability is not important?
6. What are some reasons why a 100-item test might be more valuable than a 10-item test?
7. Class exercise: Study copies of a test manual and attempt to determine its worth.

SUGGESTED ADDITIONAL READINGS

Greene, Harry A., Albert N. Jorgensen, and J. Raymond Gerberich: *Measurement and Evaluation in the Elementary School,* New York: Longmans, Green & Co., Inc., 1946, pp. 52–71.

This chapter, "The Criteria of a Good Examination," deals with validity, reliability, adequacy, objectivity, administrability, scorability, comparability, economy, and utility of tests.

Ross, C. C.: *Measurement in Today's Schools,* 3d ed. (revised by J. C. Stanley), Englewood Cliffs, N.J.: Prentice-Hall, Inc., 1954, pp. 106–135.

This chapter deals with the characteristics of a satisfactory measuring instrument. In addition to defining the terminology used in this discussion, the author makes suggestions on the uses and limitations of tests.

Roulon, Phillip J.: "Validity of Educational Tests," *Test Service Notebook,* no. 3, Yonkers, N.Y.: World Book Company, Division of Test Research and Service, 1947, 4 pp.

This free leaflet discusses validity in terms of the objectives of education and the criterion of behavior and describes how tests are designed to obtain greater validity. Relative merits of short-answer and essay tests are discussed.

Trow, W. C.: *Educational Psychology,* 2d ed., Boston: Houghton Mifflin Company, 1950, pp. 326–365.

A discussion of the terminology used in testing procedures. Reliability, sampling, correlation, validity, objectivity, and types of questions are treated. Suggestions for summarizing test results are given.

Wrightstone, J. Wayne, Josiah Justman, and Irving Robbins: *Evaluation in Modern Education,* New York: American Book Company, 1956, pp. 16–28.

In addition to the objectives for a testing program, this chapter deals with the relation of evaluation techniques to the curriculum.

CHAPTER THREE

Choosing the Right Test

If there were one best test for evaluating any one pupil trait or ability, there would be no problem involved in test selection. The one best test would have proven itself, and custom and common practice would make it widely known. However, this "happy" situation would necessarily impose some limitations. For example, the test would have to be widely applicable; it would not be adaptable to the problems of a particular school system. Users would be obligated to pay whatever price was charged for it. The publisher of the test could probably afford to be slow in rendering service to users and might even be loath to make any changes in a test so widely accepted. The necessity for test selection carries with it some advantages, then, not the least of which is the obligation of teachers to investigate tests and thus learn more about their nature, limitations, and advantages.

In order to select tests wisely, it is necessary to (1) define the purposes of the testing program, (2) select the areas to be tested in the light of the purposes, (3) apply the criteria of good tests to the tests available in the selected areas, and (4) evaluate the tests used in the light of experience as a basis for future selection. These steps will be examined in detail in this chapter.

Capitalizing on Group Wisdom

Since there is an opportunity involved in the task of test selection, several teachers should be given the privilege of participating. It is advantageous to bolster the wisdom of one or two individuals with the suggestions and advice of others, and pooling this knowledge will also help teachers to realize the values and shortcomings of tests as well as the problems involved in using them.

It has proved advantageous for the teachers in a school to select jointly the tests that will be most profitable for them locally. This is sometimes done in the larger systems by having a committee formulate the objectives of the testing program and choose the tests in the light of the purposes they are to serve. In smaller systems all teachers might well be involved in the preliminary discussion of purposes and problems. The group approach is especially advantageous when different forms of the same tests can be used in several consecutive grades, thus gaining the advantage of the criterion of comparability discussed in Chapter 2. The sixth-grade teacher, for example, can then compare the score of a pupil in his grade (on an alternate form of the test selected) with the score obtained by that pupil on another form of the same test when he was in the fifth or the fourth grade. If different tests are used, although both are valid and reliable, the results may not be comparable, and if the scores are unwittingly compared, the comparison will be misleading. Thus teachers administering both the Metropolitan and Iowa achievement tests have found that the class average is as much as half to a full grade higher on one test than on the other. The scores of individual pupils vary as much as a full grade on the two tests. Both tests are accurate, reliable, and valid; they were simply not standardized simultaneously for purposes of comparison.

The group approach also has the advantage of capitalizing

upon the experience of various teachers with different tests. Pupil reactions and typical problems in administration can be anticipated, many of which may not be described in the test manual.

DETERMINING THE PURPOSES OF THE TESTING PROGRAM

Whether tests are selected by each teacher individually for his own class or by a group of teachers for a number of grades, the first step is to determine objectives—to decide what the testing program is designed to do. Let us assume that the list would include some or all of the following objectives:

To gain insights into the social facility of the pupils as individuals
To obtain information about their aptitudes for learning in general
To obtain information about their specific talents or relative strengths
To discover their present status in subject-matter achievement
To find clues to ways of overcoming specific weaknesses
To motivate pupils to put forth consistent and serious effort

This list of objectives suggests that the tests are to be used not as ends in themselves but as *clues to the improvement of learning and instruction*. They are devices designed to facilitate each child's growth, and the results are to be used as corroborative data and as supplements to the teacher's observations.[1] An experienced teacher will know without being told

[1] This point can hardly be overemphasized. The teacher sees the total functioning of the child, not just his functioning in a test situation. The following statement by a specialist in vision illustrates this:

that the tests that are most appropriate in the fifth grade are not necessarily those that provide valuable clues in the first grade. In formulating objectives, the group must take into consideration the fact that the testing program is a whole-school program. We shall therefore approach the problem of selecting tests in terms of a minimum program for the primary grades, the intermediate grades, and the upper grades.

SIGNIFICANT AREAS TO BE TESTED

It might appear that the most important test in every grade is the intelligence test. However, as we shall see in a later chapter, rate of intellectual growth has not become steady enough in the first grade to make the intelligence test a wholly reliable indication of growth. Giving intelligence tests at this level involves the risk that a child may be branded as unintelligent because he does not understand the directions in a group test or because for some reason it is difficult for him to maintain interest. The results of one type of test, however, are much less likely to be stigmatizing after a year or two: the reading-readiness test, which many teachers prefer to the intelligence test. This device has the advantage of dealing rather specifically with an aptitude that is of immediate practical importance to the teacher and the pupil. The results are directly applicable to the question of whether reading experiences should be initiated at once or whether it would be better to spend time on a developmental readiness program. An IQ

"Don't mistrust your own observation about a child. Even a competent oculist or ophthalmologist does not have the advantage of seeing symptoms of visual difficulty after the child has been using his eyes for a prolonged period. His tests may be very good—as far as they go. The teacher sees the child in a functional situation." Evaluation of the child's vision is parallel in this sense to the evaluation of his intelligence or social adaptation.

will not yield this information; an MA would come closer to telling the teacher what he needs to know.

Intelligence tests may be used, with due reservations, in the primary grades, but some teachers prefer to wait until the third grade or even the intermediate grades. Selection of a test at this level, however, should be influenced by the experience of the teachers involved. If none of the teachers in the group has had any experience with the tests, it is wise to apply to a teacher in another system for suggestions. A letter addressed to the superintendent of schools of a city system would be turned over to competent persons (perhaps specialists in testing) who would be willing to make helpful suggestions.

After some tests have been suggested, the group should obtain the description and evaluation of these tests from the basic reference book. Oscar Krisen Buros' *Mental Measurements Yearbook*. The value of this work can be partially determined by reading a representative entry such as the following:[2]

[255]

Pintner General-ability Tests: Verbal Series. Grades kgn–2, 2–4, 4–9, 9+; 1923–46; 20¢ per manual; World Book Company.

a) *Pintner–Cunningham Primary Test.* Grades kgn–2; 1923–46; Forms A, B, C; $1.45 per 25; 35¢ per specimen test; Rudolf Pintner, Bess V. Cunningham, and Walter N. Durost.

b) *Pintner–Durost Elementary Test.* Grades 2.5–4.5; Scales 1 (requires no reading) and 2 (requires reading) may be used separately or together; Forms A, B; $2.00 per 25 Scale 1; $1.60 per 25 Scale 2; 35¢ per specimen set; (45) minutes per scale; Rudolf Pintner and Walter N. Durost.

c) *Pintner Intermediate Test.* Grades 4.5–9.5; 1931–42; revision of *Pintner Intelligence Test;* Forms A, B; $1.70 per 25; 35¢ per specimen set; $1.20 per 25 machine-scorable answer sheets; 45 (55) minutes; Rudolf Pintner.

[2] Oscar Krisen Buros (ed.), *The Third Mental Measurements Yearbook,* New Brunswick, N.J.: Rutgers University Press, 1949, p. 334.

d) *Pintner Advanced Test.* Grade 9 and above; 1938–42; Forms A, B; $1.70 per 25; 35¢ per specimen set; $1.20 per 25 machine-scorable answer sheets; Rudolf Pintner.

Following these basic data are reviews and evaluations of this test by competent reviewers. Excerpts from two of these reviews follow:[3]

Stanley S. Marzolf, Professor of Psychology, Illinois State Normal University, Normal, Ill.

The reliabilities obtained by the split-half and interform methods for the various batteries are, in the majority of cases, in excess of .90. Sources of reliability data are given in all instances.

Standardization has been based on "approximately 100,000 tests from widely separated parts of the country." Further collection of scores for normative purposes is now in progress.

The computation of deviation IQs is amply explained and illustrated. For the Intermediate and Advanced Tests a monograph which facilitates computation of IQs and centile equivalents is provided.

This series is one of the best available for school use. The tests are easy to give and score. Raw scores are easily converted to a normative form. The same score system—standard score, mental age, and deviation IQ—is used throughout the series. The attempt to make the tests comparable at all grade levels is commendable, even though empirical evidence that this has been accomplished is lacking.

D. A. Worcester, Chairman, Department of Educational Psychology and Measurements, The University of Nebraska, Lincoln, Neb.

The intermediate and advanced tests each have eight subtests. All are timed but with limits so liberal, intentionally, that they are not to be considered as speed tests. The materials of the tests are on the whole of the kind that one finds in most of the conventional intelligence tests.

Each test of the series has received careful statistical treatment

[3] *Ibid.*, p. 336.

and the statistical findings are given in the manuals. Norms for the tests are articulated with each other, making possible comparable measures at the various age levels. Scores may be interpreted in almost any way which the user may wish: standard scores, ratio or deviation IQs, percentile ranks, mental ages, or grade equivalents. Machine scoring is available for the intermediate and the advanced tests. While the task of administering these tests is somewhat greater than that for some of the tests constructed more recently, there is evidence that they have been constructed with care and may be employed with good results.

In the *Yearbook* several hundred tests are listed, classified, and evaluated; hence the suggestions of experienced users of the tests can save time and prevent the possibility of the teacher's becoming dismayed by a plethora of titles, addresses, and statistics. If the *Yearbook* is not available locally, it can probably be borrowed from the state library or the state department of education.

If it is not possible to get hold of the *Yearbook,* it is wise to obtain catalogues from the test publishers. Although this list should not be interpreted as endorsing any individual test, such addresses as the following will provide a starting point: Educational Test Bureau, 720 Washington Avenue, S.E., Minneapolis 14, Minnesota; California Test Bureau, 5916 Hollywood Boulevard, Los Angeles 28, California; American Council on Education, 744 Jackson Place, Washington 6, D.C.; World Book Company, Yonkers 5, New York; Science Research Associates, Inc., 57 W. Grand Avenue, Chicago 10, Illinois; Psychological Corporation, 522 Fifth Avenue, New York 36, New York.

The *Yearbook* and the addresses of publishers will, of course, be helpful in selecting all kinds of tests, not merely those relating to mental ability.

Achievement tests are designed to indicate the pupil's present status regarding skill and knowledge in such subject-matter areas as reading, vocabulary, arithmetic fundamentals, arithmetic operations, spelling, English usage, etc. Advanced batteries for use in the upper grades and high school sample, in addition, such areas as literature, history, civics, and geography. Norms for achievement tests are typically described in terms of age standards, grade placement, and percentile ranks. Again, these norms (or averages) represent the scores of typical third, fifth, sixth, etc. graders and are not to be considered as standards for individual children to reach or excel. Nor should the teacher regard the norm as a standard that should be achieved by his class this year. Achievement scores must be interpreted in terms of indicated pupil potential; that is, the average on achievement tests of the class *this year* may be *in part* evaluated in terms of the average obtained on a test of mental ability. What is important is that the norms provide clues for evaluating the status and progress of individual pupils. The achievement test selected should provide equivalent or comparable forms, since maximum utility will be obtained when the score a pupil makes this year can be compared with his score of a year or two ago. If a different test is used, even a test covering the same area, the feasibility of comparing them is materially reduced.

If a particular pupil does not seem to be doing so well on achievement tests as his mental-ability test "promised," an explanation may be derived from a diagnostic test. In such subject areas as reading, arithmetic, and spelling, a diagnostic test serves the purpose of locating rather specifically the difficulty the child is encountering. In reading, the difficulty may be a weak vocabulary, lack of method in word attack, or lack of experience leading to interpretative ability. The test does not tell what should be done; it simply narrows the area of search for a constructive remedial program. Similarly, in arithmetic the diagnostic test will help one find a specific area of difficulty, which might be a particular erroneous number combination, such as $7 \times 6 = 52$, or failure to understand borrowing in subtraction. Or perhaps the pupil understands the processes but does not make the correct choice of operations; that is, perhaps he does not understand the written problem. In order to detect particular areas of difficulty, the diagnostic test is divided into distinct parts which employ specific operations (addition, subtraction, etc.) and particular number combinations.

Teachers often find that special-aptitude tests are of value in understanding the "whole" child. Tests of musical aptitude, mechanical aptitude, and art may be helpful in suggesting academic approaches which will permit the pupils to experience a degree of success and thus become more strongly motivated. Language-aptitude tests, mathematics-aptitude tests, and vocational-aptitude tests are useful in academic and vocational counseling at the secondary school level.

Teachers have traditionally been, and many of them are at present, concerned mainly with the academic adjustment and achievement of pupils. However, increasingly teachers are realizing that other phases of adjustment are of equal importance. In fact, personal and social adjustment may be of even more importance immediately than academic adjustment, because in order to function well in the academic situation it is necessary that the pupil be as free as possible of personal and social problems. There are several methods of personality evaluation.[4] One of the most readily available of these methods is direct observation of behavior. Naturally, some knowledge of child and adolescent psychology, mental hygiene, and abnormal psychology contributes to make the

[4] Personality includes all that a person is and does—his capacities and abilities, achievements, and hopes. Thus intelligence and knowledge are a part of personality. However, for purposes of discussion of areas to be tested, we shall have reference here mainly to personal security, confidence, and general social functioning.

teacher's observations more penetrating and his evaluations more accurate. Rating schedules also are of real value in narrowing the range of search for possible sources of difficulty in personality adjustment. These schedules are of two kinds: one in which other pupils or the teacher rate a pupil in terms of given characteristics, and one in which the pupil rates himself in terms of given qualities or reactions. Personality questionnaires are similar to rating scales except that instead of rating one's self on a three- or five-point scale, the subject answers the questions with "Yes," "No," or "Questionable." However, the results of formal questionnaires and rating schedules must be interpreted in terms of how the pupil behaves in the classroom and on the playground.

Personality rating scales and questionnaires cover a variety of areas of functioning. Some deal with health attitudes, ethical considerations, family relationships, and interpersonal adjustments. These evaluative techniques are steadily increasing in number. Hence it is advisable that the teacher study the catalogues, tentatively select a few tests, obtain specimen sets, and then carefully read the manual to determine whether each specific test fills the needs of his situation.

APPLYING THE CRITERIA OF GOOD TESTS

After deciding what areas are to be tested and after selecting sample tests, the teacher group should study the tentatively selected tests in each area from the viewpoint of the criteria of good tests. In order to discover the relative merits of the tests in the various areas, the significant data regarding each test should be summarized or tabulated on a check list; these data, it will be remembered, may be taken from test catalogues, the manuals of directions, or the *Mental Measurements Yearbook*. A sample check list is shown in Figure 1.

The check list obviously does not automatically select the

	Name of Test	Level	Reliability	Curricular validity	Statistical validity	Norms	Usability	Time	Adequacy of manual	Ease of scoring	Cost per 25	Special features	Equivalent forms
1	Metropolitan Readiness Test	K 1st	0	1	0	%	2	70	OK	3	1.55	4	No
2	Lee-Clark Reading Readiness Test	K 1st	.92	5	0	GE	6	30	7	Easy	1.20	8	No.
3													
4													
5	New California Short-Form of Mental M.	K-1 1-3 4-8 7-10	.92	9	0	% GE	10	p o w e r	OK	11	1.20	12	No
6	Kuhman-Anderson Intelligence Test	1-12	?	?	?	MA IQ	13	45	14	Clear Easy	1.50	Brief	No
7	Otis-Quick Scoring Mental Ability Test	1-4	.68	15	.60	IQ	16	20	OK	17	1.50		2 Alpha
8	" " " " " "	4-9	.71 .86	15	0	GP	16	30	OK	17	1.10	Verbal and Non-verbal	4 Beta
10	" " " " " "	HS Coll	.90	15	.86	MA	16	30	OK	17	1.10		4 Gamma
11													
12													
13	Metropolitan Achievement Tests	1-8	.80 .97	18	0	GE AE	19	1 hr 2-40	VG	Average	1.60 2.70	20	2
14	Progressive Achievement Tests	1-14	.84 .98	21	Ade- quate	% AG	22	1-30 2-30	VG	Easy	1.75 1.90	23	3
15	Stanford Achievement Tests	2-9	.71 .84	24	25	GE AE	26	65 m 2-30	Adequate	Easy	1.35 2.70	27	2 3
16													
17													
18	The Adjustment Inventory (Bell)	HS Coll	.93		.72 .90	%	Easy	Untimed	OK	Easy	1.75	28	No
19	Washburne Social Adjustment Inventory	JHS HS	.92		.90	0	29	30- 50	OK	Average	1.60	30	No
20	California Test of Personality	12 yrs. & over	.60 .87		Vague	%	31	Untimed	32	Average	1.25	33	2
21	Mental Health Analysis	4-16	.95		Vague	%	34	Untimed	VG	Average	1.75	35	No

FIG. 1. A check list for evaluating and selecting tests. The explanation for the numbered references cited in the list is as follows:

1. High correlation with achievement in first grade.
2. Measures readiness in reading, arithmetic, and writing rather than in reading alone.
3. Easier than most tests of its kind.
4. High correlation with intelligence makes it probable that an intelligence test would be unnecessary.

5. Good screening device. Should be supplemented by observation and intelligence-test data.
6. Brief, easily understandable. Norms may be interpreted without skill in statistics. Predictive value varies with methods used in teaching reading.
7. Excellent manual. Contains bibliography valuable for teaching suggestions.
8. Heavy stress on letter symbols involved in reading.
9. Other aspects of intelligence besides "academic" aptitude are considered.
10. Tests of spatial relationships, logical reasoning, numerical reasoning, and verbal concepts.
11. Takes somewhat longer than many other tests because of breakdown into part scores.
12. Verbal and nonverbal scores.
13. Valuable because it involves less reading than many other tests.
14. Much of the explanation is in terms of the authors' experience, which is, however, considered more than adequate by reviewers.
15. Correlates well with school achievement particularly for group prediction.
16. Considered by reviewers to be somewhat weak in terms of individual predictions.
17. Ease of scoring is main feature.
18. Because of variation in courses of study, curricular validity must be determined locally.
19. Subtests cover all fundamental school subjects. Primary battery contains word and phrase recognition, word meaning, and numbers.
20. There are partial batteries for those who wish to give the test in the shorter periods indicated in the "Time" column.
21. Covers items found in the typical curriculum. Must be interpreted in the light of local emphases.
22. Superior and practical.
23. All the tests incorporate diagnostic items which should, however, be used in conjunction with supplementary data.
24. An attempt has been made to interpret scores in the light of block-promotion practices.
25. Not cited, but reviewers assert that the tests have been carefully and competently constructed.
26. Brief, simple, clear instructions to pupils. Directions for interpretation are clear and practical.
27. National norms should probably be considered seriously only in the skill areas.

28. Gives percentile rank for adjustment in terms of home, school, health, and social areas for various school levels.
29. User would need training in testing and mental hygiene.
30. Can be used for rough psychiatric screening.
31. The purposes of the test are inadequately disguised, and falsification of answers may be possible.
32. Offers some remedial approaches which, though acceptable, are somewhat superficial.
33. Subtests are: self-reliance, sense of personal worth, sense of personal freedom, feeling of belonging, withdrawing tendencies, and nervous symptoms.
34. A coding system prevents subject from discovering the exact nature of the test.
35. Calls attention of teachers to difficulties of adjustment of which they might otherwise be unaware.

test. Each test seems to have some merits and some disadvantages which are not found in others. Group discussion of relative values is advisable for the selection of the tests which are most appropriate for local purposes.

Precautions

New tests are published periodically. Some probe areas which have not previously been investigated, and others apply new or revised techniques in familiar areas. Because of the ample supply of new instruments, two suggestions are pertinent.

First, very often old tests are preferable simply because they have been previously used in the school. Teachers are familiar with them and are aware of their merits and shortcomings. Previous scores provide an opportunity to develop local norms, and the scores made in the current year are more meaningful in relation to the national norms. Unless a new test has distinctly superior features, it is often advisable to continue to use the older ones.

Second, if a new test or test battery is selected, it is wise to continue the parallel use of the old test in the same area. The results can then be compared, and the gains or losses produced by the change can be evaluated. By the same token, the new test should be given an adequate trial. It should be used for a minimum of three years, and if it is then found to be satisfactory, its continued use is justified.

Follow-up Evaluation

One aspect of the problem of test selection remains to be dealt with, even after the committee has chosen a given battery and the tests have been administered: the tests should be discussed and evaluated in terms of the experience of administering them and making use of the results. Teachers find it helpful to discuss the problems they have encountered and get the suggestions of other teachers for overcoming these difficulties. For example, such remarks as the following are likely to be made: "This test is too long for first graders." "This achievement test does not parallel the suggested course of study for the state (or locality)." "This test is so short that I doubt that it samples adequately." These remarks, however, should be viewed as precautions and limitations to be applied in interpreting test results, since all tests are likely to have their limitations. Some of the value of tests will be lost if a test is discarded because it does not fully suit all users. It is probably better to put up with some shortcomings in a test rather than dispense with the values of comparability that result from using the same test over a period of years.

SUMMARY

Choosing tests which will make a maximum contribution to the understanding of children and the improvement of instruction is a process which should involve many teachers. Even if the services of an "expert" are available, teachers should participate because (1) the work involved in choosing has educative value, (2) the school and the individual teachers should gain the advantages of pooled experience and study, (3) teachers know more about local educational objectives than experts, and (4) teachers know the needs of pupils in terms of their community background.

The first task of the group is to determine as exactly as possible the purposes which the tests are to serve or to facilitate. The kinds of tests should be named—intelligence, special aptitudes, achievement, personality inventories, etc.—and tentative lists should be suggested by capitalizing on the experience of teachers on the staff or by contacting teachers or administrators outside the system. The group should obtain sample copies of the suggested tests, together with manuals, and then compare the tests, using the manual, catalogues, and the *Mental Measurements Yearbook,* in terms of the criteria of "good" tests.

The process of test selection and evaluation does not end with ordering tests. It should be continued in the light of knowledge and experience gained during actual use of the tests. It should be remembered that, although selection is important, the really crucial issue is the interpretation and use of data. This important consideration will be discussed in Chapter 13.

STUDY AND DISCUSSION EXERCISES

1. Explain how it is that two tests covering the same subject or ability may both be reliable and valid but not be comparable.
2. Draw up a list of purposes of the testing program for the school where you teach or for some school with which you are acquainted.
3. Look up some test with which you are acquainted in the *Mental Measurements Yearbook* and see what others think of its value. Is the report such that you would like to use or continue to use it?
4. Explain the meaning of the statement, "Tests do not tell

what should be done." If they do not do this, then of what value are they?

5. Do you agree with the contention that the teacher's judgment and estimate should be used in evaluating the capacities of pupils? How does this fit with the notion that evaluations should be objective?

6. Prepare a check list similar to the one presented in this chapter. Add to it some tests in several areas and make a tentative selection of the best test in each area to fit your particular needs.

7. Why is the follow-up evaluation of the test important? How long should one keep an unsatisfactory test before sacrificing the value of year-by-year comparisons?

SUGGESTED ADDITIONAL READINGS

Buros, Oscar K. (ed.): *The Fourth Mental Measurements Yearbook,* Highland Park, N.J.: The Gryphon Press, 1953.

This book should be available to every committee charged with responsibility for test selection. Older tests are reviewed and evaluated in previous issues of the yearbook. All tests to date are indexed.

"How to Select Tests," *Educational Bulletin No. 2,* Los Angeles: California Test Bureau, 1945 (free).

This brief bulletin gives concrete advice on problems faced in test selection; it is illustrative of the good free material that is sometimes available from test publishers.

Jordon, A. M.: *Measurement in Education,* New York: McGraw-Hill Book Company, Inc., 1953, pp. 14–39.

This chapter, "Characteristics of Measuring Instruments," defines and illustrates the qualities of good tests. A knowledge of the meaning of these qualities is basic to sound test selection.

Traxler, Arthur E., Robert Jacobs, Margaret Selover, and Agatha Townsend: *Introduction to Testing and the Use of Test Results in Public Schools,* New York: Harper & Brothers, 1953, pp. 20–29.

In addition to describing the features of good tests, this chapter describes the assistance one can get on particular problems through catalogues, manuals, test-service agencies, and professional literature.

CHAPTER FOUR

How Norms Help Us Size Up Pupils

Evaluation of pupil characteristics is a pioneering and challenging task because many of the human qualities related to educational goals are not readily measurable. It is relatively simple to measure height because it is quantitative and progresses in regular units which we term inches. Weight and chronological age are equally easy to measure. For more complex qualities, however, such as personality traits, mental characteristics, and scholarship, we have no universally accepted yardstick or scale.

There was a time in history, of course, when length, weight, days, months, and years posed definite problems of measurement. There were no standards for comparison, no widely accepted units of measurement in these areas. The task of persons interested in educational measurement has in recent years been similar to that of the individuals who, long ago, established such widely accepted units of measurement as the inch, the meter, the gram, the ounce, the hour, and the month. The task in educational measurement today is to establish meaningful units for the measurement of human behavior in areas for which no adequate "yardstick" is yet available. The attempt to develop such measures has resulted in the widespread use of norms.

NORMS: MEANING AND DERIVATION

When someone tells us that a certain girl is five feet tall, we may think of five feet of linear height as an absolute measure, or we may think of persons of our acquaintance who are five feet tall. In order to make use of such a measurement, we would have to know the age of the girl. She may, for instance, be short for an adult or tall for an eleven-year-old. Hence, the significance of simple quantitative measurements depends upon comparisons and relationships.

In the area of educational measurements, there exist no absolute units such as the inch or the foot. A test score, for example, is comprised of responses to a number of test items. The items are not all exactly alike, as are standard measures such as inches; rather, they vary in nature and in difficulty.

Let us say, for instance, that Jerry has a score of 43 on an arithmetic test. What does this score mean? Were there 43 or 143 test items? Were the items related to addition, subtraction, multiplication, division, or all of these? How difficult was the test? The score of 43 becomes meaningful only when it is placed in a framework which enables us to make comparisons. If we find that 43 is one of the highest scores achieved by members of Jerry's classroom group, the score takes on a value, for the important thing is not what score Jerry made on the arithmetic test, but how his score compares with other scores *derived* from the same measuring instrument. The concept of norms is based upon such comparisons. Test scores are placed in a framework which helps us to relate scores to one another. Norms, then, are relative measures or derived scores designed to help the teacher interpret test results within a meaningful framework.

When a test is administered and scored, the first result is a *raw score,* which is ordinarily the sum of the correct responses or the total of the values assigned to the several items included in the test. The raw score, like the score of 43 which Jerry attained on the arithmetic test in the foregoing example, has no definite meaning in itself. The teacher, like the test maker, faces the problem of giving meaning to the test score.

The teacher who wishes to make Jerry's score more meaningful might ask this question: "How good is a score of 43 on this test in my classroom? Is it average, better than average, or below average?" Arranging the papers in order of size of scores from highest to lowest, he may use the middle paper as a point of reference. In this way he can evaluate a score of 43 as falling in the upper half or the lower half of the scores. Or he may establish a basis for comparison by finding the average score. In either case, he has established a *point of reference* which will give meaning to scores within this classroom group.

These procedures are in many respects similar to those employed by the professional test maker, who first establishes a sample or group as a basis for his reference scores and then administers his test to this group in order to study the results. To make the scores meaningful, he may select a score at the midpoint of the distribution of scores. This score is called the *median,* or fiftieth percentile, and it divides his distribution into two equal halves. Half the subjects scored above this point and half below.

Again, the test maker may find the average, or *mean,* of all the scores to establish a reference score. The mean is the sum of the scores divided by the number of cases, and it represents typical performance for a group. The typical score made by pupils at a grade level is called the grade norm. The basis for the norm, then, is the midpoint (median) or the average (mean). In either case, the norm is a reference point presumed to represent the level of attainment typical of the defined group.

Procedures very similar to this may be used to develop norms for any defined grade or age group or for any other special classification, such as school beginners, college freshmen, or graduate students. The norm, then, is a *reference point derived from a study of the scores of a selected group.* This group is called the standardization sample and should be explicitly defined in the manual which accompanies the standardized test.

The sampling procedures are, of course, very important to the interpretation of the results of the test for any group. The teacher will need to know whether the standardization group is in general similar to his group or in some significant way different from it. Norms on two tests are not necessarily equivalent, since the groups from which representative scores, or norms, were derived may differ. For example, in a recent report, average IQs for the same pupils in one town varied from 99.9 on test A to 107.2 on test D on four well-known intelligence tests.[1] For this group of pupils, test D appears to be relatively easy as compared with test A. The norms for these two tests are, therefore, not directly comparable so far as these pupils are concerned.

In general, in establishing intelligence test norms, IQ 100 is the average or median attainment for each age group. Thus the pupils in the example above differed markedly from the group which formed the original standardization sample, at least in ability to respond to test D.

Although the discussion above is in many respects an oversimplification of the procedures involved in the establishment

[1] Kenneth Eells, A. Davis, R. J. Havighurst, V. E. Herrick, and R. Tyler, *Intelligence and Cultural Differences,* Chicago: University of Chicago Press, 1951, p. 116.

of norms, it does appear to represent the basic principles and problems involved. The procedures in test standardization might be reiterated and expanded at this point as follows:

1. Test questions are gathered and a trial form of the test is developed.

2. The trial test is administered to a large group of pupils at the age or grade level for which the test is designed.

3. A careful study of results is conducted in an effort to select the best items, and the test is drawn up in final form or forms.

4. A large group of individuals is chosen as the basis for the derivation of test norms. Problems of grade or age levels, typicalness or representativeness, and other basic problems of classification of the sample are considered as this selection is made.

5. The test is administered to the selected group under standard conditions of directions and time allowances, as outlined in the test manual, and the scores are studied. Typical scores for various special classifications, such as age or grade, are determined, and norms are established.

6. Other problems which the test maker faces are:

   a. How valid is the test?
   b. How reliable is the test?
   c. How can scores from various forms of the test be made comparable?
   d. What kind of norms should be presented (age, grade, percentile, standard scores)?
   e. How can the results be interpreted and utilized?

Information concerning these points is generally available in the test manual.

Although many of the procedures listed above might be described in greater detail, it is clear that the standardization of a test is a long and arduous task requiring thought and a high degree of skill on the part of the test maker. It is clear, too, that norms have a very definite reference point—the group or groups that comprise the standardization sample. When the classroom teacher uses norms, he compares the test results of his pupils with the over-all results from certain specific groups. The teacher can generalize the results of testing his group as a comparison with all pupils in a specific classification only to the extent that the original group is indeed representative of the entire population in the classification he is using.

MAKING USE OF AGE AND GRADE NORMS

Age norms show the standing of the pupil by relating his test score to the score which is typical of a particular age group. Age norms are developed as follows:

The test is administered to various age groups, such as children between the ages of 6 and 12 years. A typical score (the mean or median) is found for each age group and perhaps each half year of chronological age. Suppose the results are similar to those in Table 1 (page 50). The score column gives the total range of test scores on the hypothetical vocabulary test. Typical scores for each age group are represented by the heavily lined bars in each column. These may be the medians, or midpoints, or they may be the average scores for each age group. A score of 25, then, is the six-year norm, or the score typical of the six-year group. A score of 28 is the seven-year norm, and so on. Ordinarily, tests utilizing age norms are so designed that typical scores for lower age groups are lower than those for higher age groups. Thus a series of graduated age steps or levels is established.

The crosses in Table 1 represent the distributions of scores for each age level. It will be noted that the scores *vary around the norm;* that is, not all six-year-olds achieve a score of 25

TABLE 1. AGE NORMS FOR A VOCABULARY TEST

	Age in Years						
Score	6	7	8	9	10	11	12
50							X
49							XX
48							XXX
47						X	XXX
46						XX	XXXX
45						XX	XXXX
44					X	XXX	XXXXX
43					X	XXX	XXXXXX
42					XX	XXXX	XXXXXX
41					XX	XXXX	XXXXXX
40				X	XXX	XXXXX	**XXXXXXX**
39				XX	XXX	XXXXXX	XXXXXX
38				XX	XXXX	XXXXXXX	XXXXXX
37			X	XXX	XXXXX	**XXXXXXX**	XXXXXX
36			X	XXX	XXXXXX	XXXXXXX	XXXXX
35			XX	XXXX	**XXXXXXX**	XXXXXX	XXXX
34		X	XXX	XXXXX	XXXXXX	XXXXX	XXXX
33		XX	XXXX	**XXXXXX**	XXXXX	XXXXX	XXX
32		XX	XXXXX	XXXXX	XXXX	XXXX	XXX
31		XXX	XXXXXX	XXXX	XXX	XXX	XX
30	X	XXXX	**XXXXXXX**	XXX	XXX	XXX	X
29	XXX	XXXXX	XXXXXX	XXX	XX	XX	
28	XXXX	**XXXXXX**	XXXXX	XX	XX	XX	
27	XXXXX	XXXXX	XXXX	XX	X	X	
26	XXXXXX	XXXX	XXX	X			
25	**XXXXXXX**	XXX	XX				
24	XXXXXX	XX	X				
23	XXXXX	XX	X				
22	XXXX	X					
21	XXX						
20	X						

NOTE: Crosses (x) represent frequency of scores. The heavily outlined score cell is opposite the norm or "typical" score for the age group. Hence the norm for age 6 is a score of 25.

points; some of them score higher than typical seven-year-olds. In the seven-year-old group, some children score *below* the six-year norm. This is not peculiar; it is a common feature of age or grade distributions.

Now we are ready to use our highly simplified table of age norms.

1. Suppose that June is eight years old. Her test score is 25.

Her *vocabulary age* is six years. This is interpreted as meaning that on this vocabulary test June's score is at the level typically attained by the six-year-olds in our standardization sample.

2. John's chronological age is nine years. His score is 37, which is the score typical of eleven-year-olds in our sample. His vocabulary age is eleven years on this particular test.

In this way age norms enable the teacher to compare a child's score with the level of attainment of specified age groups. In addition, this comparison is based upon specific test materials. The test we have described is based on a sampling of vocabulary items, and the scores are related to the attainment of groups of children who comprised the standardization sample. The interpretation and use of age norms must be based upon a recognition of these factors in addition to those that are common to all tests, such as validity and reliability.

The teacher will find a variety of tables of age norms accompanying the group tests which are widely employed in classrooms. Among these are mental (MA), education (EA), and reading (RA) age norms. It is possible to derive arithmetic, vocabulary, and other age norms when appropriate test materials are employed.

The *mental age,* or MA is derived from scores on tests which purport to measure intelligence, mental maturity, general mental ability, and so on. The *educational age,* or EA is derived from sets of norms for varying age groups which have been based on test results in the area of educational achievement or scholarship. *Reading age* norms are developed on the basis of tests of reading skill or attainment.

In all the above instances, the norms must have reference to (1) definite areas of ability and achievement, (2) the specific items used to sample these areas of ability or achievement, and (3) the group or groups of pupils who formed the standardization sample which purports to be representative of the pupil population at the specified age levels.

Age norms help the teacher to think about children as they are and as they compare with others. One of our serious educational tasks is to locate the pupil in the academic milieu. Where shall we start with Mary? How well can Betty read as compared with other pupils? What materials are best suited to Anne's needs and capacities? What level of achievement should be expected of Roger? Age norms are not the answers to problems; rather they serve as markers or guides which are of value in so far as their meanings and implications are clearly understood.

Perhaps the type of norm most widely used is the grade norm, particularly at the elementary school level. Grade norms are developed in much the same way as age norms, but the reference point for grade norms is, of course, grade level rather than chronological age. The procedure might be summarized as follows:

1. The test (for example, an achievement test) is administered to specified grade groups, say, grades four through eight.

2. Typical scores (medians or averages) are worked out for each grade level. Perhaps additional central scores are found for each half term at each grade level.

3. These typical, or central, scores become the norms for the grades, and intermediary points representing number of months in the grade are developed. Hence the teacher finds that a test score of, say, 68 represents a grade placement of 4.6, which would indicate that this score represents the typical performance of pupils who have been in the fourth grade for a period of six months. Grade norms are ordinarily based upon the supposition of a ten-month school year. A study of the norms tables for any achievement test which gives grade norms will indicate whether the base is a ten- or twelve-month year.

To read the table of norms, the teacher finds the pupil's raw score. Mary, for example, in the sixth grade scores 120 on a general-achievement test. A score of 120 is equivalent to a grade norm of, say, 8.3. Mary's score is typical of pupils who have been in the eighth grade for a period of three months. This decimal part of the figure (three months) is very probably an estimate or approximation, as norms are not usually worked out for each month of the school year on the basis of actual sampling; such a task would be endless. However, this norm—grade placement 8.3—helps the teacher to understand his problem with Mary in a sixth-grade class. Her scholastic attainment is obviously quite superior by comparison with the reference group (the pupils used as a basis for the standardization of the test), and she is likely to find the usual sixth-grade materials quite easy and perhaps boring. Work designed to challenge Mary would be about at the level suited to beginning eighth graders, or, at any rate, somewhat richer and more varied than that which is suitable for typical sixth graders. Thus the norm helps us to locate Mary on the academic ladder and provides a reference point in planning for her.

Perhaps grade norms are popular with teachers simply because of their familiarity with the grade system. The elementary school teacher is likely to be quite familiar with third, fourth, or fifth graders and with the quality and level of achievement of pupils in these grades, just as junior and senior high school teachers are familiar with the level of achievement of their grades. The system of grades is deeply ingrained in our educational thinking. Hence, the location of a child in terms of a grade norm gives the teacher a basis for planning regardless of the actual grade placement of the pupil.

THE MEANING OF PERCENTILE RANKS

Comparing a child with his peers is perhaps one of the most useful ways of giving meaning to a test score. Age norms, as we have seen, locate the pupil in terms of age groups but not necessarily with pupils of his own age or grade. Comparisons with others of the same age or grade are most commonly made in terms of the *percentile rank* of the score a pupil attains on a given test. Percentile ranks indicate the relative standing of the pupil in a defined age or grade group.

If, for example, Jean's score on a particular test places her at percentile 20 for fifth-grade pupils, this means that her score is better than those of 20 per cent of the fifth graders who comprised the standardization sample. However, 80 per cent of this group of fifth graders made higher scores than Jean. The norm indicates Jean's standing among fifth graders, and it must be understood that the 20 does not refer to 20 per cent knowledge of the test area or imply that Jean answered 20 per cent of the questions correctly.

The example above indicates further that the percentile norm is a *separation point* in a distribution. That is, a percentile rank of 85 is a point which separates the upper 15 per cent from the lower 85 per cent of the group. Hence, this type of norm gives us the relative rank of pupils, an indication of their relative standing in a hypothetical group of one hundred.

Among the difficulties encountered in utilizing ranking measures such as percentile norms is the fact that the ranks do not represent equal units of measurement. The foot rule, for instance, is divided into twelve inches, each identical with every other. Suppose that the inches on a ruler were not of uniform length—that the "inches" at each extreme are excessively long and those near the center excessively short, as in the diagram in Figure 2. On such a rule, the inches have different meanings as units of measurement, depending upon their location on the rule.

An analogous situation prevails in the use of percentile

ranks as units of measurement. These flexible units are "shorter" near the center of any distribution in the sense that they imply smaller differences in actual score points near the center of the distribution; they are "longer" near either extreme in the sense that score differences between percentiles are greater at the extremes. That is, in terms of actual points scored on a given test, a difference of five percentile ranks at the upper extreme—say, percentile 90 to 95—may mean a difference of twenty score points on the test. On the other hand, a difference of five percentile ranks near the center of the distribution—say, percentile 50 to 55—may mean a difference of only two or three score points.

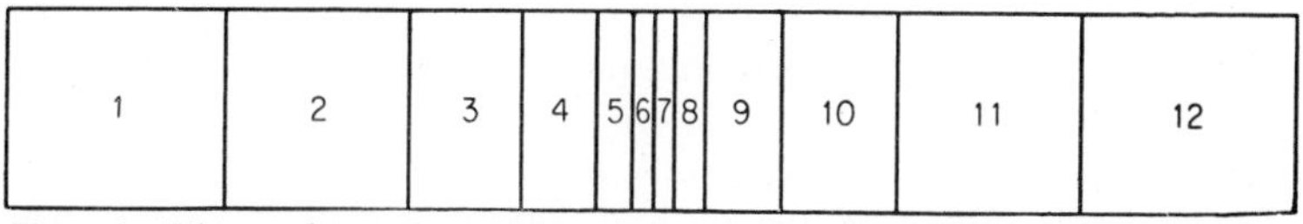

1 2 3 4 5 6 7 8 9 10 11 12

FIG. 2. Illustration of unequal units of measurement. The diagram represents a foot rule so divided that the units of measurement or "inches" are of unequal proportions.

This actual inequality of differences which appear alike when converted to percentile ranks is explained by the fact that large numbers of individuals tend to score in the middle range of a test, and few are found at either extreme. Since percentile ranks are based on proportions of the group included at or below certain points, the ranks jump rapidly wherever large frequencies occur. Conversely, percentile ranks increase slowly where frequencies are small.

To use another analogy, think of a group of a hundred persons running a race. One is outstanding and defeats the others. He is better than the other ninety-nine, and his percentile rank is 99. The person who ranks second is quite some distance behind the first, but distance does not affect his rank order. He is better than ninety-eight of the runners; hence his percentile rank is 98. The large group of average runners are probably massed at one point on the race track and reach the finish line in a group. The one who finishes fiftieth is better than fifty of the runners, so his percentile rank is 50. He has probably just barely defeated a number of others who are very close behind him, but he ranks 50 and the

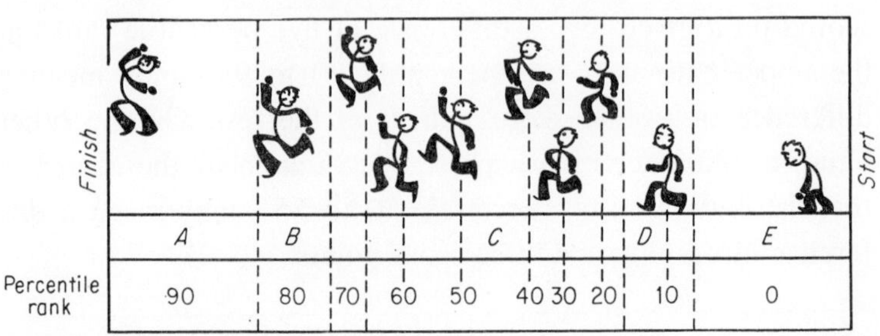

FIG. 3. The meaning of percentile ranks. Ten runners are engaged in a race. The winner, at *A*, is better than the other nine runners (90 per cent); therefore his percentile rank is 90. His percentile rank is ten "points" better than the rank of runner number two, at *B*, who attains the percentile rank of 80, since runner number two is better than eight of the ten runners, or 80 per cent. Note, however, the long distance which separates the two runners at *A* and *B*.

The runners in area *C* are grouped closely together, but each achieves ten percentile-rank "points" above the nearest succeeding runner, since each comprises 10 per cent of the total group. Ten percentile "points" at *C* appear to be the same as ten percentile "points" at *A* but give no information as to the actual distance separating the runners. This grouping near the center of a distribution, as at *C*, is a common feature of the score distributions of educational and mental tests.

next runner 49 regardless of the very short distance between the two.

At the slow extreme, perhaps one runner is trailing far behind. He is last, and his percentile rank is zero. The nearest runner in front may be far ahead of him, but that nearest one is better than only one runner, the last. His percentile rank is one regardless of the distance that separates him from the last man.

Figure 3 shows this situation for ten runners. It is apparent that percentile rank depends entirely on the number of people at a point in the distribution. Thus rank is independent of actual score value or number of items answered correctly. The teacher who utilizes percentile ranks should keep in mind the fact that these "norms" represent variable units of measure, especially when he is tempted to make distinctions among pupils on the basis of percentile-rank differences.

In spite of these characteristics, percentile norms are as valuable to the teacher as any ranking system, for they indicate the relative standing of the pupil in a defined age or grade group and thus help the teacher understand the pupil, plan for him, and develop reasonable expectations for him. They "locate" the pupil among others of his own age or grade.

STANDARD SCORES AND MEASUREMENT PROBLEMS

Standard scores represent the attempt to develop equal units of measurement. As we have seen, percentiles are in reality ranks which have no uniform reference to size of score. Standard scores on the other hand, are determined by the number of points the pupil scores rather than by his rank order in a group. Standard-score units are equal throughout the distribution.

A major problem in educational measurement is the fact that there is no such thing as an absolute zero. In other words, there is no beginning point, as there is with linear measurement. Where, for example, does intelligence begin? Is there such a thing as zero intelligence? Since such starting points cannot be established in developing measurement systems based on standard scores, a *central* point is used as a reference. This point is the *mean,* or *average,* score. In deriving standard scores, then, the first step is to locate the average score of the group.

The next step is based on the assumption that score distributions will normally follow a rather definite pattern. This pattern is called the normal curve and is represented by a symmetrical, bell-shaped curve with definite mathematical properties, as shown in Figure 4. The high parts of the curve represent the highest frequencies of scores, at *C*, *M* (the

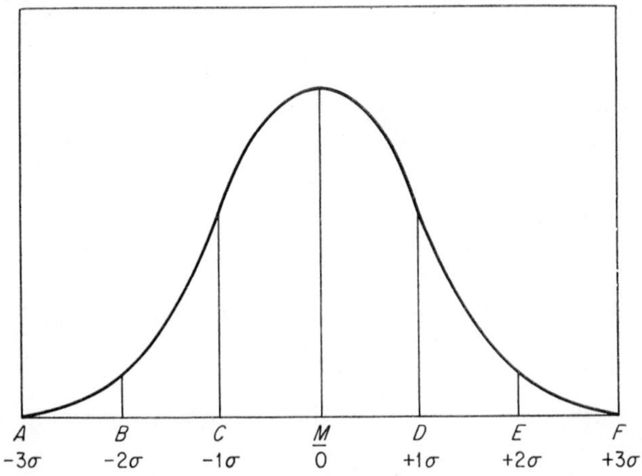

FIG. 4. The normal curve. The symbol σ represents *standard deviation,* a measure of the dispersion of scores around the *mean* (*M*) or *average.*

mean), and *D*. At *B* and *E* the shorter vertical lines represent fewer scores as we approach either extreme. At the extreme left and right, the extremely low and high ends of the scale, scores are very infrequent; this, as we have seen, is the distribution found where large numbers of persons are measured with respect to almost any characteristic. For example, suppose we consider height of adults. Very few persons are extremely short, very many are about average in height, and very few again are extremely tall. This, then, is the type of distribution we *expect* to find (or *normally* find) when adequate measures of human characteristics are applied to large groups selected at random from the population. Standard-score systems are based upon this assumption and may be developed in relation to distributions which approximate the form of this normal curve.

Assuming that the bell-shaped curve represents the normal or expected distribution of test scores, the problem resolves

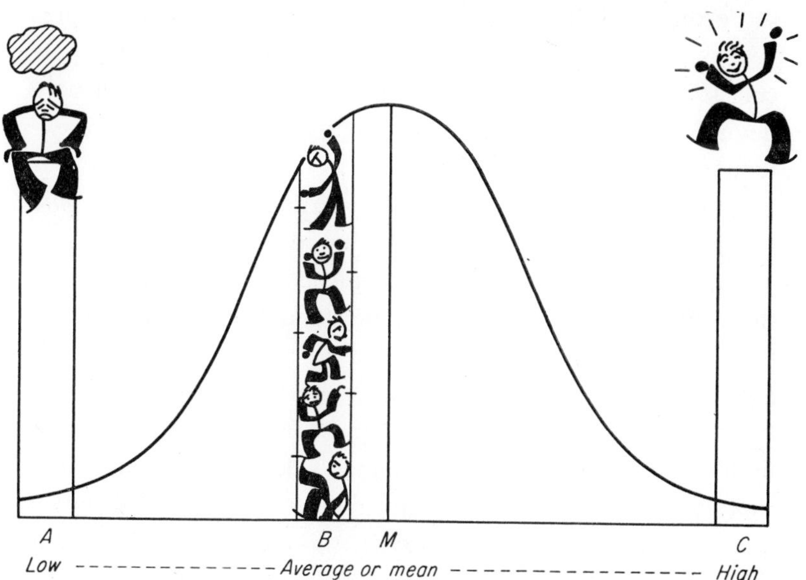

FIG. 5. Diagrammatic representation of the weighting of standard scores in terms of deviation from the mean.

itself into that of making allowances for the high frequency of scores around the center of the distribution and the low frequency at the extremes. To do this, scores near the extremes are given added weight depending upon the extent of their deviation (in score units) from the average score. The greater the deviation of the score from the center, the greater its weighting. This process gives a result analogous to that shown in Figure 5.

Five pupils receive score *B*, which is relatively close to *M*, the average score. Since score *B* does not deviate greatly from the average, this score receives little weight, even though it is the score attained by five pupils. Score *A* is near the lower extreme of the total distribution of scores. It is equivalent to score *B* in weight even though only one pupil scores at this low level. Score *C*, at the upper extreme, is also equivalent in weight to score *B*, even though only one pupil attains a score this high. This weighting of scores at the extremes prevents the difficulties of interpretation that occur in using percentile ranks, since the weighting takes into account not only deviation of the score from the average but also to some extent frequency of scores. The result is *equal units of measurement along the base line,* that is, in terms of *raw-score points.*

These units of measurement are based on the *standard deviation,* a measure of variability or dispersion of scores around the central point in a distribution. Standard deviations under the normal curve are presented in Figure 6. The mean or average is arbitrarily assigned a value of zero (no deviation from the center of the curve), and four standard deviation units have been indicated on either side of the mean (note that each standard deviation unit represents an equal distance along the base line of the curve). Opposite *A* are indicated the proportions of scores or measures which, assuming a normal distribution, may be expected to fall within each area of the curve marked off by the vertical lines. Approximately 68 per cent (roughly two-thirds) of the scores fall in the area within one standard deviation above and below the mean or average, and roughly one-sixth of the scores fall below and one-sixth above these points.

Standard scores are based on standard deviations and are centered around the average score attained by pupils in the standardization sample. A type of standard score, the T score, indicating the equal base-line units, is shown opposite B in

Figure 6 with a score of 50 representing the mean or average. The base line in this figure illustrates the fact that standard-score units are equal in base-line length. The base line here represents score points.

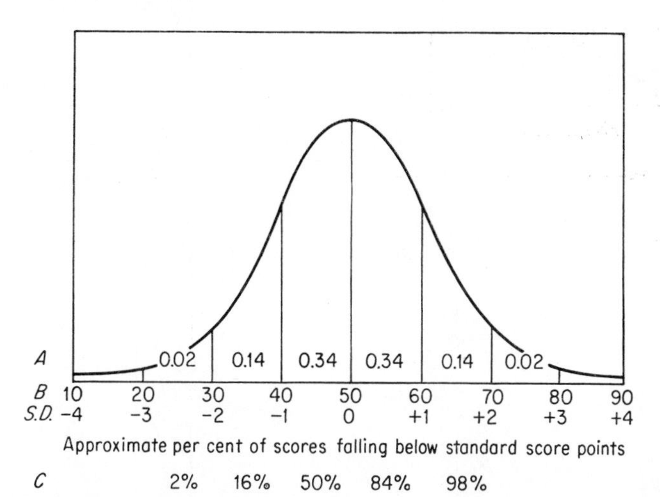

FIG. 6. Standard scores, showing equal base-line units and approximate proportions of scores included below stated standard-score points.

Opposite *A* above are shown the proportions of the population likely to receive standard scores within the limits specified. For example, approximately 14 per cent of the population are likely to receive standard scores between 30 and 40 or between 60 and 70.

Opposite *B* are listed standard-score intervals ranging from 10 to 90.

Opposite *C* are listed the per cents of the population likely to receive standard scores below the specified points. For example, approximately 2 per cent receive standard scores of less than 30, and 98 per cent receive standard scores of less than 70.

Note: The explanations above are approximate and are based upon the assumption of large or representative populations yielding distributions of scores approximating the normal distribution.

The per cent of the population likely to score below given standard scores is indicated by the numerals opposite *C*. For example, two persons out of a hundred are likely to score below standard score 30, and sixteen out of a hundred below

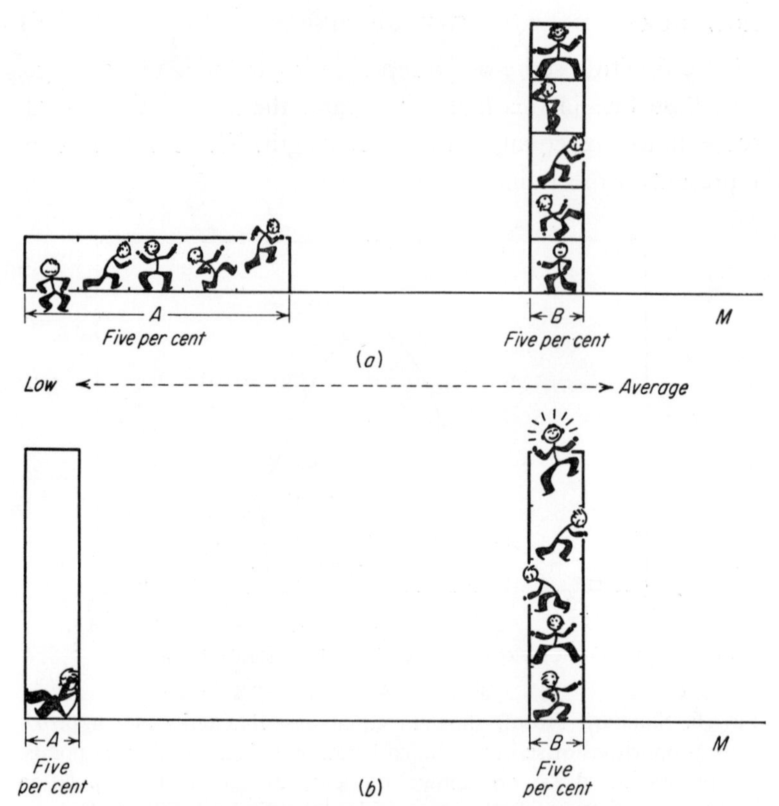

FIG. 7. Percentile ranks and standard scores.

a. Percentile (or centile) *ranks* represent *unequal units along the base line.* Where frequencies are great, percentile ranks "stretch" high and narrow. The base line represents points scored on the test. The diagram shows the effect where the group is a hundred pupils.

M is the center of score distribution. *B* is a score attained by five pupils near the center of the distribution. It represents five percentile ranks piled up above one score point. *A* is near the lower extreme. Five pupil scores are spread out over this area of five score points. Here the base line extent is five times that at *B* for the *equivalent percentile* ranks.

b. Standard scores represent *equal units along the base line.* They accommodate many or few scores retaining their unit length on this base line. The diagram shows the effect where the group is a hundred pupils.

M is the center of the score distribution. *B* is a score point near the center achieved by five pupils. It has no more weight and occupies no more of the base line (score points on the test) than score *A*, which is attained by only one pupil but is at the lower extreme of the distribution. These equal units of measurement throughout the scale result from the weighting of scores at the extremes to compensate for lower frequencies at these levels.

standard score 40. Only 2 per cent of the population exceeds standard score 70. The percentages employed here are based on the theoretical normal curve.

The uses and advantages of standard scores may be summarized as follows:

1. Standard scores represent equal units of measurement and hence facilitate comparisons regardless of the area of the distribution of scores under consideration.

2. Standard scores from different tests are comparable to the extent that they may be averaged or combined (if the assumption of normality seems to be warranted). This applies even though the tests may contain different numbers of items and one test may be more difficult than the other.

3. Standard scores are based essentially on score points on the test rather than on rank order. This facilitates interpretations in terms of ability or achievement as represented by test score and indicates relative standing in the group at the same time.

4. Mathematically, standard scores have other values. The zero point is always the mean (standard score 50 as described here). The mean is the most stable measure of central tendency, that is, the most stable central score. The range between standard scores of 40 and 50 represents one standard deviation below the mean (or average). The standard deviation is the most reliable measure of variability within the group and has many statistical uses. (See Figure 7.)

NORMS AND THE TEST MANUAL

Before giving a test, the teacher should read carefully the directions for administering it and the descriptions of norms presented in the manual of directions. It is important that the teacher follow these directions, since the norms have been developed on the basis of these specific regulations and requirements and any deviation from the required procedure may invalidate them. Pupil scores can be interpreted on the basis of the norms provided only when the test has been administered under the standard conditions set forth in the manual. The directions for scoring the test must be carefully followed, since deviations from the standard methods of scoring also will invalidate the norms.

The test manual will also include a description of the types of norms provided, and the teacher should study these descriptions carefully in order to interpret the norms correctly. For example, we have defined percentile rank as a point of separation which marks off one proportion of the group from another. In other sources the teacher may read that a pupil's percentile rank indicates the per cent of the pupils in the group that he equals or excels in score on the given test.[2] Interpretation of pupil scores will vary with the definition of norms, and it is important that the teacher study the definition given in the manual of directions for the particular test he is giving. Only on this basis are accurate interpretations possible.

In addition, the teacher must examine the test manual to discover the nature of the sample population on which the norms were based, for they will be of little value for use with pupils who differ markedly from the normative groups. For example, children of migratory workers and children in isolated or slum areas are not likely to compare favorably with the norms usually presented with educational tests.

SUMMARY

The task of persons interested in educational evaluation is to establish meaningful methods of measuring pupil status and progress relative to worthwhile educational goals. The

[2] Arthur E. Traxler, *Techniques of Guidance,* New York: Harper & Brothers, 1945, p. 182.

development of norms has facilitated educational evaluation to the extent that they give the teacher a basis for comparison of the pupil with others of specified ages or grades. The purpose of norms is to place scores on tests in a framework which helps the teacher to make comparisons or to relate scores to one another.

Norms are derived from a study of the test scores achieved by large groups of pupils of specified age or grade levels. They are measures which relate the score of one pupil to the scores of others. Among the kinds of norms frequently employed are age, grade, and percentile norms, and standard, or T, scores.

Age norms relate the individual's score to the score typically attained by pupils of a specified age group. Age norms have been developed for mental age, educational age, and reading age. Mental age is derived from scores on tests of mental maturity, mental ability, or intelligence. Educational age relates the individual's score to the attainment of age groups on tests of general educational achievement. Reading age is based upon relative attainment in skills and understandings relating to reading.

Grade norms represent the typical attainment of pupils at specified grade levels. Although they may be used with tests of aptitude or attainment, they are most commonly used in connection with tests of achievement in the basic academic fields or as a measure of general educational achievement. Grade norms help the teacher to determine the level of achievement of the pupil with reference to school grade.

Percentile norms or ranks indicate the relative standing of the pupil in a defined group such as an age or grade classification. They are rank-order measures which have no reference to size of score except as this determines rank order in a series of scores. These norms are, however, widely used, and they are meaningful and helpful, as they indicate the pupil's standing among stated groups with reference to the measured characteristics.

Standard scores represent equal units of measurement, have a wide range of application, and facilitate accurate interpretations. They relate a pupil's score to scores attained by specific groups, such as age or grade groups.

The teacher who plans to utilize the norms presented in test manuals should adhere strictly to the directions for administering and scoring the test, as the norms are derived on the basis of these standard procedures. He should also study the definitions, methods of derivation, and interpretation of the norms in order to evaluate and interpret them and to understand the implications of certain variations in definition and procedure which may apply to the specific test he is using.

STUDY AND DISCUSSION EXERCISES

1. Define the term *norm*. Indicate the essential difference between raw scores and norms.
2. In what ways may the concept of norms be misused by teachers in the evaluation of pupils in the classroom situation?
3. Anne has a mental age of ten years two months according to a group test of mental ability. What additional data would be necessary to an adequate interpretation of this derived score? Give your reasons for considering each item essential to interpretation of the test result.
4. A standardized achievement test provides age, grade, and percentile norms as a basis for interpretation of results. Cite the advantages and limitations of each type of norm presented.
5. Mary, a fifth-grade girl, achieves a score of 65 on the arithmetic section of a standardized achievement test. This score is equivalent to percentile 70. How would you interpret this score in terms of the available data?
6. Explain the difference between standard score and percentile norms. What are the particular advantages of each?
7. Differentiate between norms and standards of achievement.
8. Johnny has taken three different standardized general-

achievement batteries during the past few weeks. His scores, when converted to grade norms, differ. On battery A his achievement is at grade level 4.6, in terms of the norms for the test. On battery B his achievement places him at grade level 5.7. He scores at grade level 6.1 on battery C. Assuming that scores on all three batteries ordinarily have a high degree of reliability, try to account for the differences in performance.

SUGGESTED ADDITIONAL READINGS

Freeman, F. S.: *Theory and Practice of Psychological Testing,* New York: Henry Holt and Company, Inc., 1950.

Chapter I presents an overview of the problem of psychological measurement.

Froelich, Clifford P., and Arthur L. Benson: *Guidance Testing,* Chicago: Science Research Associates, Inc., 1948.

Chapter 3 includes a discussion of the values and limitations of norms.

Greene, Edward B.: *Measurements of Human Behavior,* New York: The Odyssey Press, Inc., 1952.

Chapter 12 presents a discussion of the interpretation of test scores.

Micheels, William J., and M. Ray Karnes: *Measuring Educational Achievement,* New York: McGraw-Hill Book Company, Inc., 1950.

Chapter 1 contains an excellent discussion of the nature of measurement with particular reference to indirect and relative measures.

Monroe, Walter S. (ed.): *Encyclopedia of Educational Research,* New York: The Macmillan Company, 1950, pp. 785–802.

A discussion of the types, comparability, and interpretations of norms.

CHAPTER FIVE

Estimating Capacity for Learning

Among the teacher's more urgent problems is that of estimating capacity for learning—of discovering what scholastic performance to expect of pupils. Is Jim learning as rapidly and as well as can be expected? Is the classroom work too easy or too difficult for Mary? What kinds of materials are best suited to Don's abilities? Is Jane's poor work in school due to lack of ability or to some other factor? These are among the everyday problems of the classroom teacher.

It is as important to discover the pupil's capacity for learning as to determine what he is learning. It is widely recognized that pupils differ markedly in ability to succeed in schoolwork and that therefore uniform standards of achievement for all are unrealistic and undesirable. No teacher expects all children to conform to a given standard in height or weight; and certainly every teacher recognizes that forced feeding, stretching, pulling, pushing, or any other kind of pressure would be entirely useless in adjusting the pupil's height to classroom standards. Although it is sometimes less obvious, educational "pressure" techniques are no more likely to equalize the learning capacity of pupils.

Recognition of the existence of individual differences implies acceptance of these differences as educational facts which form the background for the teacher's work. Indeed, a major function of testing is to enable teachers to understand and *work with* the differences that inevitably exist, such as Johnny's not learning so readily as Billy. The only satisfactory educational practice is to exert every possible effort to adapt the curriculum to the educational potentialities of individual pupils.

Adapting the curriculum to the learning potentials of individual pupils means careful study by the teacher of the aptitudes of his pupils for schoolwork. By utilizing the evidence from tests of intelligence—or tests of scholastic or educational aptitude, as they might more properly be called—the teacher gathers objective data upon which to base judgments and expectations. Tests do not give answers; they provide data that are valuable to the teacher to the extent that he uses them wisely in making judgments.

WHAT INTELLIGENCE TESTS MEASURE

The definition of intelligence is subject to a great deal of controversy involving a number of points of view. Since our purpose here is to help the teacher use test results effectively, we shall limit our discussion to the kinds of abilities that are commonly evaluated by so-called "intelligence tests." The teacher is urged to examine the tests he uses, read the manuals carefully, and decide what specific abilities are tested by the material. An intelligence-test score, like any other test score, is significant only for the materials included in the particular test, and the teacher's interpretation of the score must first of all be related to the kinds of performances required of pupils by the test.

Items commonly included in intelligence tests are designed to sample abilities such as the following:

1. Memory—immediate or delayed, meaningful or rote.
2. Ability to deal with verbal materials (vocabulary).
3. Ability to deal with spatial relationships or to orient the self in space.
4. Ability to deal with verbal relationships (analogies, opposites).
5. Ability to deal with numerical materials either as sheer facility with numbers or as ability to reason numerically or quantitatively.
6. Ability to find the guiding principle involved in tasks which may be verbal, numerical, spatial, or pictorial in nature.
7. Ability to perceive essential details, make fine distinctions, and notice similarities.

Tests of mental ability may include material on as few as three or four of the aspects of intelligence outlined above or on all or almost all of them. One test may deal primarily with verbal materials; another may require manipulation of blocks, the solution of puzzles, or the interpretation of pictures. For example, vocabulary may be tested by items such as the following, which differ in the emphasis placed upon language skills:

Words: a vocabulary test of the type which requires some reading skill. The pupil selects the one word, A, B, C, or D, which has the same meaning as the initial word.

1. big; A fair B windy C soft D large

Pictures: a test of vocabulary which does not require reading skill. The teacher pronounces the word *dog*. The pupil finds and indicates the picture which corresponds to the spoken word.[1]

[1] L. L. Thurstone and T. G. Thurstone, *S.R.A. Primary Mental Abilities, Elementary Form AH,* Chicago: Science Research Associates, Inc., 1948.

Pictures

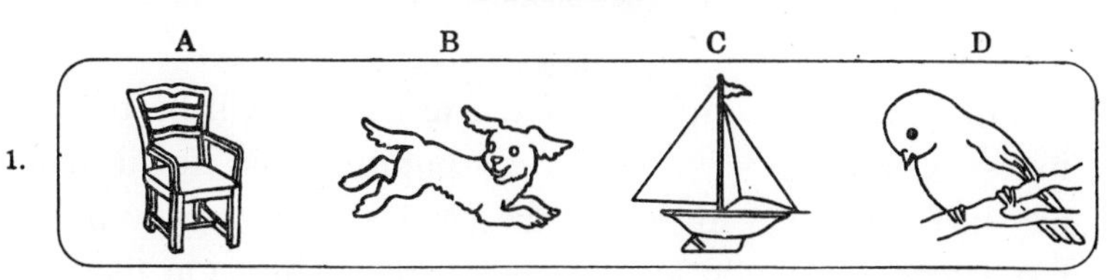

Again, reasoning ability may be evaluated by items which differ in the degree of emphasis upon verbal skills. Of the following, the word-grouping item utilizes verbal materials, whereas in the figure-grouping item language skill does not play an essential part.

Word grouping: The pupil is required to indicate the word which does not belong with the others.

A red B blue C heavy D green

Figure grouping: The pupil is asked to indicate the figure which does not belong with the group.[2]

Figure-grouping

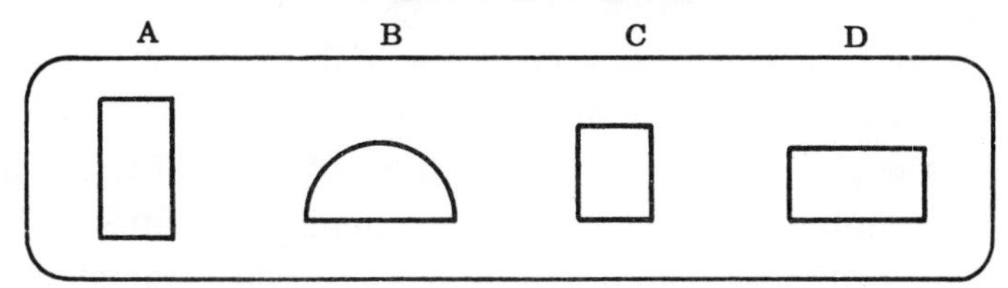

Items like the following, in which the pupil selects the appropriate analogy, may be of the language or nonlanguage type:[3]

Practice Exercise 3. ◯ is to ○ as ☐ is to : 1 △, 2 ▭, 3 □, 4 ▽, 5 ▯

. . . . [1] [2] [3] [4] [5]

[2] *Ibid.*

[3] V. A. C. Henmon and M. J. Nelson, *The Henmon-Nelson Tests of Mental Ability, Form B* (Grades 7–12), Boston: Houghton Mifflin Company, 1932.

63: *Land* is to *peninsula* as *ocean* is to: 1 gulf, 2 lake, 3 cape, 4 river, 5 island.

The particular emphasis of the test items will be reflected in the results of the tests for each pupil. Jimmy, for instance, has little facility with words and will not do very well on a test which is heavily loaded with verbal items. On the other hand, he may shine on a test which requires manipulation of materials and the solution of problems involving concrete objects or pictorial situations. But the fact that the items in the verbal test do not tap his best abilities does not mean that it is useless for Jimmy to take the test. The test will indicate Jimmy's weakness in verbal areas, and this is valuable information for the teacher, whether it is news or merely a confirmation of opinion.

The teacher who is interpreting Jimmy's test results, however, must keep in mind that a verbal test represents a sampling of only a limited number of abilities. The teacher will recognize the significance of more inclusive measures. The best way to promote Jimmy's development in verbal skills and meanings may be through the areas in which he demonstrates greatest capacity for learning. When this is the case, the teacher should seek a test or a battery of tests which gives a more inclusive picture of the pupil's capacities.

It is particularly important that a test which samples various areas of intelligence rather than probing "general" intelligence be used for adolescent students. Recent investigations have indicated that specific abilities become more sharply differentiated as the individual develops toward maturity. In statistical terms, it has been found that intercorrelations between such characteristics as memory, verbal abilities, and number facility are not so extensive in fifteen-year-olds as in twelve-year-olds. "The correlations from these various studies indicate clearly that different aspects of intelligence are being measured and that independence of mental traits, or differentiation among traits, increases with age through the adolescent years."[4] Two practical implications may be derived from these data. (1) In studying adolescents, tests of general mental ability will be less informative than tests that provide a profile of abilities. (2) As the child grows, teachers find more opportunities to capitalize upon and thus promote the development of the specific abilities as these become more clearly differentiated.

It is well, also, to understand that there are aspects of adjustment and functioning that are not measured by intelligence tests. For example, the pupil's determination to use what intelligence he has to best advantage is not measured. Health conditions and drive may have a deleterious or invigorating effect upon intellectual functioning. The paucity or richness of experience conditions the development and functioning of intellectual capacity. Experiential background is not likely to be indicated. Social intelligence—ability to get along with others without excessive emotional tension—has not yet been isolated as an aspect of intelligence, yet it does affect schoolwork and personal adjustment.

THE MEANING OF MENTAL AGE

Most intelligence tests utilize the concept of mental age (MA) as a basis for the interpretation of results. The child's test score is related to the age group of which his score is typical. For example, Betty has a raw score of 107 on a mental test. The table of norms indicates that this score is equivalent to a mental age of ten years two months. This means that Betty's score on this test is the score typically attained by children who are ten years two months of age. Betty herself may be eight or twelve years old chronologically. Her score, however, is more typical of the age group ten years two

[4] David Segal, *Intellectual Abilities in the Adolescent Period,* Federal Security Agency, Office of Education, Bulletin 1948, no. 6, p. 10.

months than of either eight- or twelve-year-olds. Betty, in other words, achieves at the ten-year two-month norm on this test and is said to have an MA of ten years two months.

In certain respects the concept of mental age is of more value to the teacher than that of IQ, which is, however, more commonly used. Mental age approximates the use of grade norms on achievement tests; that is, it relates Betty to a specific age group in mental ability. This may help the teacher to develop suitable expectations for Betty with reference to schoolwork.

The teacher may be able, on the basis of his knowledge of children at various age levels, to decide upon materials which will be suitable for Betty, regardless of her actual grade placement. Suppose that she is twelve years old and has a mental age of ten years. This does not imply that she is just like children ten years of age; in interests, experiences, social development, physique, and possibly in many respects mentally, she will differ from "typical" ten-year-olds. However, in terms of the mental abilities sampled by the test, it appears that she resembles the ten-year-old group in mentality. The index is admittedly rough, but it is perhaps the best available basis for the teacher's dealings with Betty, and it suggests some possible approaches to Betty's learning problems.

Many teachers tend to think in terms of grade groups rather than age groups. Possibly this is in part the reason for the popularity of grade norms as a basis for thinking about achievement-test results. Mental ages can be converted into mental grade placements. For example, Betty's mental age relates her, in terms of the mental-test sampling, to the ten-year-old group, and youngsters of this age are typically found in the fifth grade in school. Betty functions mentally about at the level, then, of typical fifth graders. This information gives the teacher a worthwhile starting point for his attempts to adapt the curriculum to Betty's potentialities.

Betty's mental grade placement does not necessarily indicate a fifth-grade program for her, since she may differ in many respects from typical ten-year-olds. Although the curriculum which suits her best will probably involve a level of mental functioning comparable to that expected of ten-year-olds, differences in experience and level of social development and the fact that she has been in school and has had previous contact with a wide variety of curricular materials will influence the teacher in choosing the learning materials and processes suited to Betty's needs and capacities. This decision concerning Betty's program illustrates the principle we have already discussed—that test data should be used to supplement, correct, or confirm the observations made by the teacher. The teacher must then look for evidences of interest, boredom, nervous tension, or enjoyment of suggested tasks to see how well the materials tentatively being tried are suited to Betty's needs.

The value of the mental-age concept is further illustrated by the following approximate equivalents:

Case A: The IQ of pupil A is 100. His chronological age upon entering school was five years six months; because of his birth date, he was able to enter school at a relatively early age. His MA (five years six months) indicates that very possibly he will not be ready to begin reading during his first year in school.

Case B: The IQ of pupil B is 90. He was delayed in entering school for one year because of illness. His chronological age is seven years two months; his MA is six years five months. Under ordinary circumstances pupil B is likely to be ready for reading even though his IQ is lower than that of pupil A, since mental age is more closely related to reading readiness than is IQ.

Case C: Pupil C has an IQ of 126. His chronological age is six years four months; his MA is eight years. Pupil C is likely to have little difficulty with the first-grade program in reading and may need more challenging materials than his classmates require.

The interpretations in these three cases above are clarified through the use of mental-age rather than IQ concepts. However, it must be repeated that many factors aside from tested mental ability enter into a child's readiness for learning. The possibilities suggested above should be regarded by the teacher as tentative hypotheses that may have to be changed as a result of other circumstances in the child's classroom life.

Again, the teacher must evaluate test materials carefully. Mental age is an average based upon a particular sampling of mental abilities; it may cut across few or many abilities, and it must be interpreted in terms of the test from which it is derived and the kinds of problems the test requires the pupil to solve.

THE MEANING OF IQ

The term *intelligence quotient* (IQ) is firmly established in the vocabulary of teachers. The IQ is the ratio of a pupil's mental age to his chronological age and is found as follows:

$$IQ = \frac{MA}{CA} \times 100$$

In order to compute the IQ of a pupil, the MA is derived from an intelligence test and converted into months. This term is divided by the chronological age (CA), also converted into months. The result of this computation is then multiplied by 100, thus clearing two decimal places.

By way of example, let us suppose that Billy, whose chronological age is ten years four months, has completed an intelligence test which shows him to have a mental age of eleven years one month. His IQ can be calculated as follows:

$$CA = 10\text{–}4\text{, or } 124 \text{ months}$$
$$MA = 11\text{–}1\text{, or } 133 \text{ months}$$

Using the formula given above, Billy's IQ is

$$\frac{\text{MA}}{\text{CA}} \times 100 = \frac{133}{124} \times 100, \text{ or } 107$$

It is evident that the IQ is a ratio of level of mental development to chronological age. Hence it indicates the present rate of mental development or the relative brightness of the individual. Billy, in the example above, is developing mentally at a rate slightly faster than that of the hypothetical average child, as indicated by his IQ of 107. The child whose mental and chronological ages are exactly equal has an IQ of 100. Actually, the normal rate of development or average brightness might possibly be best defined as the IQ range between 90 and 110.

Some Cautions. As we have seen, the IQ represents rate of mental development or relative brightness. The teacher should remember, however, that basically it is derived from a test score and is subject to the usual limitations which pertain to such scores. No test is completely reliable; on similar test materials a pupil may perform better at one time than at another, since he may feel better or have a better attitude toward the test at one time than at another. When he takes the test, he may be at his best with reference to some types of materials and at his worst with reference to others. Thus the test at best can only sample his abilities; it cannot give complete coverage. All this indicates that the teacher should employ at least as much caution in the interpretation of the IQ as in the interpretation of any other test score. In fact, because of the particular implications which have become attached to the concept of IQ, the need for cautious interpretation can scarcely be overemphasized.

Many persons feel that the IQ should be regarded as constant and that therefore one test result, even though it is several years old, should be sufficient evidence of the brightness of a pupil. This is far from the truth. The IQ is only roughly constant; although it does not ordinarily fluctuate widely from one test to another, it nevertheless does vary, and differences of at least ten points on the usual tests can be expected. Still larger fluctuations occur, even when similar tests are used. When tests are administered at intervals of several years, marked deviations are not at all uncommon.[5] In fact, the results of intelligence tests administered during the preschool or primary-grade period should probably be given little credence if they are over a year old. Although test results for older pupils appear to be more stable it is doubtful whether they are really dependable over any lengthy period of time.[6]

IQs derived from different intelligence tests are not comparable. The fact that two tests are labeled "mental" or "intelligence" tests does not mean that the tasks included in them are at all alike. A child may have an IQ of 107 on one test, 95 on another, and 115 on a third. Hence, to interpret any IQ the teacher should know the name and nature of the test from which it was derived. This is one of the reasons why it is desirable to use the same test with comparable forms over a number of years. This practice will tend to eliminate comparisons between measures that are not necessarily equivalent. Estimating the capacity for learning of individual pupils can be facilitated by the informed use of tests; but the estimation is not accomplished by a single test score—it is the result of properly correlating many data.

It is a recognized fact, too, that children grow at different rates and that these rates vary within individuals. This is as true with mental growth as it is with any other aspect of growth. These variations which may be due to a variety of

[5] John P. Zubek and P. A. Solberg, *Human Development,* New York: McGraw-Hill Book Company, Inc., 1954, p. 282.

[6] J. E. Anderson, "The Limitations of Infant and Preschool Tests in the Measurement of Intelligence," *Journal of Psychology,* **8**:351–379, 1939. K. P. Bradway, "IQ Constancy on the Revised Stanford-Binet from the Preschool to the Junior High School Level," *Journal of Genetic Psychology,* **65**:197–217, 1944.

factors, innate and environmental, result in sufficient variation in the IQ that the teacher must exercise care when applying interpretations to individual cases.

Environmental Influences

It is commonly assumed that intelligence is inherited. Although there is evidence that tends to support this point of view, it has been demonstrated that environmental conditions in the home and community, school attendance, and other factors influence IQ. Consequently it is perhaps wisest to consider that heredity sets limits to individual potentialities, but that these potentialities develop in response to environmental stimulation.

In judging a pupil's ability to learn, the teacher must bear in mind the fact that his opportunities to develop his abilities, at least along scholastic lines, may have been very limited. Given more stimulating environmental conditions, his measured ability might change considerably. For example, Wheeler[7] has shown that the general test level of a mountain community improved over a period of ten years during which improvements occurred in the general environment. Wellman and Pegram[8] and Skodak and Skeels[9] have shown that differences in environmental conditions are related to changes in tested intelligence.

The kind of social and economic environment from which a child comes influences his tested intelligence markedly.[10]

[7] L. R. Wheeler, "A Comparative Study of the Intelligence of East Tennessee Mountain Children," *Journal of Educational Psychology,* 33:321–334, 1942.

[8] Beth L. Wellman and E. L. Pegram, "Binet IQ Changes of Orphanage Preschool Children: A Reanalysis," *Journal of Genetic Psychology,* 65:239–263, 1944.

[9] M. Skodak and H. M. Skeels, "A Follow-up Study of Children in Adoptive Homes," *Journal of Genetic Psychology,* 66:21–58, 1945.

[10] Kenneth Eells, A. Davis, R. J. Havinghurst, V. E. Herrick, and R. Tyler, *Intelligence and Cultural Differences,* Chicago: University of Chicago Press, 1951.

Most intelligence tests tend to favor middle-class and upper-class children and to discriminate against lower-class children; that is, the test items are concerned with materials more familiar to one group of children than the other. Verbal items most markedly favor middle-class as against lower-class children, whereas nonverbal and pictorial materials discriminate least against lower-class children. This being the case, the teacher must consider the child's background in evaluating test scores. Although test results may indicate the child's ability to deal with a standard school curriculum, they may not indicate his potential ability to solve problems in areas related to his experience.

PERCENTILE RANKS

One of the most meaningful interpretations of mental-test results is that which compares the pupil with his own age group. Mental-age, as we have seen, relates the child to an age group with ability similar to his own with regard to the sampling of mental tasks included in a specific test. The IQ purports to be a more general measure which indicates relative brightness. This kind of comparison has its limitations, because an IQ of 115 at age eight is indicative of quite a different level of mental functioning than an IQ of 115 at the age of twelve or fourteen. Although the quotients are similar, the expectations of the teacher must be related to the age group to which the pupil belongs; therefore, a measure which compares the child with those of his age is more meaningful.

Comparisons with peer groups are most commonly given in the form of percentile ranks. Percentile norms indicate the relative standing of the child in defined age or grade groups; thus they provide a comparison of the child with others in a defined group. In making use of percentile norms the teacher should keep in mind that they represent variable units of measurement, especially when he is tempted to make fine distinctions in terms of others of like age.

Norms based on standard scores (see Chapter 4) provide a further means of comparing the individual with members of a specified group. Norms of this type represent points along a scale, the units of measurement being equivalent throughout the length of the scale. Certain IQ measures are based on standard scores. They provide a means of comparing the individual's ability with specified age or educational groups. Since the basic unit, one standard deviation, is similar in meaning for different tests, norms based on standard scores provide a precise basis for comparison between tests and between individuals.

USING INTELLIGENCE-TEST RESULTS

Intelligence tests, as we have seen, are valuable instruments, but their value is dependent upon competent use and interpretation. They are tools which may be used or misused. When carefully selected, administered, and interpreted, however, they provide the teacher with significant data.

The fundamental aim of the teacher is to assist each pupil to make the best use of his capacities, and the intelligence test is perhaps the best general measure of learning capacity with reference to schoolwork. This is especially true in the more academic areas such as reading, composition, arithmetic, and spelling. Mental-age scores permit the teacher to estimate the mental level at which a child is likely to work most effectively, and through the use of the IQ and percentile rank, the teacher is able to formulate expectations regarding the pupil's capacity to learn in academic areas. In the case of a new pupil or a new class, such information may be vital to the success of the program of instruction.

Intelligence-test results are useful, too, in helping the

teacher to diagnose learning disabilities. Is Johnny capable of doing better work in reading or arithmetic? Is Mary "just plain lazy," or is the work too difficult or too easy for her? Is Ronny rebellious because he is unable to work at the level expected of him, or is there some other reason for his attitude? Educational problems are seldom simple. The intelligence-test result is ordinarily, therefore, only one of several types of evidence that should be examined in reaching a decision about a learning problem. However, it is important that capacity for learning, as indicated by test results, be given due consideration.

In making more specific diagnoses, the teacher may wish to examine the pupil's ability profile. Today, many tests make such profiles available. Such instruments may provide estimates of ability in areas such as number concepts, arithmetic reasoning, and verbal or spatial reasoning. Study of the pupil's profile may help the teacher reach a tentative decision concerning specific weaknesses which may be interfering with his progress. In addition, the profile may indicate strengths which may be utilized to encourage more effective learning.

Intelligence-test results may also be utilized in grouping pupils for classroom work. The intelligence-test score is, of course, only a rough index of ability to do schoolwork; many other factors enter into and influence achievement. Nevertheless, at times the teacher may well wish to consider tested intelligence in grouping his pupils. At other times he may group them on some other basis for work on units or projects which offer a variety of tasks requiring varying levels and kinds of mental ability. In deciding upon the part which the individual pupil is to play, the teacher must consider his general-ability level and his special aptitudes as well as his interests and needs.

The teacher can derive from intelligence-test results an estimate of the range of abilities represented by his class. In a class in which the range is small, the teacher's program may be quite different from that required for a class in which the pupil group has a wide range of general ability. In other instances the teacher may find that the general ability of his group is rather low or rather high by comparison with norms. In either case his expectations for the group will be influenced by the results of the tests. Clothing which is too small or too large is usually uncomfortable, and teacher expectations which do not "fit" the group and the individual are unlikely to be comfortable and satisfying for either the teacher or the pupil.

SUMMARY

Among the more urgent and vital problems of the teacher is that of developing suitable expectations for his pupils, both as a group and as individuals, in order to adapt the curriculum to the educational potentialities of individual pupils. Tests of mental maturity, intelligence, or scholastic aptitudes, as they are variously called, offer objective evidence that helps the teacher to make sound judgments about his pupils.

Intelligence tests, to use the customary label, may give a single measure, called *general intelligence,* or may provide a profile of a series of abilities. In either case the teacher's interpretation of the test results must be based upon a knowledge of the kinds of materials included in the test and upon the kinds of mental abilities which these materials sample.

In order to give meaning to test scores, results are converted into mental ages, intelligence quotients, percentile ranks, or standard scores. Each of these derived measures has its advantages and its limitations. The mental age relates the child to an age group in mental ability. The intelligence quotient is a measure of relative rate of mental development, or of relative brightness, and represents a comparison with the population on which the test was standardized. Percentile ranks make possible a comparison of the child with others in defined age groups, ordinarily his own age group. Difficulty in the interpretation of percentile ranks derives from the fact that they represent unequal units of measurement. This difficulty is overcome when standard scores are used, and the advantage of indicating status with reference to a defined age group is preserved. In using any of these mental-test "norms," the teacher must interpret the results in terms of the test materials, the sampling of mental abilities represented, and the specific conditions of testing.

Intelligence-test results enable the teacher to help his pupils make the best use of their capacities. In adapting the school program to individual differences, mental-test results can be used to promote sound diagnosis of general or specific learning problems, effective grouping of pupils for various purposes in the classroom, and judicious gearing of expectations to the abilities of the group and the individual. However, tests are tools which may be used wisely or carelessly and ineffectively, for the value of mental-test results in classroom use is determined by the wisdom of the teacher's interpretations, judgments, and applications.

STUDY AND DISCUSSION EXERCISES

1. From your reading and from a study of group mental tests, describe the bases upon which you would select a test for use with your classroom group at a specified grade level.
2. Explain: "The results of a test of intelligence which emphasizes verbal abilities may not be completely valid for all pupils in a classroom group."
3. In some schools, ability grouping on the basis of mental-test results is used as a means of facilitating instruction. Discuss the values and limitations of mental tests as a means of grouping pupils for instruction.

4. The relationship between IQ and school achievement is positive but not strong. List a number of reasons for this apparent discrepancy between ability and achievement.

5. Evaluate the concepts of MA and IQ as partial bases for:

a. deciding on the optimum grade placement of a new pupil at the elementary school level.
b. estimating the probable readiness for beginning reading.
c. estimating an individual's chances of success in a college-preparatory program in high school.

6. Mr. S., principal of an elementary school, insists that records of intelligence-test results in the cumulative records include the name and form of the test and the date of testing. Miss B. objects to this requirement, maintaining that the MA or IQ is all that is necessary. Which point of view would you support? What are your reasons?

7. Select a test of general mental ability. Analyze the materials included in the test and describe the aspects of intelligence upon which the test results are based.

SUGGESTED ADDITIONAL READINGS

Buros, Oscar K. (ed.): *The Fourth Mental Measurements Yearbook,* Highland Park, N.J.: The Gryphon Press, 1953.
Current group tests of mental ability are listed and reviewed.

Cronbach, Lee J.: *Essentials of Psychological Testing,* New York: Harper & Brothers, 1949.
Part II of this text is devoted to a discussion of tests of ability. (See Chaps. 6 through 9 especially.)

Freeman, F. S.: *Theory and Practice of Psychological Testing,* New York: Henry Holt and Company, Inc., 1950.
Chapter 3 contains definitions and analyses of intelligence. A variety of mental tests are described in Chaps. 4 through 9.

Froelich, Clifford P., and Arthur L. Benson: *Guidance Testing,* Chicago: Science Research Associates, Inc., 1948.
Chapter 3 includes a brief account of the measurement of scholastic aptitude (pp. 20–29).

Greene, Edward B.: *Measurements of Human Behavior,* New York: The Odyssey Press, Inc., 1952.

Chapter 6 contains a discussion and description of individual tests of ability. Chapter 8 is concerned with the description of group tests of ability.

Micheels, William J., and M. Ray Karnes: *Measuring Educational Achievement,* New York: McGraw-Hill Book Company, Inc., 1950.

Chapter 2 includes a discussion of tests of scholastic aptitude. Various types of items are presented.

Monroe, Walter S. (ed.): *Encyclopedia of Educational Research,* New York: The Macmillan Company, 1950.

Pages 608–610 contain a listing and brief discussion of mental tests.

Thomas, R. M.: *Judging Student Progress,* New York: Longmans, Green & Co., Inc., 1954.

Chapter 5 is concerned with evaluation of mental ability. Illustrative materials are presented.

Torgerson, T. L., and G. S. Adams: *Measurement and Evaluation,* New York: The Dryden Press, Inc., 1954.

Chapter 4 presents a discussion of mental measurement as a part of the study of the individual.

Thurstone, L. L.: *Primary Mental Abilities,* Psychometric Monograph, no. 1, Chicago: University of Chicago Press, 1938.

Evidence that intelligence consists of a number of abilities is presented.

CHAPTER SIX

Evaluating Pupil Achievement

The assessment of achievement has long been considered a primary responsibility of the school and the classroom teacher. Traditionally assessment has been concerned with the pupil's accumulation of knowledges and skills in such areas as reading, arithmetic, language, geography, and history. However, educational goals and values are steadily changing, and concepts of measurement and evaluation are being revised. Although teachers are still concerned with the scholastic achievements of pupils, evaluation of pupil status and progress is influenced by changes in our concepts of the larger goals of education. It is being increasingly recognized that academic achievements are means to the attainment of educationally worthwhile goals rather than ends in themselves. This shift in emphasis implies revisions in the nature of measuring instruments, in the purposes of measurement, and in the utilization of the results of measurement.

THE NATURE OF ACHIEVEMENT

Aptitude for learning must be distinguished from achievement, or the actual learning accomplished. However, in order to measure aptitude for learning, which is commonly identified with intelligence, the designer of intelligence tests must use an indirect approach which involves learning or achievement. Intelligence cannot be measured directly but must be inferred from its products or its application to various types of materials. Hence, in order to accomplish his purpose, the maker of intelligence tests attempts to discover what the individual has learned in situations experienced by a vast majority of persons. Thus he presumes that all persons have had opportunities to learn in these areas and that, in the majority of instances, differences in test scores reflect differences in aptitude rather than in opportunity for learning. Another possibility open to the test-maker is to develop situations that are so completely novel that very few persons are likely to have had prior experiences in the area being tested. Hence, mental tests assess the individual's capacity or aptitude only by inference from his achievements with respect to very commonplace or very novel materials and situations. In other words, the mental test is ordinarily a measure of a very general type of achievement.

Customarily, the scholastic-achievement test differs from the general-aptitude test in that results of scholastic tests are considered to be dependent upon the acquisition of specialized skills and knowledges, usually as a result of special training. For example, the individual is provided with opportunities to learn in such fields as reading, writing, music, spelling, and arithmetic, and his achievement-test results reflect his attainments in these areas. Basic to the consideration of achievement are the ideas of opportunity to learn and attainment of skill or knowledge as a result of learning.

In an intermediate position, between and overlapping the concepts upon which aptitude and achievement tests are based, are the so-called *readiness tests,* which measure the attainment of the specific abilities, skills, and knowledges required for success in a specific course of learning experiences. Readiness tests, therefore, may tap both general and specific experience areas relating to their special purposes. The tests of reading readiness widely used in the primary divisions of the elementary schools are examples.

Achievement involves the interaction of the three factors we have been discussing: aptitude for learning, readiness or preparedness for learning, and opportunity for learning. Other influential factors also enter into the achievement concept: among these are motivation, health and physical fitness, special aptitudes or disabilities, and emotional characteristics.

MEASURING ACHIEVEMENT

Teachers have many opportunities to develop achievement tests which suit the specific purposes of their classroom situations. We shall concern ourselves here, however, with standardized tests of achievement. The special values of teacher-made tests and the methods of construction of such instruments are discussed in Chapter 12.

As we have seen, evaluation is a necessary responsibility of the teacher, and measurement *contributes* to the process of evaluation. The measurement of scholastic achievement provides the teacher with basic data which will be useful to him in over-all planning, placement of pupils, pupil guidance, evaluation of the effectiveness of instruction, development of learning situations suited to the needs and capacities of individual pupils, evaluation of special needs or disabilities of pupils, discovery of areas of particular strength, and development of remedial programs. However, achievement tests do not automatically solve educational problems, nor do they necessarily further the attainment of worthwhile educational objectives. It must be reemphasized that measuring instruments are tools whose value depends upon the skill with which they are utilized.

Among the most widely used instruments of evaluation are achievement-test batteries designed to provide a general survey of skill or knowledge attained in specific academic areas. Commonly included in these batteries are tests of reading, arithmetic or mathematics, spelling, social science, physical science, and language or literature.

The basic consideration in the selection of a battery of achievement tests is the extent to which the results of testing will reflect status or progress relative to worthwhile educational objectives. The teacher should be familiar with the achievement batteries available and should study carefully the general aspects of the educational program implied by the various tests.

The well-known test batteries are of two principal types: those that emphasize acquisition of fundamental skills, as, for example, in reading and computation, and those that emphasize acquisition of factual knowledge in content areas. A number of widely used achievement-test batteries include tests of both skills and knowledge. A test battery emphasizing development of basic skills at the elementary school level might include tests of work-study skills, reading, language arts, arithmetic skills, and spelling. The test items are oriented toward the measurement of skills and processes fundamental in the area; in arithmetic, for example, items on number concepts, problem solving, and the fundamental processes of addition, subtraction, multiplication, and division might be included.

Achievement batteries designed to measure knowledge of content may include tests in the areas of literature, social studies, science, and so on. The test items will be based on subject matter suited to pupils at the grade level for which the test is designed. At the seventh-grade level, for instance, items in social studies might concern the voyages of Columbus, American history, and the geography of North America and possibly of other continents. A "content" item asks for information such as: "When did Columbus sail for America?" "Where did he land?" Skill items in the area of social studies might involve map reading or interpretation of information given in the test.

Some achievement-test batteries provide extensive surveys of educational achievement, and others deal more intensively with a limited area. The extensive or survey type of test battery typically includes a wide variety of measures, but each measure is likely to be based on a limited number of items. The practical considerations of economy of administration time and the cost of the test are essential considerations in the development of a test battery of this type. A survey battery might include tests in all or most of the following basic areas of learning: reading, arithmetic, spelling, language, study skills, social studies, science, and literature. Such extensive sampling of educational fields is likely to preclude intensive treatment in any one area. However, the survey battery provides valuable information in a relatively economical fashion.

Other tests, as we have seen, sample intensively a limited curricular area. For example, if the teacher wishes to make an intensive study of an area such as reading skills, arithmetic, social studies, science, literature, or language, tests of more limited range provide opportunities for intensive analysis.

The teacher will wish to examine the test items in order to determine whether the various aspects of achievement are adequately sampled. He will also wish to decide whether the items require (1) use of acquired skills, (2) use of acquired facts or information, (3) information or skills suited to the curriculum his pupils have been following, (4) responses which will provide data concerning pupil progress toward the objectives which he has envisaged for his classroom group.

In many instances the classroom teacher does not have the opportunity to select the tests he would prefer; frequently he is provided with test batteries selected by someone else. This situation may not be so hopeless as it seems. Study of the tests may reveal specific areas or item groups well suited to provide basic evaluative data for his special purposes. Other aspects of the test may suggest important emphases which the teacher has overlooked.

It is worthwhile to observe the thought processes required of the pupil taking the test. In making such an analysis the teacher should inquire whether the items require (1) simple memorization of facts, (2) direct utilization of simple skills, (3) skill in obtaining factual information (as in the case of reference skills), (4) application of facts to the solution of problems, (5) ability to draw conclusions or to make inferences, (6) ability to develop generalizations, (7) ability to apply general conclusions or principles to specific situations, (8) ability to see relationships within given sets of data. Although these possibilities may not ordinarily be considered to reflect curricula in the usual sense of the term, they do represent methods of evaluating achievement relative to significant educational goals such as those concerned with the development of skill in the use of higher mental processes. Through even a cursory analysis of this type, the teacher comes closer to an understanding of the test and the philosophy which it represents.

The teacher should look upon the test as a tool which, although it may not be ideally suited to his task, may yet be far more advantageous than no tool at all. By way of analogy, one does not say that a tool has no value at all because it is merely one of many required to construct a house. The teacher would do well to consider the achievement test with the same critical eye with which the carpenter or mechanic surveys his tools. Which tool among those available is best suited to the task at hand? In the absence of the ideal tool, what possibilities are there for adapting those at hand?

Using Achievement Norms

The standardized achievement test differs from the informal classroom test in a number of important respects. During the process of standardization, the test items are subjected to critical experimentation and examination to determine their usefulness as units of measurement. Uniform procedures for administering and scoring are developed. Relative values or norms are established as a basis for interpretation of the test scores. These procedures give the standardized test certain special values unobtainable in less formal tests. However, the problems involved in standardization and large-scale publication impose limitations upon the values of such tests. Thus both standardized tests and the more flexible, informal tests serve their unique purposes in the evaluation program of the classroom teacher.

Grade Norms. The type of norm most widely used with achievement tests is perhaps the grade equivalent or grade norm. The grade norm, like other types of norms, is a reference point which the teacher uses as a basis for the interpretation of achievement-test scores. It represents neither the level of achievement to be expected of an individual child nor a standard of achievement for children at a specified grade level. The norm is merely the score which is typical of the attainment of a sampling of children at a particular grade level.

In order to derive the grade norm, the teacher scores the test and accumulates total raw scores for the several areas of the test under the appropriate headings, for example, reading, arithmetic, and language. The teacher then refers to the set of norms provided with the test and records the grade norm which each score represents. For the test in Figure 8, the sum of scores in the three areas—that is, the score over the entire test—could also be converted to the appropriate grade norm. Figure 8 represents the achievement of a fifth-grade pupil on our hypothetical achievement-test battery. The first column lists the three subtests and a space for the total score for the battery. The second column lists the raw or unconverted scores, the total number of items answered correctly in each subsection. John scored 72 points in reading, 58 points in arithmetic, 69 points in language, and, by summation, 199 points over the entire battery of tests. In the third

THE ACHIEVEMENT TEST, FORM A FOR GRADES 4–7

PUPIL: John | AGE: 10.6 | DATE: 2/3/56
SCHOOL: | GRADE: 5.6 | TEACHER:

Test	*Raw score*	*Grade norm*	*Percentile norm*
Reading	72	6.3	75
Arithmetic	58	4.0	20
Language	69	5.5	50
Total	199	5.4	47

FIG. 8. A hypothetical test situation.

column are the grade norms appropriate to John's raw scores, derived from the table of grade norms which accompanied the test.

In order to interpret these norms, which are representative of John's achievement, we must ask, "What does the figure 6.3 represent with reference to the reading test?" The reference point 6.3 typifies the performance of pupils who have spent three months in the sixth grade. Although at the time of testing, John has been in the fifth grade for a period of six months, his achievement on this test of reading is at a much higher level than the typical performance of pupils of his grade; it is more typical of sixth than of fifth graders. On the basis of the same type of reasoning, we must conclude that John is experiencing some difficulty with arithmetic, or, at any rate, *with the type of material represented in our achievement test*. His grade norm in arithmetic is 4.0, which indicates that his score on the arithmetic section of the test is typical of beginning fourth graders. His scores in language and his total scores are fairly typical of pupils at his grade level, but the breakdown of the three test areas indicates a field of acceleration in reading and an area of some difficulty in arithmetic. This interpretation is based upon comparison of John's achievement on the test with the typical attainments of pupils at various grade levels. Thus grade norms provide the teacher with a means of comparing the scores of his pupils with scores typical of pupils at specified grade levels.

Percentile Norms.[1] As we have seen, grade norms make it possible to compare scores with the performance typical of pupils at various grade levels. Percentile norms, on the other hand, indicate the relative standing of a pupil within a specified age or grade group. Norms of this type help the teacher answer the question, "How well is this pupil achieving by comparison with others of his age or grade?" This comparison indicates the standing of the pupil with reference to the group which was used as a basis for establishing the norms. It has no reference to his status within his own classroom group.

Before assigning the percentile norms for a particular set of test results, the teacher should consult the test manual and study the definitions,[2] descriptions, and directions concerning

[1] For a general discussion of percentile norms, see Chap. 4, pp. 53–57.

[2] See John C. Flanagan, "Units, Scores, and Norms," in E. F. Lindquist (ed.), *Educational Measurement,* Washington: American Council on Education, 1951, pp. 717–719, for a discussion of the problem of definition with reference to percentiles.

norms. In general, the teacher will employ the following procedures:

1. Sum the scores to derive the various totals for which percentile norms are provided in the table of norms. In the example of John in Figure 8, these might be the norms for reading, arithmetic, and language and the total achievement-test score.

2. From the tables of percentile norms for the age or grade level in question, find the norms appropriate to the raw scores attained by each pupil.

3. Utilizing the definition provided in the manual, interpret the percentile norms. For example, the manual of the test John took provides the following customary definition: "A percentile norm indicates the per cent of scores of pupils at the specified grade levels which fall below that point." John's score in reading, for example, is equivalent to percentile 75. In terms of our definition, his score is higher than that of 75 per cent of pupils at his grade level. The teacher will remember that this norm refers to the group of fifth-grade pupils whose scores on this test formed the basis for the development of this particular set of percentile norms. With this concept in mind, we can conclude that John's test score indicates a relatively superior achievement in the area of reading by comparison with fifth graders generally. Similarly, the percentile norm of 20, indicating John's relative achievement in arithmetic, points to an area of some difficulty, although his score is better than that attained by 20 per cent of pupils at his grade level. The other scores may be converted and interpreted in the same way to give us a picture of John's relative achievement status.

Age Norms. Publishers of standardized tests of educational achievement commonly provide age norms, or age equivalents, in addition to grade and percentile norms as a basis for the interpretation of test scores. The age norm is interpreted in much the same manner as the grade norm, but its reference point is the typical performance of the age group rather than of the grade group. The age norm derived from general-achievement tests is frequently termed *educational age,* or EA. Age norms related to specific subject areas may be presented as *reading age, arithmetic age,* and so on.

Age equivalents are helpful when the teacher wishes to compare the reading, arithmetic, language, or educational age of a pupil with his chronological age. They also enable the teacher to compare the mental and educational ages of pupils in his classroom. However, when two sets of results are compared—mental and achievement-test results, for example—the teacher is cautioned to remember that the norms are derived from two distinctly different tests which ordinarily have been standardized on two different groups of pupils. Again, the attainment of a pupil in one subject is likely to differ from his attainment in another. In addition, there is evidence that intelligence is not a unitary function but is comprised of a number of abilities which are not necessarily closely related to one another.[3] Thus age norms of different types are not so directly comparable as they at first appear to be.

Standard-score Scales. Although standard scores are frequently presented as a basis for the interpretation of test results, the more common practice is to utilize standard-score scales as a basis for the derivation of other types of norms.[4] That is, a standard-score scale is developed from the raw scores, and these standard scores are then used to derive age, grade, or percentile norms. Such procedures are designed to utilize some of the particular advantages of standard scores. (See Chapter 4, pp. 57–63.)

[3] L. L. Thurstone, *Primary Mental Abilities,* Psychometric Monographs, no. 1, Chicago: University of Chicago Press, 1938.

[4] See, for example, *Metropolitan Achievement Tests,* Yonkers, N.Y.: World Book Company, 1946, 1947.

RELATING ABILITY AND ACHIEVEMENT

Recognition of the fact that pupils of a given grade do not all have the same capacity to achieve in any subject area has led to efforts to group pupils in such a way as to reduce the range of individual differences and to adapt curricular materials and teaching methods to the needs and capacities of individual pupils. Evaluative procedures have been designed to relate capacity and achievement on the assumption that an achievement "expectancy" can be developed for the individual pupil or for a group of pupils.

Investigations indicate that a wide range of achievement levels is to be expected in any classroom with reference to almost any curricular area.[5] Other investigations indicate that the range of individual differences in achievement is not significantly reduced by the practice of failing slow-learning pupils.[6]

The effectiveness of grouping according to general ability in reducing the range of individual differences is of questionable value, since individuals differ so markedly in specific abilities that the over-all range of differences is not likely to be markedly reduced by such practices.[7] The conclusion of

[5] Walter W. Cook, "The Functions of Measurement in the Facilitation of Learning," in E. F. Lindquist (ed.), *Educational Measurement,* Washington: American Council on Education, 1951, pp. 10–15.

[6] Walter W. Cook, *Grouping and Promotions in the Elementary School,* Minneapolis: University of Minnesota Press, 1941. See also Cook, "The Functions of Measurement in the Facilitation of Learning," in Lindquist (ed.), *op. cit.,* pp. 11–13.

[7] Clark L. Hull, "Variability in the Amount of Different Traits Possessed by the Individual," *Journal of Educational Psychology,* 18:97–104, 1927. See also A. D. Hollingshead, *An Evaluation of the Use of Certain Educational and Mental Measurements for the Purpose of Classification,* Contributions to Education, no. 302, New York: Teachers College, Columbia University, 1928; and Marvin Y. Burr, *A Study of Homogeneous Grouping,* Contributions to Education, no. 457, New York: Teachers College, Columbia University, 1931.

investigators as summarized by Cook indicates that the extent of variation in capacity and achievement would not be markedly altered if pupils were classified by chronological age rather than by grade level.[8]

In developing measures of expectancy of achievement, it has frequently been assumed that capacity to learn, as measured by intelligence tests, is closely related to achievement status. Summaries of a number of investigations of the actual relationships between measured intelligence and achievement reveal that although some relationship is evident,[9] it is far from sufficient to be used as a basis for grouping pupils. Furthermore, the degree of relationship between measured capacity and achievement varies from one subject-matter area to another.[10] The findings referred to indicate that differences between expectancy and achievement are customary.

In the attempt to answer the question, "Is this pupil working at the level of his ability?" the teacher may be tempted to relate directly mental-age norms and achievement-age norms for the pupils in his classroom. The accomplishment quotient (AQ) has been proposed as a single index of this relationship. It is derived by dividing the age norm obtained from an achievement test (EA) by the age norm obtained from a mental test (MA) and multiplying the result by 100. The formula for derivation of the AQ is:

$$AQ = \frac{EA}{MA} \times 100$$

If the mental and educational ages of a pupil are identical, his AQ is 100. He would then be considered to be achieving

[8] Cook, "The Functions of Measurement in the Facilitation of Learning," in Lindquist (ed.), *op. cit.*, pp. 10–14. See also Quinn McNemar, *The Revision of the Stanford-Binet Scale,* Boston: Houghton Mifflin Company, 1942, pp. 26–28.

[9] J. M. Stephens, *Educational Psychology,* New York: Henry Holt and Company, Inc., 1951, pp. 228–231.

[10] *Ibid.,* pp. 228–229.

at the level of his capacity. If the MA of a pupil exceeded his EA, his AQ would be less than 100 and he would be considered to be achieving at a lower level than could be expected. If, on the other hand, the EA of a pupil exceeded his MA, his IQ would be over 100 and he could be considered to be achieving at a higher level than could reasonably be expected.

For a number of reasons, the use of the AQ in relating ability and achievement is not recommended. Among these reasons are the following:

1. It is doubtful whether the relationship between achievement in different academic areas is sufficiently high to warrant the use of a composite or average index, such as EA or AQ, for this type of comparison.
2. The AQ is unreliable.
3. EA and MA should be expressed in comparable units and in terms of norms from comparable samples if a ratio of the two is to be developed. Ordinarily this is not the case.
4. There is sufficient evidence of variation among aspects of intelligence within the individual to make the use of the general mental-age index of questionable value in predicting achievement in specific subject areas.
5. Investigations of the existing relationships between intelligence-test results and achievement-test results fail to indicate the existence of such a direct relationship as that upon which the AQ is based.
6. There is a general tendency for the average AQ of pupils of high ability to show underachievement, whereas low-ability pupils in general appear to be overachieving according to their AQs.

In comparing measured ability and achievement, the teacher should use caution in drawing conclusions from average measures such as MA and EA. Obtained differences present certain facts with only limited reliability, but these facts may help the teacher frame hypotheses as to the reasons for the difference in the case of the individual pupil. By testing these hypotheses carefully, the teacher may reach conclusions which will give him direction in his work with individuals.

THE ANALYSIS AND DIAGNOSIS OF LEARNING PROBLEMS

The total score obtained from an achievement-test battery gives the teacher some idea of the pupil's accomplishment. No analysis of specific areas of achievement is indicated; the result is analogous to the remark of the patient who tells his doctor, "I don't feel well." Such a statement of fact is of relatively little value except as an indication of a need for assistance. The medical practitioner is likely to ask questions designed to analyze the situation, such as, "Do you have pain?" "Where is the pain located?" "When do you feel this way?" "How long have you felt this way?" The answers to these questions concerning the patient's condition may result in a specific diagnosis of his problems.

Similarly, subject scores on an achievement-test battery may help the teacher locate and diagnose learning problems. An analysis of achievement in the following fundamental curricular areas is readily available to the teacher, as indicated by the title of the subtests of the *Metropolitan Achievement Test:* (1) reading, (2) vocabulary, (3) arithmetic fundamentals, (4) arithmetic problems, (5) language usage, and (6) spelling.[11]

Since norms are commonly provided for each area as well as for the entire test, such a test makes it possible for the teacher to analyze the relative strengths and weaknesses of his class and of individual pupils. Although this type of anal-

[11] *Metropolitan Achievement Tests, Elementary Battery,* Yonkers, N.Y.: World Book Company, 1948.

ysis is very general in nature, it may be useful in indicating areas requiring special emphasis. In this way, study of the test results can increase the effectiveness of the educational program.

However, detailed diagnostic procedures must be based upon a more specific analysis of test results. An analysis of the processes required in such areas as arithmetic, language, or reading indicates that numerous skills are involved. Arithmetic fundamentals, for example, involve addition, subtraction, multiplication, and division. A test in arithmetic fundamentals subdivided according to these four areas will reveal strengths or weaknesses which the teacher should take into account.

Exact diagnosis of learning problems may involve even more specific analysis of learning difficulties. For instance, the process of subtraction in itself involves a number of skills, any of which may represent a point of difficulty for the individual pupil. The following list indicates some possibilities of analysis within the process of subtraction:[12] simple combinations; borrowing; zeros; subtracting money; subtracting numerators; common denominator; whole from mixed numbers; borrowing, mixed numbers; fractions and decimals; writing decimals; and denominate numbers. Analysis of test results at this level of specificity helps the teacher to determine more exactly the particular problems his students are experiencing in the process of subtraction.

Analysis of the scores from general-achievement batteries, therefore, will provide the teacher with information in proportion to the specificity of the results. However, the number of items which involve a specific process must be strictly limited in a general-achievement test, and the results for any small group of items are likely to be statistically unreliable,

[12] E. W. Tiegs and W. W. Clark, *California Achievement Tests, Intermediate Battery,* Los Angeles: California Test Bureau, 1950.

although they may be suggestive of possible difficulties. To provide opportunity for more comprehensive analysis, standardized diagnostic tests or tests especially developed by the teacher may be utilized when a general area of difficulty has been identified or when intensive analysis of a survey test of achievement has indicated a possible source of difficulty. When pupils appear to be experiencing difficulty in a specific area of arithmetic, as, for example, in multiplication of whole numbers, the teacher may administer a test designed for intensive analysis of this area.[13] Since a test so designed provides numerous items related to each skill required in the process under study, the results are more clearly indicative of the specific difficulty the pupils are experiencing than are the results of more generalized tests.

Although this discussion has been focused upon the use of standardized achievement tests, adequate analysis and diagnosis of educational problems ordinarily involves consideration of the mental abilities, educational background, health and physical status, environment, and emotional status of the pupil. Analysis of achievement-test results, however, may play an important role in educational diagnosis and the establishment of effective instructional and remedial procedures. The value of the tests as tools in this process will reside in the skill with which the test results are utilized by the teacher in forming hypotheses to guide his work with his pupils.

SUMMARY

Perhaps the most widely used instruments of educational evaluation are achievement-test batteries, which are designed to provide a general survey of attainment of academic skills and knowledges. For the teacher, the basic consideration in

[13] L. J. Brueckner, *Diagnostic Tests and Self-helps in Arithmetic,* Los Angeles: California Test Bureau, 1955.

the selection and utilization of such test batteries is the extent to which the results of testing reflect pupil progress relative to worthwhile educational goals.

In selecting and preparing to use a standardized achievement test, the teacher should examine the organization of the test and the various types of skill, knowledge, and thought required of the examinee. This study will help the teacher to relate the results to the educational goals which he has formulated for his pupils. The test is in reality a tool which may be useful to varying degrees as an instrument providing evaluative data. Its value is largely dependent upon the skill with which it is used.

The tables of norms which accompany standardized achievement tests provide the teacher with a basis for interpreting the test results. Grade norms or grade equivalents indicate roughly the status of the pupil with reference to scores typical of various grade groups. Percentile norms make it possible for the teacher to compare the pupil with others of the same grade or age who comprised the standardization population. Age norms, or age equivalents, provide a basis for comparison of pupil performance with that of various age groups. Where standard scores are presented, the teacher is provided with scales representing equal units of measurement. Such scales are of value because they make possible comparisons among test batteries.

Although various methods of relating general ability and achievement have been proposed, such relationships are generally hazardous. Although some relationships exist between measured ability and achievement, measured ability to learn is not a sufficient base for establishing an expectancy of achievement.

The teacher may conduct analyses and attempt to diagnose learning problems at varying levels of intensity. Analysis helps the teacher to formulate hypotheses as to possible causes of learning difficulties and provides some basis for instructional procedures designed to overcome them. The more specific and reliable the analysis, the more likely it is that exact sources of learning difficulties will be located. However, diagnosis must ordinarily be based upon observations more comprehensive in nature than the results of an achievement-test battery. Intensive study of achievement-test results may, however, help the teacher derive maximum benefit from these instruments as aids to instructional planning and procedures.

STUDY AND DISCUSSION EXERCISES

1. Suggest some possible reasons why measured ability and achievement are not so closely related as might be expected.
2. Study a general-achievement battery and outline the educational philosophy it appears to represent.
3. Select a subdivision of an achievement-test battery and list the detailed skills and knowledges which pupils must possess in order to succeed in the selected test area.
4. What do you consider to be the teacher's responsibilities in utilizing standardized tests of achievement in the classroom?
5. What are some of the purposes which you as a teacher might have in mind when planning to administer a general-achievement-test battery?
6. Analyze the specific skills required of the pupil in performing any one of the following functions: (*a*) two-column addition; (*b*) multiplication of two-digit numbers; (*c*) punctuation, including quotations; (*d*) locating significant physical features on a map of South America; and (*e*) locating reference materials in an encyclopedia.

SUGGESTED ADDITIONAL READINGS

Buros, Oscar K. (ed.): *The Fourth Mental Measurements Yearbook,* Highland Park, N.J.: The Gryphon Press, 1953.
Includes a listing and evaluation of currently available tests of educational achievement.

Freeman, F. S.: *Theory and Practice of Psychological Testing,* New York: Henry Holt and Company, Inc., 1950, chap. 11.

This general discussion of the measurement of educational achievement includes a presentation of samples of the contents of representative tests in this area.

Gates, A. I., A. T. Jersild, T. R. McConnell, and R. C. Challman: *Educational Psychology,* 3d ed., New York: The Macmillan Company, 1948, pp. 543–552, 561–567.

Presents a general account of the appraisal of pupil progress through the use of tests and includes suggestions for approaches to educational diagnosis.

Goodenough, F. L.: *Mental Testing,* New York: Rinehart & Company, Inc., 1949, chap. 22.

In connection with this chapter the author presents a considered account of the problems of relating ability and accomplishment.

Greene, E. B.: *Measurements of Human Behavior,* rev. ed., New York: The Odyssey Press, Inc., 1952, chap. 7.

This chapter includes a discussion of the measurement of educational achievement and presents examples of measurement possibilities in a variety of academic areas.

Jordan, A. M.: *Measurement in Education,* New York: McGraw-Hill Book Company, Inc., 1953, chaps. 5–13.

These chapters present a detailed account of methods and instruments for the measurement of attainment in a wide variety of subject areas.

CHAPTER SEVEN

Estimating Readiness for Learning

Children differ in their readiness to undertake learning tasks. To be effective, instruction must take into account individual differences in the abilities, skills, and knowledges which are requisite to successful learning experiences. In certain curricular areas, many of these abilities, skills, and knowledges have been defined and readiness tests have been devised to measure them. Such tests provide the teacher with data about his pupils which are helpful in planning learning experiences.

READINESS AND LEARNING

The term *readiness* may be applied to any aspect of physical, mental, emotional, or experiential maturity which is requisite to a learning task. A child learns best when he is "ready." He does not learn, or learns slowly and with difficulty, when he lacks the necessary maturity.

Although the readiness concept has been most commonly applied to school beginners, it holds for all grades and age levels and for all types of subject matter. For example, it is possible to define requisite abilities, skills, and knowledges in an area as specific as two-place division at the fifth-grade level[1] or in such general areas as foreign languages, advanced mathematics, or science. The prognostic or special-aptitude tests designed to predict success in certain of these curricular areas are closely related to the readiness tests which are utilized with school beginners.

There appear to be optimal mental ages for learning such aspects of arithmetic as addition, addition and subtraction of like fractions, and long division.[2] A readiness test has been found useful in predicting success or failure in arithmetic.[3] Mental age has been demonstrated to be related to chances of success in beginning reading, and the results of readiness tests and rating scales designed to measure reading readiness indicate likelihood of success or failure in this task.[4]

These experimental results serve to illustrate the fact that a detailed understanding of the requirements of the learning task, together with an accurate evaluation of the readiness of the learner, may be very valuable to the teacher in curriculum planning. This does not mean, however, that the teacher should stand idly by waiting for the children to become "ready" for learning. Such skills as arithmetic, reading, and writing develop only as a result of learning. Carefully planned instruction can often enhance readiness for learning in such areas.[5] Evaluation of readiness is possible and readiness pro-

[1] W. A. Brownell, "Arithmetical Readiness as a Practical Classroom Concept," *Elementary School Journal,* 52:15–22, 1951.

[2] C. W. Washburne, "Mental Age and the Arithmetic Curriculum," *Journal of Educational Research,* 23:210–231, 1931. See also L. B. Ames and F. L. Ilg, "Developmental Trends in Arithmetic," *Journal of Genetic Psychology,* 79:3–28, 1951.

[3] L. J. Brueckner, "The Development and Validation of an Arithmetic Readiness Test," *Journal of Educational Research,* 40:496–502, 1947.

[4] William Kottmeyer, "Readiness for Reading," *Elementary English,* 24:355–366, 528–535, 1947.

[5] C. M. Scott, "An Evaluation of Training in Readiness Classes," *Elementary School Journal,* 48:26–32, 1947.

grams can be planned in any area of learning in which the requisite skills, abilities, and knowledges can be differentiated. The manuals of directions for readiness tests frequently offer suggestions which may form the basis for such programs.

READINESS TESTS

Like other tests, readiness tests may be general or specific in nature. In developing a readiness test, the test-maker analyzes the learning activities involved in the subject area, attempting to define the components of the background requisite to effective learning. He then designs test scales and items which provide estimates of pupil performance in these areas. As with other standardized tests, a careful study is made of the results of testing, revisions may be made in the original test, and final forms of the test are developed. Norms are then established and indications of the practical values and possibilities are presented in the manual of directions.

The *Metropolitan Readiness Tests* may exemplify a general readiness test. It was designed to measure the traits and achievements of school beginners that contribute to their readiness for first-grade instruction,[6] and it does not require the ability to read. The tests include measures of comprehension of language, including phrases, sentences, and vocabulary; visual activities involving perception of similarities; tests of number knowledge; and a copying test which provides a measure of visual perception and motor control. The authors believe that the results of the test may be of value in estimating readiness for reading, arithmetic, and writing. The manual of directions presents evidence of the value of the tests in predicting first-grade achievement as measured by the *Primary 1 Battery* of the *Metropolitan Achievement Tests.*

[6] *Metropolitan Readiness Tests: Directions for Administration,* Yonkers, N.Y.: World Book Company, 1949, p. 1.

ILLUSTRATIVE READINESS TEST ITEMS*
From the *Metropolitan Readiness Tests*

Test 3. *Information*

9. Mark the thing to travel in across the ocean.

 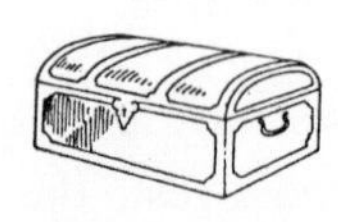  

Test 4. *Matching*

Look at the picture in the middle with the frame drawn around it. Find another picture just like it and draw a frame around it.

Test 5. *Numbers*

2. See the row of hats. Mark the middle hat.

Test 6. *Copying*

1. You are to copy every picture in this column.

* Selected from Gertrude H. Hildreth and Nellie L. Griffiths, *Metropolitan Readiness Tests, Form R,* Yonkers, N.Y.: World Book Company, 1949. (Directions adapted from the manual of directions.)

A number of tests specific to reading readiness have been devised. The Monroe *Reading-aptitude Tests* may serve as an illustration of this type of instrument.[7] The following tests, none of which require reading, are included:

1. Visual tests designed to detect perceptual reversals and to measure ocular-motor control and memory for forms.
2. Motor tests of speed, steadiness, and writing.
3. Auditory tests which indicate abilities in word discrimination, sound blending, and auditory memory.
4. Articulation tests designed to evaluate speed and level of articulation ability.
5. Language tests which include measures of vocabulary, classification, and sentence ability.
6. Laterality tests which indicate hand, eye, and foot preference.

Administration

The following rules should be carefully observed in giving a test:

1. The teacher should be thoroughly acquainted with the tests and with the detailed instructions and directions given in the test manual before attempting to administer the tests.

2. The test should be given in a quiet room and interruptions and disturbances should be avoided during testing time.

3. Small children should be tested in small groups.

4. It is important to test children at a time when they are not fatigued or overly excited. Pupil attitudes in the testing situation are an important consideration in interpreting test results. It is therefore necessary to do everything possible to ensure a cooperative attitude on the part of the pupils being tested.

5. Where group tests are used, the testing should be done

[7] Marion Monroe, *Reading-aptitude Tests*, Boston: Houghton Mifflin Company, 1935.

by the children's own teacher. This is especially important in the case of young children, who are sometimes disturbed by the presence of unfamiliar persons.

6. Short testing periods are necessary for young children. It is preferable to test over several short periods rather than to attempt to administer the entire test at one long sitting.

7. Pupils should be seated comfortably and in such a manner that they are not easily disturbed by one another.

8. In testing small children, the names and other data required should be filled in by the teacher before the testing begins.

9. The printed directions for administering the test should be followed implicitly, since any marked deviation from these instructions is likely to invalidate the results.

Interpreting the Results

Norms are provided as the basis for interpretation of the results of readiness tests. These norms may be of various types. For example, the norms for the Monroe *Aptitude Tests* are presented in the form of percentile ranks. Norms of this type are presented for the total test and for each of the five scales, which include measures of visual, auditory, motor, articulatory, and language abilities. As a result of experience in using the test in connection with other measures, Monroe suggests interpretation of the results in terms of probable student status as superior, average, or retarded. She also proposes methods calculated to overcome a variety of difficulties which pupils might encounter in beginning reading.[8]

A somewhat different approach to interpretation makes use of raw scores, presenting the "probable per cent of failure" in terms of the test results.[9] Still another test manual presents

[8] Marion Monroe, *Manual of Directions, Reading-aptitude Tests,* Boston: Houghton Mifflin Company, 1935.

[9] J. M. Lee and W. W. Clark, *Manual of Directions, Lee-Clark Reading-readiness Test,* Los Angeles: California Test Bureau, 1943.

percentile ranks, letter ratings, and readiness status and offers interpretations of letter ratings and readiness status.[10]

As we have seen test scores and norms provide valuable information, but interpretations of test results must be based upon a recognition of the limitations of the measuring instrument. Readiness tests provide information covering a limited range of abilities and skills. Other factors which enter into readiness for a learning task must ordinarily be estimated by means of other devices or by observation. Furthermore, since it is difficult to get accurate test results with young children, the results of readiness tests used with preprimary or primary-grade children should be interpreted with due regard not only for the limitations of the instrument but also for the difficulties of testing young children.

UTILIZING THE RESULTS OF TESTING

In actual practice, readiness-test results provide the teacher with data that are valuable when used in conjunction with other information about the children in his classroom. This additional information might well include evaluations of mental age, emotional and social adjustment, health, vision, hearing, speech and language development, experiential background, ability to solve problems, sense of sequence and relationships, attention, memory, motor ability, handedness, and eyedness. When used in conjunction with such data, readiness-test results may be useful as (1) an aid in estimating the readiness of a pupil to do the work included in the area of testing; (2) an aid in grouping pupils for instructional purposes; (3) an aid in analysis of instructional needs of a preparatory nature; (4) an aid in estimating the strengths and weaknesses of pupils in areas fundamental to the learning

[10] G. H. Hildreth and N. L. Griffiths, *Metropolitan Readiness Tests,* Yonkers, N.Y.: World Book Company, 1948.

task; (5) a guide to the teacher in adapting instruction to the needs of the group and the individual; and (6) a source of significant data useful to the teacher in planning work with pupils.

Readiness tests provide at least a partial basis for estimating the pupil's chances of success in a particular area of learning, for diagnosing specific weaknesses, and for helping the teacher to plan a course of preparatory learning. That is, if a pupil achieves a relatively low score on a test of word comprehension, he would benefit from a program of experiences designed to increase ability in this area before he begins a reading program. A low score on a test of knowledge of numbers or number concepts indicates the need for experiences in this area preparatory to studying arithmetic. Low scores on tests of vision or hearing may indicate the need for special medical examinations or for a program designed to improve visual or auditory skills.

Although many of the skills required by school curricula may be developed to some extent by carefully planned instruction, readiness is in part a matter of maturation rather than of learning, and maturational factors are only in part amenable to instruction. Hence the teacher may discover that certain pupils in his group appear to be unable to profit significantly from a program directed toward preparation for a learning task. Certain general skills, however, may be improved where the activities involved are geared to the child's capacity. The development of such skills may be enhanced through activities designed to encourage:

1. Alert listening.
2. Ability to follow instructions and directions.
3. Keenness of observation, as in discrimination of likenesses and differences, perception of form, quantity, size, color, and so on.

4. Questions, conversations, evaluations, judgments, and sharing of experiences.
5. Development of meanings through varied planned experiences.
6. Active attention, recall, and organization of meaningful materials.
7. Development of skills of observation and interpretation of pictures, events, and materials.
8. Development of skills in problem solving, planning, and construction.
9. Development of motor skills related to the various learning tasks.

Harrison[11] has proposed that reading readiness may be influenced by instruction which fosters:

1. Extension of meaningful concepts.
2. Extension of spoken vocabulary.
3. Accurate enunciation and pronunciation.
4. A desire to read.
5. Correct use of simple sentences.
6. Ability to do problematic thinking.
7. Ability to keep a series of events in mind.

Carter and McGinnis[12] present the following list of activities to facilitate reading readiness:

1. Looking at picture books and telling stories suggested by the pictures.
2. Dramatizing children's stories.
3. Telling short stories in response to questions.
4. Listening to children's stories and poems.
5. Telling, in response to questions, what happened in a familiar story.

[11] M. Lucile Harrison, *Reading Readiness,* rev. ed., Boston: Houghton Mifflin Company, 1939, p. 6, Fig. 1.

[12] H. J. L. Carter and D. J. McGinnis, *Learning to Read,* New York: McGraw-Hill Book Company, Inc., 1953, pp. 63–64. By permission.

6. Making scrapbooks of pictures taken on a vacation trip; telling group of trip.
7. Looking through magazines for interesting pictures and later telling original stories about them.
8. Bringing interesting books and phonograph records from home to be shared with the group.
9. Sharing juvenile books with others; understanding that books belong to children and that they may be used by them.
10. Telling of one's own experiences before a group.

Although these suggestions for preparatory activities have reference specifically to reading, they may, in principle, be applied to other areas of instruction. For example, activities designed to stimulate children's interest in and develop meaningful concepts related to arithmetic could include dramatizations, play stories, games, story telling, picture interpretations, and manipulation of concrete materials, all involving quantities. In the fields of social studies and science meanings are developed in terms of experiences which can be preparatory as well as directly instructional in nature.

The teacher, however, will recognize that certain aspects of readiness cannot be learned but are dependent upon maturational characteristics. That is, there is a period in a child's development when it becomes possible for him to undertake certain tasks; prior to this time, these tasks may be difficult or perhaps impossible. Training in the absence of the required maturation is not effective, and a child may be as unprepared for some aspects of a readiness program as he is for the learning task which is envisaged as the outcome of the training. However, school is not necessarily a loss for those children who seem to be markedly below the stage of readiness for some types of learning; they may be gaining in social skill and in familiarity with new surroundings or broadening their experiences so that when they do become ready for reading and arithmetic they will have somewhat fewer concomitant adjustments to make.

SUMMARY

Children differ in many characteristics that influence their readiness to undertake the variety of learning tasks involved in the school curriculum. In certain areas of learning, particularly in the areas of reading and arithmetic, the specific tasks have been defined and tests have been devised to measure the extent to which the child possesses the required skills. Such tests are generally called readiness tests, and most of them have been devised for and used with school beginners. The concept of readiness, however, does not necessarily apply to this age group alone, nor to only one or two areas of learning.

Ideally, teacher estimates of readiness should include mental, motor, social, and emotional maturity as well as the specific abilities, skills, and knowledges required for the learning task. It has been demonstrated, however, that the results of readiness tests are predictive of success in such areas as reading, and that readiness programs designed to prepare the child for the learning task to come do increase the child's chances of success.

In his selection of a readiness test the teacher should be guided by the needs of his group. The extent to which the test will enable the teacher to analyze the skills, abilities, and achievements involved in learning the skill will be an important consideration. The teacher should create the best possible conditions for administering the test and should follow the standard directions implicitly if the results are to be interpreted in terms of the norms and classifications included in the test manual. Typically, readiness-test manuals provide the teacher with many suggestions for the interpretation and utilization of results.

If test results are to be used for more than screening purposes, the teacher may plan a program of learning experiences designed to develop the skills and knowledges which will prepare the child for the more formal instruction to follow. But many factors other than specific skills will probably enter into the teacher's consideration in planning such a program, since maturational factors may impose a limitation upon the effectiveness of specific instruction.

STUDY AND DISCUSSION EXERCISES

1. Outline as specifically as you can the skills which you feel are involved in one of the following activities: writing, addition of simple fractions, map reading, library reference, use of the dictionary, or some other specific learning task in the area of your interest.
2. What activities are you able to devise which might represent a readiness program for the learning task which you have analyzed above?
3. Indicate the characteristics which you would study in estimating a child's readiness for reading. Suggest the possible significance of each in relation to the child's chances of success in your reading program.
4. In what ways might the results of selected reading-readiness tests be utilized in developing a readiness program for school beginners?
5. Suggest reasons for using mental tests as part of the readiness battery. If possible, validate your conclusions by reference to the literature on readiness.
6. It has been suggested that teacher ratings are predictive of readiness. On what bases would you rate a child as to his possible chances of success in beginning arithmetic?

SUGGESTED ADDITIONAL READING

Adams, F., L. Gray, and D. Reese: *Teaching Children to Read,* New York: The Ronald Press Company, 1949.

Chapters 4, 5, and 6 present a discussion on the nature and development of reading readiness. A reading-readiness check list is presented in chap. 4.

Buros, Oscar K. (ed.): *The Fourth Mental Measurements Yearbook,* Highland Park, N.J.: The Gryphon Press, 1953.

Pages 566–575 present information concerning general readiness and reading-readiness tests.

Carter, H. J. L., and D. J. McGinnis: *Learning to Read,* New York: McGraw-Hill Book Company, Inc., 1953.

Chapter 5 includes a discussion of activities designed to prepare children for reading.

Greene, E. B., *Measurements of Human Behavior,* rev. ed., New York: The Odyssey Press, Inc., 1952, pp. 99–103.

These pages present a discussion of measures of reading readiness.

Greene, H. A., A. N. Jorgensen, and R. Gerberich: *Measurement and Evaluation in the Elementary School,* New York: Longmans, Green & Co., Inc., 1942.

Chapter 15 contains a discussion of readiness tests.

Harrison, M. Lucile: *Reading Readiness,* rev. ed., Boston: Houghton Mifflin Company, 1939.

This book deals with the problem of reading readiness, describing tests and presenting suggestions for readiness programs.

Hildreth, G.: *Readiness for School Beginners,* Yonkers, N. Y.: World Book Company, 1950.

Chapter 3 contains suggestions for exploring general readiness of school beginners. Chapter 4 includes a discussion of readiness tests and their uses.

Monroe, W. S. (ed.): *Encyclopedia of Educational Research,* New York: The Macmillan Company, 1950.

Pages 879–880 present a discussion of results of research in readiness for reading, spelling, handwriting, and arithmetic.

Wood, B. D., and R. Haefner: *Measuring and Guiding Individual Growth,* Morristown, N.J.: Silver Burdett Company, 1948.

Readiness and readiness tests are discussed in chap. 9 of this readable text.

CHAPTER EIGHT

Appraising Personality

Educational tests are customarily classified as ability, achievement, or personality tests. The teacher must bear in mind, however, that fundamentally these different categories represent simply different vantage points; the various tests provide different views of the pupil. Intelligence or aptitude is intimately related to achievement, and both intelligence and accomplishment are limited aspects of the total personality of the child. In short, all techniques of measurement and evaluation are approaches to the understanding of personality. Thus, personality appraisal is treated here in a separate chapter only for the sake of convenience, for the totality which is the child can be fragmented only in textbooks and in academic discussion.

THE MEANING OF PERSONALITY

Personality is a term which designates the person as he behaves in his characteristic milieu. It embraces what he is, was, and can or will be; it is what he hopes to be, loves, hates, fears, and is confident of, and how he works and plays. Because of the inclusiveness of the concept, intelligence tests and achievement tests are at best *approaches* to the understanding of the total personality, and we shall deal here only with the facets of personality that are especially important in the conduct of school life.

Many of the significant aspects of personality concern relationships with others. Ways of adjusting to others, ways of relating oneself to them, ease of communication, and trust or distrust of both intimates and strangers are significant aspects of personality. To measure this tangible and important facet of personality, test makers have devised social-adjustment questionnaires and inventories and personality schedules containing a large proportion of questions that sample interpersonal relations. The popular concept of personality concerns this social aspect almost exclusively: the word is commonly taken to mean attractiveness to others; a person who is almost automatically liked by others is said to have a "wonderful personality." This social phase of personality is indeed important; the creative genius must communicate his ideas to others, and to the extent that he fails to do this he is popularly thought to have a "poor" personality. Similarly, the person who can establish easy contacts with others, even if he is of limited intelligence, is said to have an effective personality. Limiting personality to sociability has certain advantages where testing is concerned, but, as will be shown in the section entitled "Personality Inventories," some difficult technical problems arise in evaluation.

The following definition of personality emphasizes sociability: personality is the total pattern of behavior and behavior tendencies as they affect others; it is the adjustment of the individual as it affects others. Such a definition introduces a difficult problem in the evaluation of personality—namely, the fact that the teacher's evaluation of the pupil, or any person's evaluation of another, is dependent upon *the perception of*

the evaluator. One's description of another reveals, at least to some extent, what one is himself. This is true not only in verbal descriptions but also in instruments designed to appraise personality. Specifically, an instrument for giving an indication of adjustment reflects such factors as the interests, scholastic background, and experience of the author of the device. It is extremely important to keep this in mind as we deal with personality appraisal, because it will help us to exercise the proper restraint in interpreting the instruments that purport to measure so multifaceted a concept as the human personality.

Some specialists define personality as a degree of consistency—the extent to which a person may be depended upon to behave in specific ways in his day-to-day conduct. Others refer to this degree of consistency as "character." The distinction is academic, however, because in the larger sense, character, like intelligence and achievement, is one of the many aspects of personality. Regardless of whether we call it character or personality, the element of consistency is important. In fact, the whole object of personality appraisal is to predict what the individual is *likely* to do—how he is likely to behave, what situations probably will upset him—so that we may help him more effectively. If it were not for this consistency, there would be little chance of predicting probable reactions. Thus the purpose of instruments for appraising personality is to determine those consistent elements by asking the subject or persons who know the subject what his responses to certain situations have been. His future actions are predicted on the basis of his answers.

Personality refers to inner, unobserved motives and proclivities as well as to external, observable behavior. The importance of the "inner man," the "private world" of the individual, is indicated by the fact that a substantial amount of mental ill health, or personality disintegration, is justifiably attributed to the individual's lack of understanding of his "true self." Misunderstanding between persons is often due to the difficulty of communication between these inner but basic and fundamental selves. Hence, another significant approach to the study and understanding of personality is the acquiring of clues to the nature of these hidden aspects of attitude and conduct.

Misconceptions in Appraising Personality

Some obvious misconceptions concerning personality need to be briefly mentioned. Many people still fail to recognize the fallacy of categorizing or "typing" personalities without allowing for "in betweens," in spite of the conclusive evidence of psychology and sociology. The idea that there is a relationship between hair color and temperament has been found to be erroneous, yet one frequently hears personality interpreted according to this misconception. The fact that there is no connection between personality characteristics and inherent racial factors has been demonstrated in psychology and anthropology, but one still hears unenlightened references of this type to Negroes, Mexicans, Japanese, and other groups. Sometimes character traits are associated with religious differences, i.e., the selfishness of the Jews. Data from careful research point to the fact that correlations between race or religion and character traits are so low as to render invalid any inferences regarding individuals that are derived from such generalizations. It is well known that, aside from cultural factors, the differences between races are slight. The safe conclusion is that differences between races and religious groups are much slighter than are the differences within them.

The fact that one cannot judge personality from appearance remains for many teachers mere academic knowledge, for teachers still refer to "bright-looking children" or "obvious dullards." There are two reasons why teachers should avoid appraising personality on the basis of appearance. First, there are clinical "types" of mental defect, such as Mongolism, cretinism, hydrocephalism, and microcephalism, which have recognizable facial and bodily characteristics. But these recognizable features are not present inside the range of what are considered to be normal individuals. Thus we will miss the mark if we use appearance as the criterion when working with typical school children. Second, teachers, like other persons, tend to read into what they see what they want to see; hence, their judgment of personality, even after a period of acquaintance, must be cautious.

The belief that there is an accepted norm for personality development is a misconception. Some educational and psychological literature creates the impression that extrovertism and sociocentric behavior should be the norm—norm in this case meaning a standard. Other competent scholars emphasize that "it takes all kinds"—that there is a place in society for both the extrovert and the introvert and for all those who come between the extremes. Some pupils are well adjusted even though they are not highly social or outgoing individuals. In a democracy, it is recognized that different individuals make their contributions to the total welfare of society in different ways. The school might well take the position that the development of uniqueness (within limits, of course) is a definite responsibility. Hence, as teachers we should not necessarily encourage all boys to be athletes, and we need not necessarily worry about girls who do not seem to enjoy dancing. Such differences among pupils need not disturb us so long as they do not display symptoms, or patterns of symptoms, of less-than-desirable adjustment. The defect of some standardized tests of personality is that their norms seem to imply that deviation from a hypothetical average is necessarily an undesirable thing.

Another problem in dealing with personality is the difficulty of defining traits. For example, different interpretations are placed on "honesty," "application," "dependability," and "adequacy of feelings of personal worth." This difficulty contrasts with the difficulty of defining intelligence. Intelligence has many facets, but most of them are recognized as aspects of intelligence. However, when personality traits differ in degree, they may become something else. Thus, self-reliance is an extension of dependence, but if it develops still further it becomes selfish egotism. As one outgrows submission, he becomes ascendant, but if the characteristic develops still more, the individual is called domineering and with further development of the trait, tyrannical. Thus personality testing deals with varying degrees of different but intimately related traits. As difficult as it is to accept a measurement of intelligence as being valid and reliable, it is still more difficult to place credence in personality tests, since trait definition is even more elusive than definition of abilities.

A misconception reflected in many tests is that personality is static. The fact is that personality is both complex and variable. People not only experience gradual change, but their actions are variable within a few moments. This principle does not conflict with consistency in personality; the variability of behavior has been partially described in the statement that the manifestation of a trait is specific to a situation. For example, a person may be honest when it comes to shunning the use of his neighbor's answers on an examination, but he may not be honest when it comes to returning extra change he has received at the ticket window of a movie. One may be neat in the care of his room at home but exceedingly careless with the appearance of the spelling and arithmetic papers he presents to the teacher. Thus in using adjustment inventories it is well for teachers to bear in mind the difficulties involved in getting an accurate picture of "the total situation."

The Fallacy of Types

There seems to be a well-nigh universal temptation to classify people. Such opposites as the good and the bad, the white and the black, the new and the old, the traditional and the progressive are indicative of this tendency. One of the early attempts at classification was a differentiation of body types and an attempt to parallel these types with personality characteristics. E. Kretschmer postulated three major types of body build with corresponding personality attributes—the pyknic, the asthenic, and the athletic. Periodic follow-up studies have indicated that the "types" are actually continuous and therefore the classification is futile. Despite the experimental evidence, there are periodic recurrences of schemes for typifying. Dominance-submission and introversion-extroversion are not far from such older categories as sanguine, choleric, and phlegmatic. The attractiveness of the practice of "typing" personalities is exemplified in the remarks of teachers characterizing pupils as being normal or abnormal, academic or mechanically minded, and friendly or hostile.

As we have seen, evaluating personality on the basis of appearance is dangerous precisely because of the element of truth involved. Similarly, "typifying" is dangerous because of the degree of validity inherent in the descriptions; there *are* introverted, sanguine, academically gifted, and mechanically apt persons. But there are also many people between the two extremes, and there are those who possess some of two or more characteristics, and there are different manifestations of a given trait in various situations. It follows that measures or evaluations of personality based on a bimodal, trimodal or even multimodal distribution should be interpreted with studied caution. Although such questionnaires or scales have certain values, those values do not necessarily reside in the fact of classification. We may be aided in our understanding of children by these personality measures, but it is not because the pupils have been "typed."

PERSONALITY RATING SCALES

A rating blank, scale, or schedule is a formal set of questions asked of one person about another or a self-rating form in which the individual checks certain questions about himself. The questions are answered in terms of the degree to which the individual has the trait or does the act described in the question. Thus, the question may be, "What is his (or your) attitude when facing difficult schoolwork?" Answers may be arranged along a continuous line with a mark indicating divisions between very poor, poor, average, good, or excellent. Such evaluations are, however, considered to be too vague to be maximally useful, and descriptive phrases are believed to lead to greater accuracy. Thus the item, "How effectively does he apply himself to an activity?" is answered in a weighted scale, allowing a certain number of points for each answer. These answers range from "(1) Shifts about in random fashion," through "(3) Sticks to an activity until something more interesting is presented," to "(5) Voluntarily pursues an activity for two or more days consecutively." Many of the more recent rating scales use the more precisely descriptive approach, which has the advantage of strengthening the objective element in the scale.

Rating scales are available for classroom use from the nursery and kindergarten level through the college level and are sometimes used in business and industry. By means of them, many different aspects of personality can be investigated: there are, for example, scales measuring ascendance-submission, behavior maturity, self-adjustment, delinquent and predelinquent behavior, attitudes, interests, and social adjustment. Sometimes the schedule includes several kinds of situations under a single heading; for example, an adolescent rating schedule includes fear, family emotion, family authority, feeling of inadequacy, nonfamily authority, maturity, escape, neurotic traits, and compensation.[1]

Teachers who wish to use personality rating scales are advised to consult the current volume of the *Mental Measurements Yearbook,* where they will find descriptions of the kinds of behaviors which are supposed to be analyzed and the levels for which the schedules are specifically designed. More pertinent still, the instruments have been critically examined and carefully evaluated by scholars in the measurement field. The reading of these appraisals will help teachers to come to an evaluation regarding each scale which will enable them to use the results most accurately and effectively.

A number of precautions must be observed in using personality schedules; some of these were anticipated earlier in the chapter. (1) It is just as difficult to formulate a precise definition of the traits that are evaluated by means of the scales as it is to define personality. (2) There are no widely accepted norms for what should constitute desirable behavior. (3) The "specificity" of behavior makes it unlikely that the demonstration of a particular trait in one situation will be an accurate sample of that same trait as it might appear in another context. (4) The element of and danger from subjectivity is an ever-present complicating factor. The last seven words in the following statement, taken from an evaluation in the *Mental Measurements Yearbook,* are probably pertinent to all the scales and inventories available at present: " . . . being little better or worse than the average person-

[1] *Cowan Adolescent-adjustment Analyzer: An Instrument of Clinical Psychology,* Salina, Kans.: Cowan Research Project, 1946.

ality questionnaire of its kind, this inventory makes up for none of the serious limitations still inherent in these instruments."[2]

The necessity for caution in the use of an instrument should not cause teachers to repudiate it entirely. Rating scales can be used to advantage if teachers will observe the following precautions: (1) Children should not be labeled predelinquent, neurotic, or poorly adjusted as a result of their scores or standing on a rating scale. Because of the likelihood of change and growth, the importance of the subject's mood when he answered the questionnaire, and the possible influence of the mood of the person who interprets the results, the scores should not be placed in a permanent record folder. The questionnaire may, however, be used by the teacher for a temporary and tentative evaluation. (2) Specific items on the questionnaire may serve to direct the teacher to a further investigation of behavior in a particular area; that is, an atypically answered item may suggest other questions that will lead to a better understanding of the individual. (3) The teacher should bear in mind that the rating scale does not constitute a diagnosis. It may supply some data which will make effective diagnosis possible, but in the final analysis the individual items on the scale and the total score must be interpreted by the user of the scale. (4) The data obtained from the rating scale should not be regarded as conclusive or infallible. Rather they should be regarded as supplementary information which provides a test of the validity of data or conclusions obtained from the teacher's observation of the child.

The need for the exercise of these precautions is indicated in the following statement:[3]

[2] Albert Ellis in Oscar K. Buros (ed.), *The Third Mental Measurements Yearbook,* New Brunswick, N.J.: Rutgers University Press, 1949, p. 69.

[3] Laurance F. Shaffer in Buros, *op. cit.,* p. 56.

Such devices vainly seek the pot of gold at the end of the rainbow: a simple, cheap, foolproof method for studying human personality. Teachers, administrators, and school counselors who are tempted to consider the use of such devices would be benefited by a psychological insight into the fact that their own great need to do something about personality problems leads them to the delusion of accepting instruments of very low objective value.

Rating schedules must be used with consideration for their inherent limitations; hence conclusions based upon them must be temperate and tentative.

PERSONALITY INVENTORIES

A personality inventory is a questionnaire on which the subject checks his reactions to a number of specifically described situations. He may be asked how he typically reacts, how he thinks he would feel in specific situations, or whether certain events have occurred in his life. Examples of each of these types of questions are: "Do you cross the street to avoid meeting someone whom you dislike?" "At an automobile wreck, would you get sick at the sight of blood?" "Have you been knocked unconscious by a blow on the head?"

Many other situations and classes of situations are "plumbed" in an inventory. No one question is considered crucial; it is the total response to all the questions—the pattern of the answers—that is considered significant. If the results are not interpreted too specifically, the general trend of personality orientation indicated is helpful, but as in the case of rating schedules, the temptation to label or classify should be avoided, even though the enthusiastic test maker may himself have classified the results.

Some of the difficulties involved in devising instruments to probe personality have already been suggested. Among these difficulties are (1) the vagueness of the term, (2) the fact that the personality orientation of the test maker creeps into the questions he asks, (3) the lack of a well-defined norm for social and personal behavior, and (4) the variability of behavior in diverse situations.

Subjectivity endangers several aspects of personality measurement: not only is the interpreter of the test subjective, but so inevitably is the individual taking the test. This aspect of personality testing is of importance to us here because, thus far, a negative view of personality testing has been presented in this chapter, and the teacher has the right to ask, "If inventories and scales are so subject to criticism, should they be used at all?" Actually, the subjective nature of inventories and scales points up the advantages of what are called projective techniques, as we shall see later.

As we have seen, each personality is a "private world." As the individual grows and develops he learns certain tricks for protecting himself from "the slings and arrows of outrageous fortune"—for defending himself from the psychological and physical batterings which even a protected existence entails. Critics of extreme behavioristic psychology have pointed out that individuals do not react to stimuli in a simple, mechanical fashion; rather, each individual has a unique response. The late J. S. Plant described this private world as follows:[4]

> Between the need of the child and the sweep of social pressures lies a membrane—a sort of psycho-osmotic envelope of transcending importance. . . . One should never think of this as a tangible, material structure. It is rather a property of that part of the personality which is in touch with the environment.
>
> It is only through the operation of the envelope that we can get at the problem of meaning—what anything "means" to the indi-

[4] James S. Plant, *The Envelope,* New York: The Commonwealth Fund, 1950, pp. 2–3. By permission of the Harvard University Press, publishers.

vidual. . . . Certainly one of the most brilliant of the psychoanalytic contributions has been the theory that one sees the world only as he can afford to see it—that the material of the environment is sensed by the personality only in terms of the problems which it is trying to work through.

This "envelope" which protects the individual from hostilities and contributes to his uniqueness is in turn protected by the individual, who practices a measure of self-concealment. Often when he does wish to reveal himself he is unable to think clearly enough about his feelings to verbalize or describe these inner workings.

Thus, in terms of objectivity, questionnaires suffer from two inescapable shortcomings: (1) the inability of the individual to evaluate with accuracy his own feelings, and (2) the individual's desire to keep his feelings to himself. A third shortcoming operates certainly in the upper grades and at the high school level, and perhaps even earlier; (3) the desire deliberately to mislead others. The motive for such behavior may not be negative; it may simply be a desire to please the teacher, for example.

Inventories, like scales, should be used only with a proper regard for their limitations. They can be used to supplement other measures and observations and to help the teacher investigate and gain some understanding of a particular area of adjustment, such as schoolwork and family or peer relations. Atypical responses on a questionnaire may serve as a point of departure for a fruitful interview. The teacher should remember, however, that the scores on an inventory do not constitute a diagnosis. The following statement applies to several personality measures that attempt to define behavior precisely and categorically: "The worst features of the tests, in the opinion of this reviewer, are the elaborate suggestions to teachers for the treatment of conditions claimed to be revealed by the scores, profiles, and even individual item responses.

When not clearly dangerous, these procedures are stereotyped, superficial, and lacking in clinical sense."[5]

INFORMAL APPROACHES TO PERSONALITY EVALUATION

Some approaches to personality assessment are valuable because they are admittedly subjective and users cannot escape the pervasiveness of the subjectivity. Because of the obvious presence of the personal element, there is much less danger that the tester will think he has an accurate measure of personality than might be the case with scales and inventories in which norms have been cited. These fruitful methods of personality evaluation are (1) anecdotal records, (2) teacher-pupil conferences, and (3) staff meetings.

The anecdotal record is an attempt to "catch" the child in a word picture when he is his typical or average self. The teacher describes without attempting evaluation or interpretation, a particular youngster as he is performing some characteristic action. The anecdote is designed simply to indicate to the teacher, at a later date when evaluation of the child's growth is desired, what the child was like at a certain time. The child's next teacher may use the anecdote, *along with other data,* to get a more complete picture of the child as he has been in the past. Certain precautions should be observed in making and using anecdotal records, however; the described action should be a *typical* one (teachers sometimes make the mistake of picking the strange or bizarre action to record), and interpretive and evaluative terms should be avoided in the wording of the behavior descriptions. A good method for making an anecdotal record is to decide at the beginning of the day to record the behavior of Albert B. at ten o'clock and the behavior of Patricia L. at 2:30. In this

[5] Douglas Spencer in Buros, *op. cit.,* p. 58.

way the teacher can gradually acquire anecdotes of typical behavior for each pupil in his group. The outcome might be something like the following:[6]

September 30. Jackie has been paying special attention to Elsie the past few days. He put a piece of bubble gum on her desk, put his hands into his pockets, cast his eyes up to the ceiling, walked a few steps away, whistling between his teeth. Elsie took the gum, raised her eyes, lowered them, said nothing; but Jackie seemed satisfied. He has been trying to give her clean notebook paper every day.

October 6. The class chose Jackie and Mort to keep our part of the grounds this week. Both stayed in at recess, so the girls picked up the paper for them. Mort asked what to do about being grounds monitor. Jackie said: "If the kid is littler'n you, make him pick it up. If the kid is bigger'n you, report him to the teacher."

Teacher-pupil conferences in which *the teacher does a great deal of listening* are an excellent way of gaining understanding of a pupil's personality. In these conferences the teacher should play the role of "counselor with" rather than "adviser to." A questionnaire may tell how a person typically acts or how he has behaved in the past, but a conference in which the teacher listens at least part of the time will produce much more information about why the pupil behaves as he does. The difficulty with the technique is that teachers tend to give too much advice, although analysis of their successful experiences in working with pupils shows that solutions were discovered only after they had gained, through listening, an understanding of how the pupil felt about his difficulties. At every age, pupils talk freely with teachers who are patient listeners. Often teachers are in such a hurry to get results that

[6] Helen Bieker in *Fostering Mental Health in Our Schools,* 1950 Yearbook, Association for Supervision and Curriculum Development, Washington: National Education Association, 1950, p. 189.

they fail to encourage the development that will help the pupil to understand his own personality.

One relatively unexplored but highly fruitful way of securing a better understanding of individual children is the conference composed of a small number of teachers. In these conferences, a teacher mentions the name of a pupil he would like to help *on a professional basis*. Teachers who have had the pupil previously will be able to suggest helpful approaches to and reveal their insights into his problems. Frequently teachers who do not know the pupil concerned will make important contributions to such conferences, since a teacher's experience and knowledge can sometimes be most fruitfully brought to bear when he does not know the pupil. One of the authors has tried this technique frequently by reading data on a particular case to a group of teachers; the suggested approaches to the problem involved have often been practically the same as those suggested by psychologists on the basis of the test data and interviews.

These informal approaches (anecdotal records, teacher-pupil conferences, and teacher conferences) are especially valuable because they do not promise a miraculous conclusion. They are admittedly subjective; hence there is more likelihood that appropriate allowance will be made for subjectivity. The advantage of these techniques over formal instruments is that teachers can base their subjective judgments and evaluations on objective data.

PROJECTIVE TECHNIQUES

As we have seen, personality is, at least in part, the private world of the individual. To the extent that this is true, one must, in order to understand the vast realm of emotional experience, study the individual when he is off guard. Various projective techniques provide fruitful approaches to this aspect of personality. Many projective techniques have the double advantage of providing some degree of therapy during the process of study or analysis, for as the child carries on the activities that will be observed and interpreted, he is also getting rid of some of the tension that is complicating life for him.

A projective technique involves a situation which is meaningless, ambiguous, amorphous, or neutral. What the person being tested does or sees in these meaningless circumstances is not dictated by external questions, directions, or demands; his actions are an expression of himself. The meanings which he believes are present in the pictures or stories are meanings which he puts there himself.

One of the earliest and most widely used projective techniques, the Rorschach test, presents a series of ink blots such as could be made by allowing a drop of ink to fall upon a paper from a height and folding the paper over in such a way as to produce symmetrical halves. Some of the blots in the series are black, some have many colors; being formless, they represent nothing. The subject is asked what he sees in them; what he reports is, obviously, a projection of himself. The scoring and interpretation of the Rorschach blots are involved, extensive, and time-consuming processes which require highly specialized training. Research is still going on, but there is no indication at present that this process will become a routine classroom technique. The untrained individual must be warned against the dangers of uninformed and irresponsible interpretation of responses to projective techniques.

Other projective techniques include a cloud test, in which each member of the group tells what he sees in a pictured cloud formation, much as children describe their castles in the air; a sentence-completion test, in which the subject is presented with the first part of a number of sentences and is asked to complete them in any way he sees fit; and a story-completion test, in which part of a story is read to the subject, who is then asked to tell what happened in the rest of the tale.

Play techniques consist of giving the child a few toys to play with and observing what he does with them, or what he has the toys and dolls do. An important element in play techniques is a high degree of permissiveness (i.e., the child is made to feel that there are no important compulsions or restraints being placed upon him) which cannot practically be made a part of the classroom situation. However, the principles of play techniques are useful to the teacher in that the child gives a picture of his inner self when he is engaged in spontaneous play, either alone or with others. By cautiously interpreting this behavior and evaluating it against other data, the teacher can see more clearly specific aspects of the child's personality. The teacher might well be advised to see that interference with what to the adult are objectionable aspects of play is held to a minimum, thus allowing the child some chance to "spill over" with some of his hostile or frustrated feelings.

Some practices which, when used informally, we should perhaps not call projective techniques can be put to immediate use by teachers in understanding personality orientations. One of these is free or creative writing. The pupil is encouraged to write whatever he likes—stories, poems, biographies, or articles—and criticism of content and composition is kept to a minimum. When sound rapport exists between teacher and pupil, trends will frequently appear in the writing that will serve as diagnostic aids to the teacher. No great reliance should be placed on single bits of writing; it is the recurrent theme that is important. Since some youngsters have difficulty in thinking of what to write, suggestions may be made: My Favorite Pastime, My Pet Peeve, My Ideal Boy Friend, My Kind of Father, etc. As with play techniques, data from free writing should be interpreted cautiously and should be regarded as supplementary information.

Fingerpainting is a favorite technique of many classroom teachers for getting revealing glimpses of pupils from the beginning of their school experience. Some pupils are reluctant to participate, and even this reluctance, in conjunction with other information, may be revealing or suggestive of personality trends. The kinds of color, the kinds of strokes, and the degree of freedom of movement and care employed all may give the teacher clues to the meaning of behavior. The authors do not recommend direct interpretation of these features of the paintings, however; they are clues only. Quite apart from analysis, many teachers have found that children talk more freely when they have a picture to which to point; that is, a child may be unable to discuss a feeling such as a resentment, but he may be able to paint it and describe what he has painted.

Working with clay is another projective technique. As with paint, the characteristic way of dealing with the medium, the vigor of movement, and the degree of satisfaction or discontent with the product are all elements that might be involved in the interpretation.

The advantage of projective techniques, in the main, is that they have not become routine, stereotyped, and standardized. There is, of course, the danger that the user will project himself into the interpretations and conclusions, but the teacher who attempts to interpret what he sees in a child's writing, play habits, and art processes and products fully realizes that the interpretation is wide open to error; consequently he is careful in its use. Such data, cautiously used, may frequently be more helpful in the evaluation of personality than the results of standardized instruments that give apparently accurate statistical interpretations of data that are necessarily subjective and approximate.[7]

SUMMARY

All instruments for measurement or evaluation are in reality used as approaches to the understanding of some aspect of personality. The word *personality* is an inclusive term embracing actions, inner feelings, and what others think of one. It is obvious that a thing so complex and ever-changing cannot readily be measured in a mathematical sense. The difficulty of evaluation, however, should not lead the teacher to a repudiation of the available instruments. Rather, an understanding of the complexity of the problem should underscore the need for proper caution and reservation of final judgment.

Rating scales are designed to systematize judgments or observations regarding oneself or others. The shortcomings of the scales are that they are subjective and must of necessity be limited by the particular questions asked—the things the scale maker thinks are most significant. If the teacher uses them with these limitations in mind, they provide useful corrective or corroborative information. If, however, conclusive judgments are based on the attractive norms, the results will be unfortunate for many pupils.

Personality inventories are subject to limitations similar to those of rating scales. They have their place in evaluation schemes, where they may be used as the starting point for an interview or as supplementary data. If the teacher finds himself attracted by the statistical norms which sometimes accompany such tests, he would do well to heed the words of

[7] Another approach to the understanding of personality—functioning in a group, or sociometry—will be examined in Chap. 8. This technique is available to classroom teachers without any outlay for equipment save perhaps a book which explains in detail some of the problems involved in the approach.

George G. Thompson: "[It] is surprising (in the face of this preponderance of negative research findings) that these personality questionnaires should continue to be so widely used in school and youth-guidance organizations!"[8]

Some recent developments in personality evaluation give indications of overcoming some of the defects of older measures. Inclusively, these tools are called projective techniques. They include art, free writing, and spontaneous play used for the purpose of gaining an understanding of children. One explanation of the value of these instruments is that they are admittedly subjective and approximate. They unearth clues or furnish supplementary data. Specifically, although one would not be justified in concluding from a child's drawings that he has a mother fixation, one can discover signs of emotional tensions that should be more carefully studied in home visits, interviews, and further psychological investigation.

The evaluation of personality is an inescapable responsibility of the school, since evaluation must precede constructive help. The instruments available today for evaluating personality are tools for increasing the accuracy of the teacher's perception, just as the stethoscope increases the accuracy of the doctor's diagnosis. The fact that personality instruments are imperfect indicates only that they should be used with appropriate regard for their shortcomings, for they provide a means of arriving at a tentative evaluation of certain aspects of the child's personality.

STUDY AND DISCUSSION EXERCISES

1. What is the significance for teachers of the statement, "When one describes the personality of another, he reveals himself"?
2. Point out some instances in typical everyday conversations

[8] George G. Thompson, *Child Psychology,* Boston: Houghton Mifflin Company, 1952, p. 614.

which indicate the tendency to classify persons as personality types.

3. Study the reviews of three or four well-known personality inventories, using the *Mental Measurements Yearbook.* Do the reviews reflect or contradict the views presented in this chapter?

4. Formulate a list of suggestions which would help teachers to use their own subjective evaluations of pupils more constructively.

5. Consult the *Education Index* and find and report on some articles published in the last six months having to do with the use of projective techniques by classroom teachers.

6. Which would you consider to be more important for a boy having difficulty in social adjustment at school—a factual study of home and community or an interview which reveals how he feels about his home and community?

7. Evaluate this statement: Personality is formed in the first six years of life.

SUGGESTED ADDITIONAL READINGS

Bernard, Harold W.: *Mental Hygiene for Classroom Teachers,* New York: McGraw-Hill Book Company, Inc., 1952, pp. 297–362.

Three chapters deal with the role of writing in the release of tensions and interpretation of personality, with art as an approach to understanding personality, and with play and drama as classroom techniques in pupil understanding.

Bieker, Helen: "Using Anecdotal Records to Know the Child," in *Fostering Mental Health in Our Schools,* 1950 Yearbook, Association for Supervision and Curriculum Development, Washington: National Education Association, 1950, pp. 184–202.

This is a condensed account of the aims, techniques, and advantages of the anecdotal record. It provides background material which prepares one to experiment for himself.

Cattell, Raymond B.: *Personality,* New York: McGraw-Hill Book Company, Inc., 1950, chap. 4.

A scholarly description and evaluation of various techniques for testing personality. The discussion points up the difficulties inherent in the problem of personality assessment.

Kaplan, Louis, and Denis Baron: *Mental Hygiene and Life,* New York: Harper & Brothers, 1952, pp. 52–80.

This chapter discusses the origin and meaning of personality. The uniqueness of personality, rather than the division into types, is described.

Klopfer, Bruno, Mary D. Ainsworth, Walter G. Klopfer, and Robert R. Holt: *Developments in the Rorschach Technique,* Yonkers, N.Y.: World Book Company, 1954.

This book contains a detailed description of the technique and theory of Rorschach tests. It will be of interest to the student who wishes to specialize in clinical testing.

Olson, Willard C.: "Personality," in Walter S. Monroe (ed.), *Encyclopedia of Educational Research,* rev. ed., 1950, pp. 806–817.

The greater part of this article is devoted to a critical examination of the uses and shortcomings of methods for appraising personality. An extensive bibliography for further study is included.

Thompson, George G.: *Child Psychology,* Boston: Houghton Mifflin Company, 1952, chap. 14.

Approaches to the evaluation of personality are discussed in terms of the theoretical constituents of personality and the kind of development that seems to be culturally expedient.

CHAPTER NINE

Evaluating Classroom Social Relationships

In the classroom, the child is brought into contact with other children in a social situation which influences his academic achievements and his personal and social adjustment. One of the important tasks which face the child of school age is the development of satisfying relationships with his peers. Adequate relationships minister to the child's need for social acceptance and the approval of his age mates. The child's attitude toward life and learning in the school situation may be either favorably or unfavorably influenced by the nature of the social climate of the classroom. School learning cannot be isolated from the social setting in which it occurs.

FACTORS RELATED TO SOCIAL ACCEPTANCE

Investigations of social acceptability among children of school age have pointed to a number of considerations which are of importance to the teacher. Children tend to select their friends from their neighborhood and classroom groups[1] and

[1] M. V. Seagoe, "Factors Influencing the Selection of Associates," *Journal of Educational Research*, **27**:32–40, 1933.

on the basis of similarity in chronological and mental age.[2] Physical condition, proficiency in playground activities, and neuromuscular skill play a significant role in social acceptability during the school years.[3]

Social acceptance is also related to scholastic achievement. For example, "best-liked" children are typically superior to unpopular children in scholastic ratings and in reading achievement.[4] It has been demonstrated, too, that children tend to choose as friends those classmates who are somewhat similar to themselves in mental age and scholastic achievement.[5] Children who have been retarded in school are frequently among the unchosen individuals in the group and are likely to display problems in social and emotional adjustment.[6]

Social acceptance in the classroom is related to the personal and social characteristics of the individual. Popular children are typically more self-confident and emotionally stable than unpopular children[7] and evidence a greater degree of outgoing energy.

Thus the social status of a child among his peers is related to developmental characteristics and environmental factors. The fact that a child's acceptance status tends to remain rela-

[2] R. Pintner, G. Forlano, and H. Freeman, "Personality and Attitudinal Similarity among Classroom Friends," *Journal of Applied Psychology,* **21**:48–65, 1937.

[3] B. Grossman and J. Wrighter, "The Relation between Selection-Rejection and Intelligence, Social Status, and Personality among Sixth-grade Children," *Sociometry,* **11**:346–355, 1948.

[4] M. C. Hardy, "Social Recognition at the Elementary School Age," *Journal of Social Psychology,* **8**:365–384, 1937.

[5] D. S. Belden, "A Study of the Nature of Social Structure" (unpublished), Division of Research and Guidance, Los Angeles County Schools, 1942.

[6] A. A. Sandin, "Social and Emotional Adjustments of Regularly Promoted and Nonpromoted Pupils," *Child Development Monographs,* 1944, no. 32.

[7] D. Baron, "Mental-health Characteristics and Classroom Social Status," *Education,* **69**:306–310, 1949.

tively constant from year to year[8] indicates that problems of social acceptance represent an area in which guidance is needed and which should be an important concern of teachers and parents. The relationships between social acceptability and scholastic and personality factors indicate that questions of promotion or nonpromotion, acceleration, reorganization of classroom groups, changes of school, neighborhood, or classroom may represent crucial decisions from the point of view of adjustment and learning.

STUDYING SOCIAL RELATIONSHIPS

In the course of his everyday activities the teacher has many opportunities to observe children working and playing together. When such observations become systematized and purposeful, the data which they provide are likely to become increasingly valuable. Scientists have developed a number of techniques designed to systematize the study of social relationships. One of these techniques, the sociometric method,[9] is designed to facilitate the study of individuals in groups and is readily applicable to the classroom situation. The method involves the selection of associates for group activities. In the classroom, for example, pupils may be asked to choose seating companions, group leaders, associates in specific activities, guests for parties, and so on. Various techniques of recording, charting, and evaluating such choice patterns have been developed.

In group situations, certain patterns of attraction, neglect, and rejection develop among individuals. In classroom groups,

[8] M. E. Bonney, "The Relative Stability of Social, Intellectual, and Academic Status in Grades II to IV and the Interrelationships between these Various Forms of Growth," *Journal of Educational Psychology,* **34**:88–102, 1943.

[9] J. L. Moreno, *Who Shall Survive?* Washington: Nervous and Mental Disease Publishing Company, 1934, pp. 12–14.

for instance, some children become the focal points of attraction and their company is eagerly sought by many members of the group. Other children may be overlooked when associates are selected, and still others may be actively rejected as companions. The social "climate" of a classroom is profoundly influenced by the pattern of interrelationships which prevails among members of the group. One classroom group may be drawn together by numerous attractions which extend throughout its membership; this situation facilitates united, cooperative effort. Another group may be comprised of mutually exclusive subgroups; in such classes the possibilities for cooperative group activities are minimized.[10] The sociometric method enables the teacher to obtain information concerning the pattern of relationships which forms the social "climate" in which pupils live in his classroom.

The Sociometric Question

In the sociometric method, pupils are asked to choose the associates they would prefer for a specific situation. The question might be, "Which three of your classmates would you prefer to have as your best friends?" This is a general question which implies no forthcoming action. A more specific question ideally would imply subsequent action: "We have decided to have a puppet show. Which of your classmates would you prefer to work with in preparing the show?" The teacher should design sociometric questions in such a way as to elicit valid or real preferences. Choices are likely to be most valid when the situation is real and meaningful and when the pupils are assured that the choices will be acted upon. The following question, for example, meets these criteria: "You are seated now according to a plan which seemed convenient. You have now had a chance to become acquainted with each other and perhaps would like to be seated near someone of your own

[10] Hilda Taba et al., *Diagnosing Human-relations Needs,* Washington: American Council on Education, 1951, p. 71.

choice. Which (two, three, four) of your classmates would you like to have seated near you? You will be seated near at least one of the persons you choose." In this statement, the situation, the purpose, and the number of preferences allowed are all specified. Finally, assurance is given that the results will be utilized.

The following principles will help the teacher in framing sociometric questions:

1. Give pupils a good reason for listing their preferences.
2. Present your plans for utilizing the choices.
3. Plan and word the directions carefully so that pupils will understand clearly what is wanted.
4. State the question in such a way that pupils fully understand it.

The sociometric question should be formulated in terms of the actual situation and the purposes of the teacher. However, the list of questions which follows may suggest some areas which provide meaningful situations:

1. Which of your classmates do you prefer to have seated near you?
2. Some of you are having difficulty with your work. Which boys or girls do you choose to help you?
3. We are going to plan a field trip. Which boys or girls do you prefer to work with on the planning committees?
4. We have planned a project in social studies. Which boys or girls would you like to have as members of your group?
5. We are going to select groups for games on the playground. Which of your classmates do you prefer as members of your group?
6. The other day we decided to hold a class picnic. Which boys or girls do you choose as members of the planning committee?
7. We plan to have a class party. We will be seated in groups around tables for lunch. Which of your classmates do you wish to have seated at your table?

8. A group of pupils is to plan a program for a parent-teacher meeting. Which of your classmates should represent our class on the planning committee?

The following suggestions will help the teacher in the preparation and administration of sociometric questions:

1. Utilize realistic and meaningful choice situations which bear a definite relationship to the activities of the group.

2. Word the question in such a way that the pupils understand its purposes and significance.

3. Have a few pupils prepare a list of the first and last names of the members of the group. The lettering should be large enough so that all the pupils can read the names.

4. Allow sufficient time for pupils to record their choices.

5. Have pupils list their choices on a small sheet of paper or a 3- by 5-inch card. Each pupil should sign his paper or card so that he may be identified. It helps to have a sample of the choice blank presented on the chalkboard. A suggested form for recording sociometric choices is presented in Figure 9.

6. Indicate precisely the number of choices which each pupil is to make. The number of choices requested will vary with the sociometric question, the purposes of the teacher, and the practical problem of the amount of time available for tabulation and evaluation of the results. Certain authorities suggest three choices by each pupil as the most practical number.[11] Other investigators indicate that larger numbers of choices result in increased validity.[12] The age of the pupils is a further consideration, since children in the primary grades typically choose fewer associates than children in the middle and upper grades.

7. Explain the range of choice. Ordinarily choices are limited to members of the classroom group exclusive of the

[11] *Ibid.*, p. 76.

[12] E. Eng and R. L. French, "The Determination of Sociometric Status," *Sociometry*, **11**:368–371, 1948.

YOUR NAME. Beverly A.
(first) (last)

GRADE. 3 DATE. May 15, 1957.

SCHOOL. P.S. 14

TEACHER. Miss Smith.

QUESTION: With whom would you like to work on our project in social studies?

CHOICES.

	First Name.	Last Initial.
1.		
2.		
3.		
4.		
5.		

FIG. 9. Suggested form for recording sociometric choices, showing two sides of the choice blank.

teacher. In certain situations the range of choice may be wider or more limited. The teacher should specify whether or not pupils who are absent are eligible for choice.

Scoring and Tabulating the Results. In many instances it is not necessary to weigh or give score values to the choices. In such cases the pupil's sociometric "score" is the total number of choices he receives from members of the group. In other cases the teacher may wish to consider the order of preference and assign arbitrary score values to choices in terms of the rank of the choice, as first choice, second choice, third choice. For example, in a situation where five choices are requested, a first choice might be assigned five points, a second choice four points, a third choice three points, and so on. Such scoring is arbitrary and does not necessarily reflect the actual value or intensity of the preference. Where a system of weighted scores is to be used, however, the directions to pupils should include the request that associates be listed in order of preference.

The tabulation sheet should contain a complete record of the results of the sociometric test. It should include all the data needed to identify the group, the date of the test, the nature of the question, the number of choices requested, the method of scoring, and other information (such as the number of pupils absent on the day of the test) which may be important in interpretation of the data in the record. The tabulation plan represented in Figure 10, which presents the complete record for a sample group, is one of a number of methods which meet these requirements:

1. Essential data are indicated at the top of the sheet.

2. The tabluation sheet is blocked off in cells, one row and one column for each pupil in the group. First names and initial of last names are listed across the top and down the side of the tabulation sheet.

3. Girls and boys are listed separately in alphabetical order according to initial of last name. A vacant row and column separate the two lists. This type of listing helps in the analysis and interpretation of the results.

4. The columns represent preferences indicated on the question blanks. Choices are entered in the cell where the column under the name of the pupil chosen is intersected by the row opposite the name of the chooser. For example, Bev-

SOCIOMETRIC TABULATION SHEET

Question. With whom would you like to work on our project in Social Studies?

No. of choices. 5

Scoring. first choice-5 points; second-4 pts.; third-3 pts.; fourth-2 pts.;

Date of Test. 4/15/57

School. P.S. 14. (city or town)

Grade. Third

Teacher. Miss Smith.

Choices Received. ⟶ / Choices By.	Beverly A.	June B.	Shirley B.	Janet D.	Laura G.	Dolores K.	Sharon L.	Lynn M.	Leona N.	Jackie S.	Carol T.	Patricia W.	David B.	Peter B.	Bob C.	Cameron F.	Tommy G.	Norman K.	Jerry M.	Jerry N.	Ernest R.	Terry T.	Dennis T.	Paul V.	Jimmy Y.
1. Beverly A.		3	1		5		2	4																	
2. June B.	5		4		1		3	2																	
3. Shirley B.		1		4	5		2	3																	
4. Janet D.		3	4				5															2			1
5. Laura G.		1	5	3			2					4													
6. Dolores K.					1		2		4		3		5												
7. Sharon L.		2	1	3	4			5																	
8. Lynn M.	4	1	2	5			3																		
9. Leona N.						3		2		4	5	1													
10. Jackie S.			5	4	3		2					1													
11. Carol T.	1	5			3		2		4																
12. Patricia W. (absent)																									
13. David B.		1															3				2		5		4
14. Peter B.															4	3				5				1	2
15. Bob C.														5			1	3				2			4
16. Cameron F.																	3	4		2		1			5
17. Tommy G.		1						5										3	4		2				
18. Norman K.																2	4		1			3			5
19. Jerry M.		4						1									5					2			3
20. Jerry N.														5		3			2				1		4
21. Ernest R.													3			5	2	4						1	
22. Terry T.																	2		1				3	4	5
23. Dennis T.		5	2					1														3			4
24. Paul V.																	2	3			5		1		4
25. Jimmy Y.		2											1			3					4	5			
A. Total Score	10	29	24	19	22	3	23	23	8	4	8	6	9.	10	4	16	22	17	8	7	13	18	10	6	41
B. 1. First choices	1	2	2	1	2		1	2			1		1	2		1	1			1	1	1	1		3
2. Second "	1	1	2	2	1			1	2	1		1			1		1	2	1		1			1	5
3. Third "		2		2	2	1	2	1			1		1			3	2	3				2	1		1
4. Fourth "		2	2				6	2								1	3		1	1	2	3			1
5. Fifth "	1	5	2		2			2				2	1				1		2			1	2	2	1
C. Total Choices received	3	12	8	5	7	1	9	8	2	1	2	3	3	2	1	5	8	5	4	2	4	7	4	3	11

FIG. 10. Sociometric tabulation sheet.

erly A. (first column) is chosen as an associate by June B. The figure 5 under Beverly and opposite June indicates that this is a first choice.

5. To facilitate tabulation of choices, the choice blanks (Figure 9) can be arranged in the order in which choosers' names appear on the tabulation sheet. Each choice can then be listed along the rows under the name of the pupil chosen. The score value of each choice is indicated if score values are used.

6. The sociometric "score" of each pupil is derived by summing the columns, as indicated opposite *A* in Figure 10. For example, Beverly's sociometric score is 10, the sum of the score values in the column under her name.

7. If the teacher wishes, he may also indicate the number of choices of each rank and the total number of choices received by each pupil. These figures are shown opposite *B* and *C* in Figure 10.

The tabulation sheet presents a summary statement of the results of the test, indicating the choice status of the pupils. In our example, Jimmy Y,, with 41 points, leads the group in sociometric score. The leading girl is June B., with 29 points. No pupil is unchosen, but the lowest scores are those of Dolores K. (3 points) and Jackie S. (4 points) among the girls and Bob C. (4 points) among the boys.

The tabulation sheet may be easily preserved for future reference and comparisons, and it is a basic work sheet for the teacher who plans to further analyze the results of testing. From the tabulation sheet, sociograms may be developed as a means of further clarifying relationships within the group.

The Sociogram

The sociogram is designed to portray graphically the choice relationships which are recorded on the tabulation sheet. The method presented here makes use of the target diagram as a

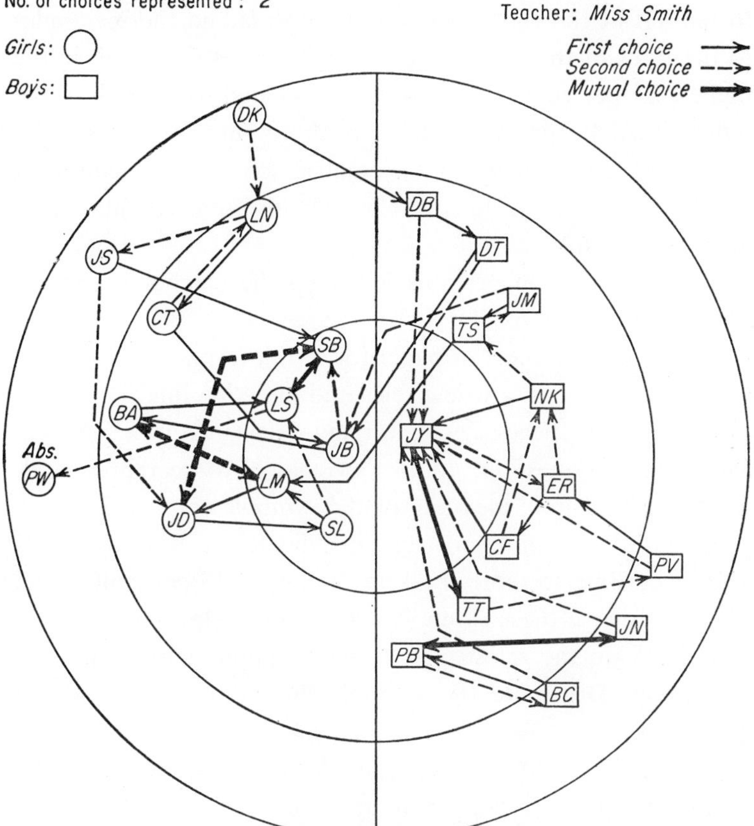

FIG. 11. Sociogram representing interrelationships among pupils in the third grade as indicated by their responses to the question, "With whom would you like to work on our project in social studies?" First, second, and mutual choices are represented.

PUPIL: Dolores K. GRADE: 3 SCHOOL: *P. S. 14* (*City or town*)
SEX: F AGE: 8-8 DATE: 4/15/57
QUESTION: "With whom would you like to work on our project in social studies?"
CHOICES: 5 SCORE VALUES: 5, 4, 3, 2, 1 (in terms of rank of choice)

means of representing sociometric data in graphic form. This type of sociogram is based on a series of concentric circles bisected vertically, as shown in Figure 11. The small circles to the left of the center line represent girls and the rectangles to the right of the line represent boys. Pupils who rank in the highest 25 per cent of the group are located, by initial, in the inner circle. In the outer circle are those pupils who comprise the lowest 25 per cent in sociometric score. The location of pupils within the various circles roughly approximates their sociometric rank.

The following suggestions will help the teacher prepare a sociogram of this type:

1. Use a large sheet of paper for a trial form.

2. Draw the concentric circles and bisecting line.

3. Fill in the necessary identifying data (i.e., grade, school, date, teacher, question, number of choices to be represented, score values if any, meaning of the symbols employed).

4. Within the innermost circle indicate the boys and girls who, according to score, rank in the upper 25 per cent of the group. Disperse these symbols within the circle.

5. Indicate the relative positions of pupils within the second circle. Distribute the symbols throughout the available space.

6. Locate the pupils with the lowest sociometric scores within the outer circle. These symbols should ideally be located so that lines can be drawn directly to the symbols in the central circle.

7. Draw lines representing the direction of the first choices of pupils in the group, using arrow tips to indicate direction of choice, as in Figure 11. The number of lines can be reduced by using a single line with double arrow tip and bar to indicate mutual choices.

8. Indicate second choices similarly by using a dotted or colored line. Other levels of choice may be indicated if the teacher wishes.

9. Study the trial sociogram for ways to relocate symbols in order to improve the clarity of the diagram and estimate the number of choices which can be satisfactorily depicted for the group.

Sociograms are of great assistance to the teacher in studying relationships among pupils. The following list suggests some of the advantages they offer:

1. Relative sociometric ranks are revealed graphically.
2. Directions of choice and extent of mutuality of choice are indicated.
3. Heavy concentrations of choice are revealed.
4. Choices which run across sex lines are clearly indicated.
5. The teacher can readily identify individuals and study their choice relationships with others in the group.
6. Possibilities for grouping pupils in a psychologically meaningful way are portrayed.
7. The popular individuals, the unchosen, mutual pairs, and subgroups are graphically depicted.

For example, the following noteworthy features are revealed concerning the group studied in Figure 11:

1. There are more girls than boys in the circle representing high choice status.
2. Choices of boys are heavily concentrated on Jimmy Y. Choices of girls show greater dispersion.
3. Boys in this group frequently select girls as working companions, but girls seldom select boys.
4. By comparison with the total number of choices depicted, the number of mutual choices is relatively small.
5. There are indications of some rather closely knit groups, particularly in terms of first choices.
6. No pupil, with the exception of D. K., a girl, fails to receive either a first or second choice. This would seem to indicate relatively good relationships throughout the group. A further indication of a good dispersion of attractions is seen in the chaining of choices, as with P. V., E. R., C. F., and J. Y.

A further method of graphic representation is presented in Figure 12, which depicts the choice relationships of an individual pupil, Dolores K. The direction of choice is again represented by arrow tips, and the score values of choices are indicated near the inner circle. For example, Dolores gives her first choice (5 points) to D. B., one of the boys of the

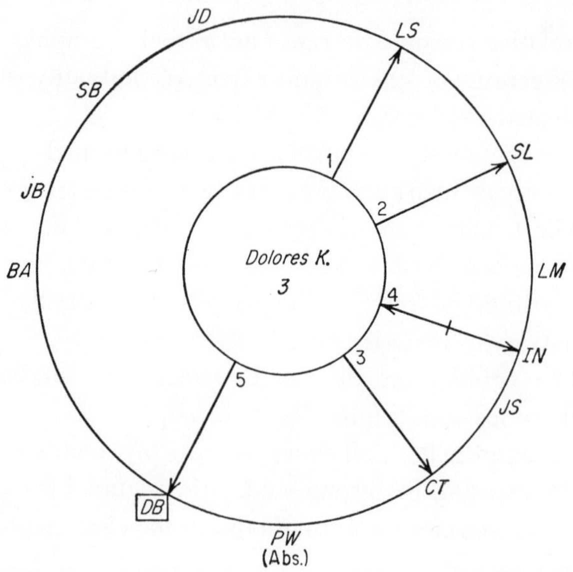

FIG. 12. Diagrammatic representation of the sociometric relationships of Dolores K.

group. She gives her second choice (4 points) to I. N., and is the third choice (3 points) of I. N. The mutuality of choice is indicated by double arrow tips and bar. This type of diagram helps to clarify the choice relationships of individuals whom the teacher may wish to study further and is useful in working out committee and other classroom groupings.

ANALYZING AND INTERPRETING RESULTS

Some of the interrelationships within a group are readily discerned in the results of sociometric testing. Still other sets of relationships are not so clearly defined but may be clarified by various techniques of representation and analysis. The sociogram and the diagrammatic representation of the choice relationships of individuals offer possibilities for clarification and analysis of the data.

The teacher will undoubtedly study the results by means of questions which apply to his unique situation. The following questions may serve as leads in developing this type of analysis.[13]

1. Do the choices center upon a few pupils, or are they relatively well dispersed. In our example, almost 20 per cent of the choices received by boys of the group are centered around Jimmy Y. The teacher may wish to consider possible reasons for the popularity of individuals with high choice status. Such pupils may play important roles in determining classroom morale and leading the activities of the group.

2. Are there pupils who receive no choices? Typically there are "isolates" in every class. The proportion of unchosen children is ordinarily highest in the kindergarten and the first two grades. In the third-grade group we have been discussing, there is no child who is unchosen and only one pupil, Dolores K., who fails to receive either a first or second choice. In a two-choice situation, Dolores would be considered an isolate. Observation of unchosen children may reveal behavioral or other factors which interfere with their acceptance by their peers and may suggest ways in which teachers can help these pupils establish themselves as accepted members of the group.

3. Do choices cross sex lines, or is there a rather definite cleavage between girls and boys? During the first three years of school there is generally less cleavage between the sexes than in the succeeding three years. In the case of our third-grade group, cleavage along sex lines is especially marked in

[13] Adapted in part from Taba et al., *op. cit.,* pp. 83–86.

the case of the girls. This pattern is fairly common during the early school years and is an aspect of boy-girl relationships which is an important consideration in the grouping of pupils during this period.

4. Is there a satisfactory degree of mutuality in the choice patterns? Mutuality of choice is ordinarily likely to indicate satisfying relationships. However, in some instances pupils may pair off to form small, tightly closed groups. In our example, a considerable degree of mutuality is evidenced when all choices are considered. Furthermore, considerable "chaining" is evidenced, which seems to be indicative of a series of attractions which run through and knit together the groups of boys and girls. For instance, although a triangular chain relationship of first choices links S. L., L. M., and J. D., the pattern of second choices indicates that members of this group have good relationships with others of their classmates.

The above suggestions offer some basic possibilities for study of the results of sociometric testing. The teacher will undoubtedly note other relationships which are of special interest to him; for example, we may look for the choice patterns that he expected to find. It is also profitable to look for the unexpected; in fact, a most common reaction of teachers using the sociometric design for the first time is surprise at seeing relationships which they had not previously realized. Frequently, for example, the teacher may find that a pupil is more or less popular than he had expected; or he may find lines of attraction taking unexpected directions or intensities. Such events merit special study and may increase the teacher's understanding of his pupils.

Utilizing Results

The feelings and attitudes, attractions and repulsions which pervade the group inevitably influence the learning activities of the classroom. Sociometric data may enable the teacher to develop more satisfying, meaningful, and effective learning situations, since they reveal who the preferred leaders and associates of the pupil group are. When accompanied by first hand observation of the pupil leaders, a knowledge of the leadership roles of pupils is helpful in developing morale, in the management of the classroom, and in the development of psychologically meaningful pupil groups.

Recognition and observation of pupils who receive few choices or none at all may alert the teacher to group or individual problems. The teacher who has identified pupils of this type and who is aware of their preferences in the group is frequently able to help such pupils attract the attention and respect of others. This can sometimes be accomplished through judicious grouping or through capitalizing upon a special skill or hobby to bring a pupil into the group.

In classes in which pupils are organized into almost mutually exclusive groups, sociometric-test data may indicate linkages by means of which the teacher can encourage more expansive patterns of social interaction. The pupils' choice patterns also suggest possibilities for improved group activities and the formation of more harmonious working groups.

The first step in putting sociometric data to work is to act upon the results in terms of the purpose for which the test was given. If the test question referred to seating arrangement, the class should be reseated in a pattern closely approximating the choice patterns revealed by the test. Ordinarily, some compromises will be necessary. If the question referred to the formation of working groups, such groups should be organized on the basis of the findings. Again, ingenuity will be required in working out acceptable compromises. The following suggestions may help the teacher utilize test results:

1. If possible, give the unchosen pupil his first choice.
2. When choices are mutual, give the pupil his highest reciprocated choice.

3. If the pupil has chosen only individuals who have not chosen him in return, give him his first choice as an associate if there is a possibility that he will be accepted by this individual.

4. Do not place any pupil with a pupil who may actively reject him.

5. In forming groups on the basis of the results of sociometric tests, provide each pupil with an associate of his choice. If possible, organize groups in such a way that their members are linked together by the choice patterns.

6. Provide for leadership which will be recognized and accepted by group members.

The sociometric test is a tool which provides the teacher with information regarding the interrelationships of individuals in the group. Like other test results, this information is of greatest value when it is used in conjunction with data obtained from other sources. It gives impetus to the teacher's observations of the social interaction of pupils, and it may form the basis for the development of meaningful and satisfying social and learning experiences in the classroom.

SUMMARY

The classroom is a social situation which has a significant impact upon the learning activities and social development of pupils. The sociometric test provides a means of studying the social interactions of persons in groups. The individual taking the test is asked to select one or a number of companions for a situation in which social relationships are important. Choices are tabulated; graphic representations may be developed for the group or for the individual, and the results may be utilized as a basis for grouping pupils for the specified situation or activity.

The utilization of sociometric devices in the classroom provides the teacher with information regarding (1) the acceptance status of pupils in the group, (2) the lines of attraction among pupils, and (3) cleavages within the group. This information can be of value in grouping pupils for work or play, in studying the problems of individual pupils, in developing pupil leadership in classroom activities, and in the improvement of relationships among members of the group. Sociometric data help the teacher create the appropriate social setting for learning.

STUDY AND DISCUSSION EXERCISES

1. Present some reasons why teacher and pupil choices of leaders for classroom activities sometimes differ. What values do you see in pupil selection of classroom leaders and associates?
2. List some classroom situations which might form the basis for sociometric questions.
3. What values might the teacher derive from the use of sociometric questions which refer to extraclassroom situations?
4. What particular advantages might a teacher who is new to a classroom group derive from sociometric data? What difficulties might such a teacher find in the interpretation of the data?
5. What advantages are there in keeping records of the results of successive sociometric tests?
6. If a classroom is available to you, arrange to administer a sociometric test. Develop a sociogram on the basis of the results.
7. What methods might the teacher use to find an explanation of the results of sociometric testing?

SUGGESTED ADDITIONAL READINGS

Blair, G. M., R. S. Jones, and R. H. Simpson: *Educational Psychology,* New York: The Macmillan Company, 1954.

Chapter 18, pp. 472–478, presents a brief discussion of the sociometric method.

Jennings, H. H.: "Sociometric Grouping in Relation to Child Development," chap. 15 in *Fostering Mental Health in Our Schools,*

1950 Yearbook, Association for Supervision and Curriculum Development, Washington: National Education Association, 1950.

This chapter is a readable and authoritative account of the nature, purposes, and values of the sociometric method as it applies to the classroom situation.

———: *Sociometry in Group Relations,* Washington: American Council on Education, 1948.

This study is devoted to a description of the sociometric method and enlarges upon its uses and applications in the classroom situation.

Moreno, J. L.: *Who Shall Survive?* Washington: Nervous and Mental Disease Publishing Company, 1934.

This text includes a description and an account of the rationale of the original experimentation which introduced the sociometric method.

Northway, M. L.: *A Primer of Sociometry,* Toronto: University of Toronto Press, 1952.

This booklet presents a detailed account of the sociometric test and of methods of organizing and presenting the results. A discussion of interpretations and uses is included.

Taba, H., E. H. Brady, J. T. Robinson, and W. E. Vickery: *Diagnosing Human-relations Needs,* Washington: American Council on Education, 1951.

Chapter V presents an excellent account of the procedures involved in the use of the sociometric method.

Thomas, R. M.: *Judging Student Progress,* New York: Longmans, Green & Co., Inc., 1954.

Chapter 9 describes the sociometric technique as a basis for the evaluation of social relationships in the classroom.

CHAPTER TEN

Studying Interests and Attitudes

Interests and attitudes offer clues to the understanding of the behavior of the individual, since both are closely related to emotional life. They determine essential aspects of motivation and can facilitate or interfere with the efficiency of learning in the classroom, for a learning program geared to the interests of the pupils becomes vital and meaningful to them. Favorable attitudes toward the school, the learning task, the teacher, and the group facilitate the pupil's attainment of worthwhile educational goals. Adverse attitudes, on the other hand, are likely to result in discord, apathy, rebellion, truancy, and other behavior that interferes with the attainment of desirable educational objectives.

Interests and attitudes are learned. Individuals develop attractions or aversions as a result of environmental opportunities, personal needs, and experiences. For example, the individual may develop a favorable attitude toward reading or an aversion to reading in accordance with the opportunities, satisfactions, failures, or frustrations with which reading becomes associated in his experience. If the pupil has developed positive attitudes, his energy can be readily directed toward reading experiences. If he has developed negative attitudes, he is likely to avoid reading situations.

Parents and other individuals in the child's immediate environment influence the development of his interests and attitudes. Hence, attitudes toward school and school experiences, racial and religious groups, teachers, and other children are frequently created before the child reaches school age. The teacher's task of knowing the pupil and working with him is facilitated by adequate understanding of his attitudinal and interest patterns.

METHODS OF STUDYING INTERESTS

The investigation of pupil interests may be carried out by means of observation techniques, interviews, direct questions, a check list, or an interest inventory. Studying interests by observation offers certain advantages over the use of interviews or inventories, since it permits the teacher to study his pupils under conditions which are natural rather than artificial. The classroom affords many and varied opportunities to observe behavior; the method of observation can be adapted to many situations, and records can be kept over long periods of time. Planned and purposeful observation is likely to arouse the teacher's interest in and increase his understanding of pupil behavior.

However, the teacher must be aware of the limitations of observational methods. If the observations are carried on with reference to too many situations or too many pupils at one time, they may become extremely time-consuming. Probably it is wisest to begin by keeping relatively complete records on a few pupils who present motivational problems. When this procedure is used, the observations may well be used to supplement data derived from other, less time-consuming methods of studying interests.

Further limitations of observation as a method of studying the child are its subjectivity and the need for skill on the part of the teacher. The attitudes of the teacher, the range of situations in which he observes behavior, the significance he attaches to specific incidents, and the degree of objectivity he attains in recording behavior all influence the validity of the observations.

Interviews offer possibilities for the study of interests, since pupils are ordinarily eager to discuss hobbies and other activities which are of interest to them, when they find an adult who appears to be interested, understanding, and willing to listen attentively. Pupil interests form a good basis for beginning an interview which may actually have some purpose other than to investigate interests. The teacher may acquire information about feelings and attitudes as he encourages the pupil to talk about his after-school activities, his favorite games or play activities, his hobbies, trips he has taken, his most interesting experiences, the books he likes, his favorite radio or television programs, movies he has enjoyed, and so on. Such interviews ordinarily prove fruitful in developing friendly relationships and increasing understanding of pupil feelings and attitudes as well as locating interests. Interviews of this type help the teacher to plan experiences for pupils which will utilize their interests advantageously.

In order to save time and gather data from the entire classroom group at one time, the teacher may wish to ask pupils to describe their preferred activities or to name their favorite school subjects, games, hobbies, reading material, or recreational activities. Written reports of this type provide the teacher with a wealth of information which may be utilized to good advantage in the classroom.

The more formal type of interest questionnaire may also help the teacher to know his pupils better. The questionnaire has the advantage of providing an economical method of gathering the desired data, but the method is subject to certain limitations. For instance, the questions may or may not be meaningful to the pupil in terms of his experience and information; and he may or may not be willing to cooperate fully in indicating his real preferences. The questionnaire, however, may include a wide range of statements related to interest and hence may represent a broad coverage of interest possibilities. The teacher may develop questionnaires to serve his specific purposes, or he may use a suitable published questionnaire. Interest inventories have been developed to facilitate the study of preferences among vocations, academic areas, extracurricular and recreational activities, and personal and social activities. The accompanying examples have been selected from a few published inventories to indicate some of the methods and instruments that have been devised for the study of interests.

A relatively informal listing of seventy-four interests and activities accompanies the *California Test of Personality*.[1] The directions and a few items will serve to indicate the general nature of the inventory.

Interests and Activities. First look at each thing in this test. Make a circle around the "L" for each thing that you like or would like very much to do. Then make a circle around the "D" for things you really do.

1. L D Play the radio
2. L D Read stories
3. L D Go to the movies
4. L D Read comic strips
5. L D Work problems
6. L D Study history

* * *

70. L D Go to parties
71. L D Go to dances
72. L D Be an officer of a club

[1] W. W. Clark, E. W. Tiegs, and L. P. Thorpe, *California Test of Personality*, Los Angeles: California Test Bureau, 1942.

73. L D Be a class officer
74. L D Go camping

The items of the inventory are arranged according to the amount of activity involved, proceeding from the more individual and passive interests to those which are predominantly social and active in nature.

Very few interest-test materials for elementary school pupils have been published. However, among the few published inventories of children's interests is one entitled *What I Like to Do,*[2] which is designed for pupils in grades four through seven. The authors suggest that the inventory may be useful as an aid in (1) curriculum development, (2) selection of instructional materials, (3) parent conferences, (4) understanding of individual differences among pupils, (5) planning for pupils in instructional, recreational, and educational areas, and (6) pupil guidance.[3] The interest areas covered are: art, music, social studies, active play, quiet play, manual arts, home arts, and science. Interest profiles provide percentile norms for boys and girls from grades four through six. Pupil responses are indicated by a cross in answer boxes under *No, ?,* or *Yes* for each item. The following are illustrative sample items:

Would You Like to . . .

	No	*?*	*Yes*
1. Eat ice cream	____	____	____
2. Play "Crack the Whip"	____	____	____
3. Walk in the woods	____	____	____
4. Sleep in a tent	____	____	____

The Strong *Vocational Interest Blank*[4] is an example of a carefully standardized interest inventory. Separate forms are

[2] Louis P. Thorpe, Charles E. Meyers, and Marcella R. Sea, *What I Like to Do: An Inventory of Children's Interests,* Chicago: Science Research Associates, Inc., 1954.

[3] Thorpe et al., *Examiner Manual for What I Like to Do: An Inventory of Children's Interests,* p. 3.

[4] E. K. Strong, Jr., *Vocational Interest Blank,* Stanford, Calif.: Stanford University Press, 1938.

available for men and women. The individual is asked to indicate whether he likes, dislikes, or is indifferent to each of a list of occupations, amusements, school subjects, activities, and groups of persons. Included also are scales in which activities are ranked in order of preference and scales in which a comparison of interest between two items is requested. The inventory includes a self-rating of abilities and characteristics. The individual checks "L," "I," or "D" (like, indifferent, or dislike) for (1) *occupations* such as advertiser, architect, army officer, artist; (2) *amusements* such as golf, fishing, tennis; (3) *school subjects* such as algebra, agriculture, arithmetic, art; (4) *activities* such as repairing a clock, making a radio set, interviewing clients; (5) *people* such as progressive people, conservative people, energetic people, people who borrow things. Scores on the blanks indicate whether or not the subject has patterns of interests similar to those of persons who are engaged in given occupations. The Strong inventory has been found to be useful as one source of data in counseling with high school and college students relative to academic and vocational choices.

The *Occupational Interest Inventory*[5] represents a somewhat different approach to the study of occupational preferences. The individual is asked to indicate his preferences among paired activities such as the following:[6]

1

A. Deliver groceries or meat to homes.

D. Wrap articles in the shipping department of a store.

8

B. Raise pedigreed dogs, horses, or other animals.

C. Operate lathes, drill presses, or planes.

[5] E. A. Lee and L. P. Thorpe, *Occupational Interest Inventory*, Los Angeles: California Test Bureau, 1944.

[6] *Ibid.*, *Intermediate Inventory*, Form A.

16

D. Direct the sales policies for a large store or firm.

E. Write stories or articles for important magazines.

Scores on the *Occupational Interest Inventory* are related to six fields of interest: personal-social, natural, mechanical, business, the arts, the sciences. Scores are also available for types of interest such as verbal, manipulative, and computational. The last section of the inventory is designed to identify the level of the individual's interest which may be associated with tasks at the routine level, the skilled levels, or a level which requires expertness, skill, judgment, and perhaps supervisory or administrative responsibilities. The test appears in forms adapted to the upper elementary or junior high school age and to the high school, college, and adult levels.

The *Kuder Preference Record*[7] appears in two forms, vocational and personal, which differ in emphasis and purpose. The vocational inventory provides a profile of scores in ten interest categories: outdoor, mechanical, computational, scientific, persuasive, artistic, literary, musical, social-service, and clerical. The personal form of the *Preference Record* is similar in format to the vocational form. It provides scores for different types of personal and social activities such as working with ideas, being active in groups, avoiding conflicts, directing or influencing others, being in familiar and stable situations.

The Kuder inventories utilize a forced choice technique in which the individual checks the best and least liked of three possibilities presented in each item. For example, the individual indicates the most and least preferred of the following:[8]

[7] G. F. Kuder, *Kuder Preference Record,* Chicago: Science Research Associates, Inc., 1948.

[8] *Kuder Preference Record, Personal Form AH,* Chicago: Science Research Associates, Inc., 1948.

a. Visit an art gallery
b. Browse in a library
c. Visit a museum

An inventory of a somewhat different type is the *Dunlap Academic Preference Blank.*[9] This is a check list designed for use with pupils from grades 6 to 9. It consists of ninety words and phrases representative of eight academic areas of elementary schoolwork. Pupil responses indicate liking, dislike, indifference, or absence of familiarity with the various areas.

Interest-test scores have generally been found to possess a relatively high degree of reliability. Administration of the tests to seventeen-year-old students, to college students, and to adults has demonstrated that the scores have a considerable degree of stability.[10] However, the interest scores of high school students are not so stable as those of older individuals.[11]

The constructive use of interest inventories requires an appreciation of the limitations of the instruments. The teacher should bear in mind the following limitations: (1) Answers depend on the individual's present status. Since interests grow out of experience, it is possible that future interests may develop in other directions. It is entirely possible that success in some activity which the pupil is required to pursue may engender an interest; it is also possible that such required participation, especially if the student is not successful in the

[9] J. W. Dunlap, *Dunlap Academic Preference Blank,* Yonkers, N.Y.: World Book Company, 1940.

[10] E. K. Strong, *Vocational Interests of Men and Women,* Stanford, Calif.: Stanford University Press, 1943. See also A. E. Traxler and W. C. McCall, "Some Data on the *Kuder Preference Record,*" *Educational and Psychological Measurement,* **1**:253–268, 1941.

[11] L. Canning, K. Van F. Taylor, and H. D. Carter, "Permanence of Vocational Interests of High School Boys," *Journal of Educational Psychology,* **32**:481–494; 1941.

activity, may inhibit the development of interest. (2) Published inventories do not necessarily include the whole range of possible interests. The score indicates simply that of all the interests represented on the inventory the subject is most interested in a given area, not that this area is necessarily his greatest interest. If another area had been represented, his highest score might be different. (3) The tests do not indicate potentiality. If a person has not yet engaged in a given activity, his responses simply indicate that at present he has not become interested. There is no indication that familiarity will not generate interest.

The interest inventory does, however, provide an effective means of gathering data within short periods of time and serves as a tool which may be helpful to the teacher in a variety of ways. At the secondary school level, interest-test results provide useful data in educational and vocational guidance, where test results are best used in conjunction with interviews designed to assist the student to reach suitable decisions. For guidance purposes the results of interest tests should be used in conjunction with other information in reaching a decision. Basing academic and vocational advice solely on the results of questionnaires is hazardous. As a starting point for an interview, however, these instruments are commendable, and the results of such tests are useful at the elementary and secondary school levels in curriculum and instructional planning and in working with pupils who present behavioral or motivational problems.

METHODS OF STUDYING ATTITUDES

Attitudes are predispositions or tendencies to react in certain characteristic ways toward objects, creatures, individuals, institutions, races, religions, or practices. Attitudes may be studied by means of observation, interviews, ratings, and various types of attitude and opinion scales. The teacher will find the study of pupil attitudes rewarding because it yields increased understanding of pupils and assistance in the planning and conduct of the instructional program and the evaluation of educational outcomes in terms of program objectives.

Observation. Observational methods may be utilized as a means of gathering behavioral data from which pupil attitudes may be inferred. However, the method is subject to definite limitations. Personal attitudes and biases are likely to influence teachers' interpretations of behavior. For this reason it is advisable to record observed behavior as accurately and objectively as possible over a period of time before attempting interpretations. Since situational factors influence behavior, the record should include: (1) a reference to the specific situation, (2) a description of the circumstances associated with the behavior, and (3) a factual statement of the behavior observed. Over a period of time the teacher may gather a series of records from which valid inferences regarding behavior and attitudes may be drawn. The following points are fundamental to the development of adequate observational (or anecdotal) records:

1. Note the setting in which the behavior occurred, e.g., the classroom, the playground, the halls.
2. Record the activity in progress, e.g., the class, extracurricular activity, special program, or period between classes.
3. Note special circumstances, e.g., the individuals involved, prior events which may have been influential, plans or directions, if any, which were operating at the time.
4. Describe the behavior concisely and factually without interpretative terms such as "bad," "mean," "good."
5. Sample behavior over a period of time.

6. Interpret cautiously on the basis of the objective data which have been recorded. The behavior description and the interpretation are not combined.

These requirements suggest that it is probably best to begin by selecting one or two pupils for intensive study rather than attempting to record the behavior of a considerable number.

Attitude Scales. A number of attitude scales have been developed, using, for the most part, one of two basic methods. One of these approaches, devised by Thurstone, involves the placement of statements upon a continuous scale from extremely favorable to extremely unfavorable. Each item or step on the scale is assigned a carefully developed weighted-score value. The subject indicates the statements with which he agrees and disagrees, and a score is derived. Representative statements from the Thurstone scale for measuring attitudes toward communism are:[12]

A. Communism is the solution to our present economic problems (9.1).
B. Both the evils and benefits of communism are greatly exaggerated (5.4).
C. Police are justified in shooting down Communists (0.3).

Statement A presents a view highly favorable to communism. Statement C represents extreme dislike, whereas statement B is considered to reflect a relatively neutral attitude. The median scale value of the statements checked by the subject determine his attitude score on the scale.

Utilizing the technique outlined above, Thurstone and others have devised scales for the measurement of attitudes toward war, the Negro, the Constitution, the law, freedom of speech, labor unions, the treatment of criminals, and so on.

[12] L. L. Thurstone, "Attitude toward Communism," *Scale No. 6, Form A,* Chicago: University of Chicago Press. (Copyright, 1931, by the University of Chicago Press.)

Utilizing a similar technique, Remmers and others[13] have developed general scales designed to measure attitudes toward any person, group, institution, or practice. Excerpts from "A Scale for Measuring Attitude toward Any Institution," developed by Ida B. Kelly and edited by Remmers, will indicate the nature of these scales:

1. Is perfect in every way.
5. Represents the best thought in modern life.
9. Is a strong influence for right living.
12. Is valuable in creating ideals.
16. Aids the individual in wise use of leisure time.

The subject is asked to check each statement with which he agrees. The results of the Remmers scales are comparable to those of the more specific scales of Thurstone.[14]

Among the many scales developed by Remmers and his associates are scales which indicate attitudes toward:

1. Any disciplinary procedure (V. R. Clause).
2. Any elementary teacher (M. Amatora).
3. Any practice (H. W. Bues).
4. Any school subject (E. B. Silance).
5. Any proposed social action (D. M. Thomas).
6. Any teacher (L. B. Hoshaw).
7. Any vocation (H. E. Miller).

Another procedure for the measurement of attitudes has been proposed by Likert.[15] In the Likert scales, each statement represents either a favorable or an unfavorable attitude.

[13] H. H. Remmers and N. L. Gage, *Educational Measurement and Evaluation,* rev. ed., New York: Harper & Brothers, 1955, pp. 387–389.

[14] H. H. Remmers, "Generalized Attitude Scales: Studies in Social-psychological Measurements," in *Studies in Higher Education,* no. 26, Lafayette, Ind.: Purdue University, 1934, pp. 7–17.

[15] R. Likert, "A Technique for the Measurement of Attitudes," *Archives of Psychology,* **22** (140), 1932.

Strength of reaction toward each item is indicated along a scale running from strongly agree to strongly disagree. Favorable attitudes are reflected in high scores and unfavorable attitudes in low scores. Each item is carefully selected and tested. The procedures used in developing the Likert scales are not so time-consuming as those required for the Thurstone scales, yet the Likert scales appear to be equally reliable.[16] The Likert method requires subjects to respond to all items of the scale and has some advantages in terms of possibilities of analysis of the results.

The *Scale of Social Distance* developed by Bogardus[17] is an instrument designed to indicate attitudes toward persons of various nationalities and races. Seven degrees of closeness are represented in the statements of the subject concerning his willingness to admit members of a national or racial group to (1) close kinship by marriage, (2) his club, (3) his street as neighbors, (4) the same occupation as himself, or (5) citizenship in his country; (6) as visitors only to his country; or (7) to exclude them from his country. Although the scale was designed for the study of attitudes toward racial and national groups, the method is readily adaptable to the study of attitudes toward members of a variety of religious, social, political, and vocational groups.

In a study of the development of attitudes toward the Negro, Horowitz[18] used pictures of Negro and white boys. Pupils from kindergarten through eighth grade were first asked to rank the pictures in order of preference. Next they were asked to use the pictures as a basis for the selection of com-

[16] R. Likert and others, "A Simple and Reliable Method of Scoring the Thurstone Attitude Scales," *Journal of Social Psychology,* **5**:228–238, 1934.

[17] E. S. Bogardus, "Measuring Social Distance," *Journal of Applied Sociology,* **9**:299–308, 1925.

[18] E. L. Horowitz, "The Development of Attitude toward the Negro," *Archives of Psychology,* **28** (194), 1936.

panions for various situations and activities. For example, children were selected as classmates, captain of the ball team, luncheon companions, party guests, members of the gang, neighbors, and so on. Pictures of social situations involving the two races were also presented to afford further opportunities for expressions of attitudes. Horowitz found that prejudice appeared at an early age and that attitude development is relatively consistent for groups and for individuals.

An interesting approach to attitude assessment appears in Minard's study of racial attitudes.[19] Statements were written involving situations which would place individuals in close proximity to members of such racial or national groups as Filipinos, Chinese, Mexicans, and Negroes. The situation might center around neighborhood residence, team or club membership, and so on.

Attitudes toward the self, classmates, home, school, or persons in authority are frequently indicated in pupil responses to personality inventories. For instance, an analysis of the responses of a boy to selected items of the *California Test of Personality*[20] may suggest that he considers his classmates to be mean, willing to cheat, unreasonable, unfair, and willing to take advantage of him whenever possible. Clues of this nature provide a basis for understanding his behavior.

Attitude scales have been criticized because of the absence of objective evidence of their validity; there is frequently no ready means of checking the individual's verbal report. The subject may wish to conceal his real attitudes or may not be aware of them. However, responses to attitude scales and studies of attitudes, when critically and cautiously interpreted, provide the teacher with pertinent information concerning

[19] R. D. Minard, "Race Attitudes of Iowa Children," *Studies in Character,* **4** (2), University of Iowa, 1931.

[20] W. W. Clark, E. W. Tiegs, and L. P. Thorpe, *California Test of Personality,* Los Angeles, Calif.: California Test Bureau, 1942.

the prevailing attitudes of pupils toward school subjects, individuals, groups, and practices, and changes of attitude produced by presentations, discussions, interviews, or other techniques. Teacher evaluation of attitudes is in actuality almost a necessity, since many of our most worthwhile educational goals are related to the development of pupils' attitudes. We call these goals character development, citizenship, moral and ethical behavior, or social cooperation.

APPLICATIONS IN THE CLASSROOM

Interests and attitudes are perhaps generally thought of as sources of motivation for learning. However, motives, values, attitudes, interests, and ideals which are socially acceptable and personally satisfying are not only valuable as supports for academic learning but represent valid educational goals in themselves. In the evaluation of the educational growth of pupils, the development of interests and attitudes deserves careful consideration.

A study of pupils' interests by any of the techniques suggested may provide the teacher with information useful in:

1. Understanding pupils.
2. Discovering motivational possibilities.
3. Relating teaching to pupils' interests and experience.
4. Studying and evaluating pupils' interest changes.
5. Helping pupils to: (*a*) become aware of their interests, (*b*) evaluate their interests, and (*c*) increase their understanding of themselves.
6. Stimulating thought and discussion among pupils concerning the implications of their interests.

Investigations of attitudes provide the teacher with data which may be significant in a number of respects. Such data may enable the teacher to:

1. Attain an increased understanding of pupils.
2. Attain deeper understanding of pupil behavior.
3. Develop curricular, field, social, or civic experiences related to major educational goals.
4. Evaluate pupil behavior on a broader basis than that of subject-matter attainment.
5. Study attitude change as the result of directed experiences.
6. Assess the relative effectiveness of various teaching methods and techniques as a means of influencing pupil attitudes.

Data derived from careful studies and evaluations of interests and attitudes will be of value in compiling cumulative records and in accurate reporting of educational attainments not represented in achievement-test results. For example, such characteristics as cooperation, self-control, self-confidence, tolerance, optimism, leadership, respect for the rights of others, respect for the contributions and ideas of others, and such attitudes as those toward civic affairs and authority form an essential part of the evaluation of pupil progress and attainment. A sincere attempt on the part of the teacher to develop adequate bases for judgment with respect to such characteristics as those listed above could be expected to improve the teacher's understanding of pupil behavior and his evaluation of pupil status and progress.[21]

SUMMARY

Interests and attitudes are essential aspects of the emotional and behavioral life of the individual and are essential in motivation and learning. The assessment of interests and

[21] For a list of educational objectives and suggested means for evaluating them, see J. W. Wrightstone, "Measuring the Attainment of Newer Educational Objectives," *Sixteenth Yearbook of the Department of Elementary School Principals,* Washington: National Education Association, 1937, pp. 493–501.

attitudes is an important aspect of the evaluation of pupil progress and attainment with respect to important educational objectives.

Interests can be studied by a variety of methods: observation, direct questions, check lists, and interest inventories. A variety of instruments provide means of gathering data concerning a broad range of pupil preferences with regard to school subjects, activities, forms of recreation, hobbies, and vocations.

Attitudes can be investigated by means of observations, anecdotal records, interviews, ratings, and attitude and opinion scales. Data concerning pupil attitudes may contribute to the understanding of pupils, the planning and conduct of the instructional program, the evaluation of pupil attainments, and the development of adequate records and reporting practices. A number of scales are available for the study of significant attitudes. In his use and interpretation of these scales, the teacher should consider the method utilized in the development of the scale.

Data concerning pupil interests and attitudes may contribute significantly to the educational program with reference to instruction, evaluation, planning, recording, and reporting.

STUDY AND DISCUSSION EXERCISES

1. In what ways is it valuable for the teacher to understand techniques for the measurement of interests and attitudes?
2. Select an interest inventory and suggest specific ways in which its results can be of value to the classroom teacher.
3. List a number of attitudes which you feel are closely related to the effectiveness of classroom learning. Describe one of these attitudes in specific behavioral terms. How might the teacher study this attitude among pupils in his classroom?
4. Select a published interest inventory. Outline the bases for its development and utilize these to discuss the possibilities of interpretation of scores which might be derived from this inventory.

5. Indicate as specifically as you can the contributions which teacher investigations of pupil interests and attitudes can make to (*a*) teacher understanding of pupil behavior, (*b*) the development and maintenance of cumulative records, (*c*) pupil-teacher conferences, (*d*) parent-teacher conferences, and (*e*) reports of pupil progress.

6. Observe pupils in social situations in the classroom and out of the classroom and write behavioral descriptions. Make a record of the social attitudes which appear to be represented in the behavior observed.

SUGGESTED ADDITIONAL READINGS

Cronbach, L. J.: *Essentials of Psychological Testing,* New York: Harper & Brothers, 1949.

Chapters 15 and 17 include descriptions of methods and instruments used in the assessment of interests and attitudes, with suggestions for the applications of results. Chapter 18 is concerned with observation as a method of studying behavior.

Greene, E. B.: *Measurements of Human Behavior,* rev. ed., New York: The Odyssey Press, Inc., 1952.

Chapters 20 and 21 are devoted to the measurement of interests and attitudes and contain descriptions of instruments and discussions of methods of assessment.

Jordan, A. M.: *Measurement in Education,* New York: McGraw-Hill Book Company, Inc., 1953.

Chapters 16 and 17 present an account of interest and attitude measurement. Chapter 16 includes a list of published interest inventories.

Remmers, H. H., and N. L. Gage: *Educational Measurement and Evaluation,* New York: Harper & Brothers, 1955.

Chapter 13 presents a discussion of the nature, organization, and significance of attitudes, and chap. 14 contains a discussion of methods of studying attitudes and interests.

Super, D. E.: *Appraising Vocational Fitness,* New York: Harper & Brothers, 1949.

Chapters 16, 17, and 18 are devoted to a detailed description of the nature and measurement of interest; the emphasis is primarily vocational.

CHAPTER ELEVEN

Rating Techniques in Pupil Evaluation

Some of the most important results of education cannot be evaluated by the usual paper-and-pencil tests: the acquisition of effective work habits and study skills, for example, and the development of acceptable social attitudes and behaviors. Good work habits, cooperativeness, industry, responsibility, and citizenship are commonly listed on report cards and cumulative records and are recognized as standard educational objectives. Rating methods are among the possibilities of evaluating pupil progress toward these educational goals. This chapter describes means of summarizing and recording teacher ratings and suggests ways of improving the methods which the teacher may use.

PROBLEMS IN THE USE OF RATING METHODS

As we have seen, tests are tools to provide data upon which to base estimates and judgments. A rating represents an estimate or judgment regarding a pupil characteristic, based on the teacher's observations of the pupil. Test results imply, in the nature of the items, certain definitions of intelligence, achievement, readiness, and so on, and these definitions form a point of reference for the interpretation of test results. On the other hand, a rating on citizenship may have no such definitive point of reference. A teacher or parent may well ask, "What does the rater mean by *citizenship?* On what kind of data is his rating based?" Ratings typically are highly subjective in nature. They tend to reflect the characteristics of the rater to almost as great an extent as they do those of the individual being rated.

The most common sources of error in ratings are inadequate or inconsistent definition of traits, fixed patterns of rating, and halo effect. A further problem is lack of consistency between several ratings of the individual on the same trait.

Perhaps the key problem in the interpretation of ratings is the definition of the rated characteristic. Suppose that teachers A and B are rating pupils on cooperation. The definition utilized by teacher A may involve a large measure of obedience or emphasize cooperation with the teacher. Teacher B may evaluate the same trait almost entirely on the basis of ability to work cooperatively with other pupils. Ratings of the same pupils by these two teachers would bear no necessary relationship to one another. At the same time, a parent attempting to interpret the ratings might have in mind a definition of cooperation which differs markedly from those of the two teachers. Unless traits are clearly defined, ratings may be meaningless.

The *fixed pattern* is a common source of error in ratings. Some raters, for example, are inclined to be consistently overgenerous in their judgments. This has been termed the *generosity error*. A second, and smaller, group of raters demonstrate a consistent tendency to underrate, and still others are prone to rate almost everyone as average regardless of existing differences. The resulting ratings reflect the characteristic evaluative tendencies of the rater and may have little reference to the actual characteristics of the individuals being rated. Figure 13 illustrates the possible effects of such rating patterns with respect to a hypothetical class of twenty students. Teacher A rates 45 per cent of these pupils as "excellent" or "superior"; he is relatively generous in his ratings. Teacher B is apparently unable to differentiate among a majority of the pupils, since he places 70 per cent in a single category in the

TRAIT: COOPERATIVENESS

Scale	Excellent %	Superior %	Good %	Fair %	Poor %
Teacher A	20	25	40	10	5
Teacher B	5	10	70	10	5
Teacher C	5	10	30	35	20

FIG. 13. Per cent of a hypothetical class of twenty pupils placed by three teachers under each of five levels of a scale for rating cooperativeness.

center of the scale. This is an instance of the "average" error. Teacher C rates 55 per cent of the group as "fair" or "poor," illustrating the error of underrating. These ratings would be difficult to interpret apart from a knowledge of the raters and their characteristic rating patterns.

The *halo effect* is a further common source of error in ratings. The teacher forms a general impression concerning the pupil, and his ratings of the pupil's traits are as likely to be representative of this general impression as they are of the specific characteristic being rated. For example, Mary may have a pleasing appearance and manner. Teacher ratings of such traits as dependability, emotional stability, and cooperativeness may be influenced favorably by the teacher's general impression of Mary rather than by her actual status with respect to the specific characteristic being evaluated. Unfavorable general impressions may lead to equally unrealistic trait evaluations. The influence of the halo effect is illustrated in Figure 14.

Inconsistencies frequently appear in repeated ratings of a characteristic. That is, two teachers rating a pupil on a given

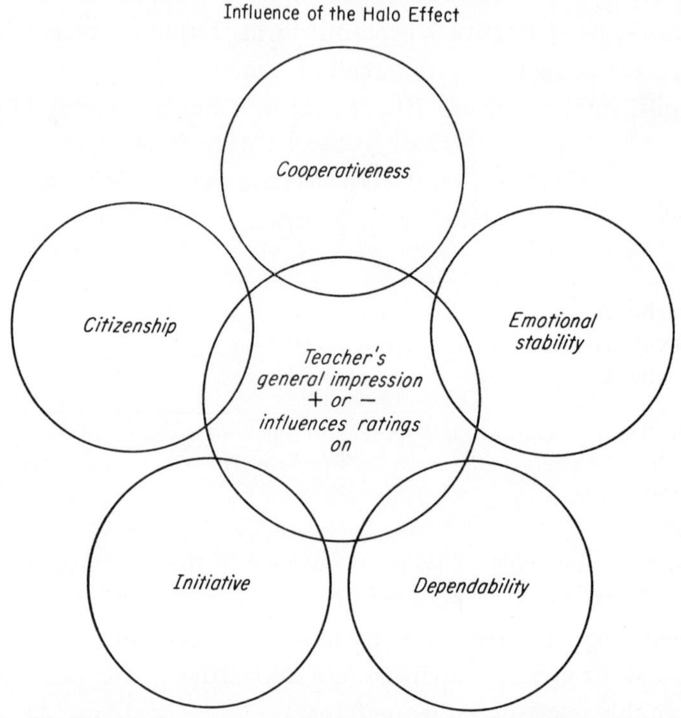

FIG. 14. Schematic representation of the pervasive influence of halo effect on ratings on specific characteristics.

characteristic may vary markedly in their evaluations. Again, a teacher may change his rating of a given pupil even in a short space of time. This lack of consistency or reliability poses a problem with respect to the interpretation of ratings. By way of analogy, consider the situation which develops when two sets of comparable mental- or achievement-test scores give entirely different pictures of the same person. Is the difference a result of the type of test used? Can it be explained in terms of differences in the two testing situations?

Was the subject in poor physical health or emotionally upset at one of these times? How can the differences be explained? Similarly, interpretation is difficult when ratings of the same person differ with respect to identical characteristics. Among the reasons for inconsistencies may be the characteristics of the rater, factors in the situation in which ratings are developed, the nature of the characteristic being evaluated, the extent of opportunity to observe the individual, and changes in the individual over the period of time between ratings. There are many possible explanations.

Ratings based on casual or incidental impressions are notably unreliable, but ratings based upon careful and systematic observations of well-defined characteristics can be quite reliable. Again, certain characteristics are more reliably evaluated by rating methods than others. Ratings of traits which can be observed objectively are typically most reliable. Ratings of general characteristics and traits which involve interaction with others tend to be least reliable.[1] For example, traits such as cooperativeness and integrity are relatively difficult to evaluate by rating methods.

ORGANIZATION OF RATING SCALES

The usual rating scale presents the rater with a set of characteristics (such as initiative, responsibility, and social effectiveness) which are to be evaluated. These traits may or may not be defined. The rater is asked to assess individuals by checking a point on a scale representing a level or degree of the trait. The list that follows indicates various ways in which the levels or degrees may be indicated:

1. By means of *numbers:* 1, 2, 3, etc.
2. In terms of *frequency* of occurrence of the trait: always, usually, seldom, never.

[1] H. L. Hollingworth, *Judging Human Character,* New York: Appleton-Century-Crofts, Inc., 1922.

3. By *qualitative* terms: excellent, superior, good, fair, poor.
4. By terms which refer to *relative* status, e.g., relative to others: outstanding, above average, average, below average, inferior.
5. By *descriptive* terms which apply to each level or step, e.g.:
   a. Recognized as a leader; assumes leadership willingly.
   b. Accepts leadership when specifically requested to do so.
   c. Avoids leadership.
6. By means of *coded numbers or letters:*
   1 or A represents excellent.
   2 or B represents above average.
   3 or C represents average.
   4 or D represents below average.
   5 or E represents inferior.

Each of these types of organization of rating scales may be of value as a means of providing the teacher with a frame of reference or a guide, provided the type of organization is suited to the trait being rated and the purposes which the rating is designed to serve. For example, Schedule A of the *Haggerty-Olson-Wickman Behavior Rating Schedules* utilizes an organization based on the frequency with which a type of behavior occurs. Four levels of frequency are indicated for each of the fifteen traits listed. A weighted score or quantitative value has been established for each rating. This quantitative value is based on the seriousness and frequency of occurrence of the behavior among school children (Fig. 15).[2]

[2] M. E. Haggerty, W. C. Olson, and E. K. Wickman, *Haggerty-Olson-Wickman Behavior Rating Schedules, Manual of Directions,* Yonkers, N.Y.: World Book Company, 1930.

Behavior Problem	*Frequency of occurrence*				
	Has never occurred	Has occurred once or twice but no more	Occasional occurrence	Frequent occurrence	Score
Disinterest in school work	0	4	6	7	
Truancy	0	12	18	21	

FIG. 15. Organization of Schedule A of the *Haggerty-Olson-Wickman Behavior Rating Schedules,* indicating basis in frequency of occurrence and showing weighted scores.

Schedule B of the *Haggerty-Olson-Wickman Scales* combines descriptive categories and quantitative values. The weighted scores of Schedule B have been assigned on the basis of relationships between ratings on each of thirty-five traits and the behavior tendencies listed under Schedule A.[3] Figure

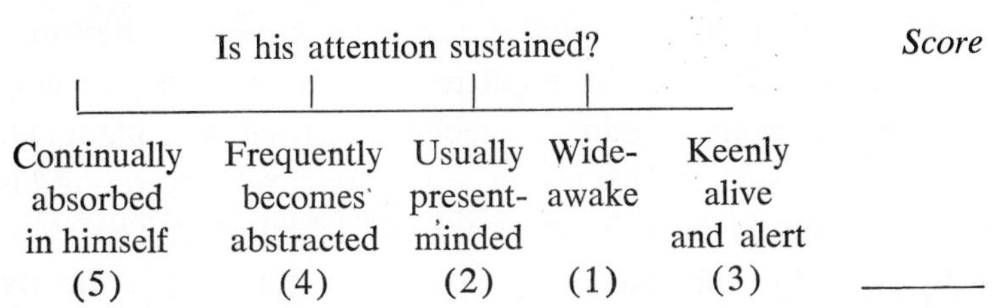

FIG. 16. Organization of Schedule B of the *Haggerty-Olson-Wickman Behavior Rating Schedules.* Descriptive categories are accompanied by weighted score values.

16 illustrates the organization of Schedule B. These schedules represent an attempt to assign meaningful quantitative values to rating categories; they also illustrate the definition of scale steps in terms of frequency of occurrence and descriptions.

[3] *Ibid.*

IMPROVING RATINGS OF PUPIL CHARACTERISTICS

In the use of rating devices there is no substitute for conscientiousness, skill, and objectivity on the part of the rater. However, work with rating instruments indicates that evaluations based on these devices may be improved through the following procedures:

1. Selecting carefully the traits which are to be evaluated.
2. Defining the traits.
3. Describing the traits.
4. Establishing a basis for judgment.
5. Establishing scale steps.
6. Organizing the rating instrument.

1. *Selecting the traits.* In selecting a list of traits to be evaluated by rating methods, the teacher should consider the purpose of the evaluation and the extent to which each trait is related to educational objectives. Carefully developed ratings of significant pupil characteristics provide essential information in the evaluation of pupil status and progress. Such ratings will increase the value of pupil records and reports and may play an important role in the teacher's instructional planning.

The traits selected for use in a teacher-developed rating instrument should be (*a*) relatively few in number, (*b*) critically related to the teacher's purposes in rating, (*c*) as clearly differentiated as possible, and (*d*) capable of clear and precise definition, preferably in terms of observable behavior.

2. *Defining the traits.* A majority of the characteristics which the teacher evaluates by means of ratings may be defined in a number of different ways. Since teacher ratings may be a means of providing information to other persons, such as the pupil, parents, or other teachers and professional persons, it is important that the rated characteristics be defined carefully, objectively, and specifically. Such definitions are

necessary to interpretation of the evaluation represented by the rating. Probably the ratings that lend themselves best to accurate interpretations are those that can be described in terms of observable behavior, for many traits (e.g., "cooperativeness") are subject to a number of possible definitions depending on the individual who interprets the term. However, the teacher can clarify his intention by means of a recorded definition such as the following: "*Cooperativeness:* The pupil's ability to work harmoniously with his classmates in classroom activities and projects."

Certain advantages are achieved through the use of this type of definition. The ratings refer to classroom activities which can be observed by the teacher. There is no implication that the rating applies to the pupil's behavior in situations in which the teacher has limited opportunity to conduct systematic observations. Again, the reference applies to cooperation with other pupils rather than cooperation with the teacher.

The pupil traits listed on report cards and other rating instruments are often inadequately defined on the report or schedule. In such instances it is usually advisable for the teacher to decide upon a clear definition and to record it.

3. *Describing the traits.* As we have seen, a clear definition of traits is helpful in rating. However, definitions are general descriptions or summary statements, and ratings are more likely to be reliable and meaningful when they are based on specific behaviors which serve as indicators of the characteristics being assessed. For example, having defined cooperativeness, the teacher lists pupil behavior which is related to the definition. The teacher's worksheet might look like this:

Cooperativeness: The pupil's ability to work harmoniously with his classmates in classroom activities and projects.

Behaviors:

1. Participates actively in group planning, work, and discussion.
2. Brings materials and ideas to class to share with others.

3. Listens to the ideas and experiences of others.
4. Respects the opinions of others.
5. Shares his opinions with members of the group.
6. Abides by the decisions of the group.
7. Works with class officers, committees, and group leaders.
8. Does not needlessly disturb the work of others in the group.
9. Carries his share of responsibility for the work of the group.

Such a list of behavioral indicators provides a relatively tangible basis for the observation and evaluation of the characteristic.

4. *Establishing the basis for judgment.* Judgments with respect to any characteristic may be either absolute or relative. The statement, "This object is five feet high," illustrates an absolute judgment. Linear and quantitative measures of length, height, weight, etc., are based on standard units which give them a common meaning. A rating scale involving absolute judgments asks the rater, in effect, such questions as "Is he cooperative? To what degree?" This is probably the type of rating scale most commonly used. However, one might ask whether all raters use the same standard or unit of measurement as a basis for their judgments.

In utilizing relative methods, the rater decides whether the pupil is relatively more or less cooperative than others. The comparison may be limited to members of an age group, grade level, or classroom group. Interpretations based on ratings of this type specify or imply the limitation that the pupil is being compared with others of a group. Thus the ratings of pupils will be dispersed around the level of average or typical performance for the specified group. The technique is roughly similar to that involved in the development of "norms"; that is, the pupil is rated in terms of his status with respect to his group rather than in terms of a "standard" or "expected" level of attainment. The rating scales presented in Figure 17, prepared for the Springfield, Missouri, Senior High School, are examples of relative scales.

*Behaviors Which Indicate That One Is "Considerate of Others"**

Teacher____________________ Pupil____________________

"Average" means that the pupil exhibits the behavior indicated to about the same degree as the average pupil of his grade level.

	Much below average	Below average	Average	Above average	Much above average
1. Shares materials willingly and properly					
2. Observes normal courtesies in personal relationships with others					
3. Participates in and makes positive contribution to group activities					
4. Returns materials to proper places after use					
(Other behaviors; write in and rate)					

*Behaviors Which Indicate That One Is "Not Considerate of Others"**

Teacher____________________ Pupil____________________

"Average" means that the pupil exhibits the behavior indicated to about the same degree as the average pupil of his grade level.

	Much below average	Below average	Average	Above average	Much above average
1. Interrupts others who are speaking					
2. Doing such things as cleaning fingernails, cleaning out purse, combing hair, etc., while other students are making reports					
3. Crowding ahead of others in lunch line, while coming into or leaving classroom					
4. Cutting across, shoving, or crowding in corridors					
5. Loud and boisterous in corridors					
(Other behaviors; write in and rate)					

* Springfield, Missouri, Senior High School, 1949 (mimeographed).

FIG. 17. Examples of rating scales.

A special type of relative scale is the "man-to-man" scale. In developing this type of instrument the teacher selects certain pupils as "standards" for the various steps of each trait scale. One pupil is selected to represent each step of the scale, and others are rated by comparison with these "standards." This method of establishing a basis for judgment appears to have definite possibilities for classroom use.

5. *Establishing scale steps.* A further procedure in establishing the basis for judgment is developing categories, levels, or steps which represent the scale for each trait. Ordinarily we think of any trait variable (such as energy, enthusiasm, or initiative) as essentially continuous. In practice, however, a number of areas or "units" are established along the trait scale as a matter of convenience rather than fact. For example, a scale for enthusiasm might be represented as follows:

Enthusiasm:

Completely indifferent	Extremely enthusiastic

The continuous line represents the range from, say, zero enthusiasm to the highest extreme of the trait. But it would be difficult accurately to rate pupils along a continuum of which only the extremes are described. The following arrangement is more useful because five specific steps are described along the continuum.[4]

Enthusiasm:

Indifferent	Rarely shows enthusiasm	Sometimes enthusiastic	Usually has pep and vigor	Works with great enthusiasm

The number of steps included in a scale will be determined, in part at least, by the purposes for which the ratings are to be used and by the nature of the trait. In general, however, if

[4] *Summary Behavior Rating Scale, Springfield* (Missouri) Senior High School, 1949 (mimeographed).

too few steps are included in the scale, it will not accurately reflect trait differentiations among individuals. Too many steps, on the other hand, may make the task of the rater cumbersome or make differential judgments difficult. As with other evaluative devices, the purpose of rating scales is to differentiate among individuals in terms of specified characteristics. More refined and specific differentiations ordinarily represent a more adequate basis for interpretation and evaluation.

6. *Organizing the rating instrument.* Rating instruments are customarily organized according to one of four general plans: (*a*) the check list, (*b*) the coded scale (using coded numbers or letters), (*c*) the graphic form, and (*d*) the descriptive scale.

The *check list* presents the rater with a list of characteristics or behaviors to be checked off if they appear to apply to the person being rated. The "Behavior-observation Record" (Figure 18) is such an instrument, developed to help teachers understand the behavior of their pupils.

The *coded* scale is commonly used in pupil report cards. Typically, it employs numerals or letters which are described in one section of the card. Following each rated characteristic, the code number or letter (frequently a "grade") is indicated to represent pupil standing. The following excerpts from the "Primary Pupil Progress Report" of the Corvallis Public Schools (Figure 19) are illustrative of such organization.[5] The brief statement of philosophy will perhaps indicate the basis for the letter and number codes used in connection with this particular pupil report card. The numerals opposite reading items represent the pupil's academic status in the subject as interpreted under "Subject-matter Evaluation." The letters opposite the citizenship items indicate the pupil's status with respect to each of the listed traits.

[5] "Primary Pupil Progress Report," Corvallis Public Schools, Corvallis, Ore.

BEHAVIOR OBSERVATION RECORD

To understand behavior, it is important to observe the pupil's reactions on the playground, in the neighborhood, and at home. Check words or phrases that describe the behavior of the pupil as you have observed it. Please feel free to individualize the report as much as possible by adding descriptive comments. If you know of reasons for the conditions you check, please jot them down at the right of your answers.

Is this pupil physically strong?

_____ Is strong and active
_____ Seldom tires
_____ Has ordinary endurance
_____ Is listless, easily fatigued

Does he have good work habits?

_____ Completes what he starts
_____ Is able to evaluate his work
_____ Capable of sustained attention
_____ Needs urging to stay with a task
_____ Is easily discouraged
_____ Seldom completes the job
_____ Easily distracted

Does he get along with other people?

_____ Is a successful leader
_____ Works and plays well with others
_____ Earns recognition
_____ Prefers to work by himself
_____ Is destructive
_____ Has bad temper when thwarted
_____ Is quarrelsome
_____ Is overaggressive
_____ Is easily led
_____ Often lies to get out of difficulties
_____ Is disobedient to teachers
_____ Has few friends
_____ Is disliked and avoided by others

What is his usual disposition?

_____ Cheerful, happy
_____ Kind and sympathetic
_____ Self-controlled, calm
_____ Quiet, reserved
_____ Impulsive
_____ Stubborn
_____ Moody

FIG. 18. *Behavior-observation Record,* used in the San Diego Public Schools (San Diego, 1949).

Corvallis teachers believe that each child's progress should be reported to him and his parents at least three times each year. They also believe that each pupil should be evaluated in terms of his individual growth and progress and in terms of his achievement in academic work. In order to do this dual evaluation task, two different sets of symbols and meanings are required.

Individual Evaluation

A—Pupil is using all his ability.
B—Pupil is using nearly all his ability.
C—Pupil is using about half of his ability.
D—Pupil is using less than half of his ability.
E—Pupil is using almost none of his ability and is making very little individual progress.

Subject-matter Evaluation

1—Pupil's achievement and position in this subject are excellent.
2—Pupil's achievement and position in subject are above average.
3—Pupil's achievement and position in this subject are average.
4—Pupil's achievement and position in subject are below average.
5—Pupil's achievement and position in this subject do not meet the standards for this subject.

READING	*First report*	*Second report*	*Third report*
Reads with understanding......	2		
Reads well to others..........	3		
Shows ability to attack new words	2		
Enjoys stories and poetry......	3		
EFFECTIVE CITIZENSHIP			
Follows directions promptly....	B		
Makes good use of free time....	B		
Completes work..............	A		
Takes care of property........	C		
Accepts criticism.............	B		
Displays good sportsmanship...	D		
Uses courtesy in manner and speech....................	C		
Cooperates in classroom.......	C		
Controls own freedom.........	C		

FIG. 19. Primary pupil report card.

In the *graphic* type of rating scale, checks are placed along a line. Steps in the graphic scale may be presented numerically, as coded letters or numbers, or as descriptive phrases. The following item is illustrative of the graphic organization utilizing descriptive-trait categories:[6]

3. Is his attention sustained?

Distracted: Jumps rapidly from one thing to another	Difficult to keep at a task until it is completed	Attends adequately	Is absorbed in what he does	Able to hold attention for long periods

The graphic presentation permits relatively rapid assessment of the results of the rating.

Descriptive rating scales may be organized in a variety of ways. The distinctive feature of this type of scale is that descriptions indicate the various scale steps. The item for rating "attention" in the preceding paragraph combines the graphic and descriptive forms of presentation. The descriptive scale may also be organized as follows:[7]

B Does he need frequent prodding or does he go ahead without being told?

_______ Seeks and sets for himself additional tasks

_______ Completes suggested supplementary work

_______ Does ordinary assignments of his own accord

_______ Needs occasional prodding

[6] Haggerty et al., *ibid.*

[7] Adapted from *American Council on Education Personality Report, Form B,* Washington: Committee on Personality Traits, American Council on Education (mimeographed).

_______ Needs much prodding in doing ordinary assignments

_______ No opportunity to observe

The ordering of the steps constitutes a problem in setting up rating categories for each trait. In many scales, *constant alternatives* are used; that is, a set of steps is established which applies to all traits included in the scale. The levels represented may be "Excellent, good, fair, poor"; "Always, usually, frequently, seldom, never"; "Outstanding, above average, average, below average, inferior"; and so on. Coded number or letter forms of organization typically utilize constant alternatives.

In general, ratings are likely to be more accurate if the steps of the scale for each trait are set down in *random order*. That is, the "good" and "poor" ends of the scale used in the graphic form may be alternated in random fashion. This procedure encourages the rater to examine each descriptive statement and minimizes the tendency to check one or the other side of the rating sheet continually.

USING RATING DEVICES IN SCHOOLS

As we have seen, rating pupils is one of the teacher's customary responsibilities, for ratings are required for report cards and school records. Techniques have been designed to improve ordinary rating devices such as report cards, and these techniques may be utilized for a variety of educational purposes.

Ordinarily, the task of reporting pupil status or progress presents difficulties for the teacher. Should the pupil be graded on the basis of "standards" or "expectations" for his grade? On the basis of improvement or growth? Of a comparison with others of his grade? These questions concern the main problem of the establishment of a basis for judgment. Where established procedures exist in schools, evaluation may be improved through clear statement of purpose, definitions of traits, and clarification of the basis for judgment. Presentations by teacher committees and discussions in staff meetings provide a means toward the development of common understandings essential to meaningful evaluations.

Report forms, of course, must be interpreted by parents. It is therefore advisable that the traits evaluated on reports be clearly defined as to the meaning and significance of ratings. Printed statements and discussions related to the development and use of report cards are often helpful in increasing parent understanding of the ratings.

The teacher may utilize rating devices for a variety of useful purposes in the classroom. A few of the possible areas of usefulness are:

1. Study of the work habits and skills of pupils.
2. Study of pupil behavior in specified group activities (such as games, field trips, committee work).
3. Evaluation of performance or products (as in handwriting, art work, speech, shop work, oral reading).
4. Pupil self-evaluation with respect to specified traits, activities, and interests (such as cooperation on a field trip, work habits, study skills, contributions to the class).

The following suggestions are designed to serve as a guide to the teacher in the development and use of rating devices.

1. In developing the device (scale or check list), relate it to educational objectives.
2. State clearly the behaviors which are to be observed and rated.

3. Rate one trait at a time. Whenever possible, it is advisable to rate all pupils on one trait before going on to the next.
4. Examine ratings for indications of lack of distribution. Although frequencies should be greatest around the center of each trait scale, ratings should be dispersed over the length of the scale.
5. Limit the number of traits which are to be considered in any one device.
6. Rate a pupil only after adequate observation of the specific characteristic which is being evaluated.

SUMMARY

Rating devices represent a convenient means of compiling data which provide a basis for the evaluation of pupils. Ratings are typically subject to certain errors, but their limitations can be minimized by (1) careful selection, definition, and description of the characteristics to be rated, (2) establishment of a clear basis for making differential judgments, and (3) organization of the scale to provide a meaningful dispersion of ratings for each trait.

The traits selected for use in a rating instrument should be relatively few in number and should be adapted to the purposes for which the ratings are to be used. They should be clearly defined and described, preferably in terms of observable characteristics. The traits may be assessed on the basis of either absolute or relative judgments. Rating instruments are ordinarily organized in the form of (1) a check list, (2) a coded number or letter device, (3) a graphic scale, or (4) a descriptive scale.

Rating devices serve a variety of purposes in the school and classroom. Grading systems, report cards, and cumulative record forms involve the rating process. The teacher may develop rating instruments to study and evaluate a wide range of pupil behaviors and attitudes, and to the extent that he improves his ability to develop and utilize instruments of this type, his program of evaluation will be less tied to those educational objectives which are more readily assessed by means of the usual paper-and-pencil tests.

STUDY AND DISCUSSION EXERCISES

1. List educational objectives important in your teaching which cannot be measured by paper-and-pencil tests.
2. Discuss the merits and limitations of absolute and relative measures as they apply to rating instruments.
3. What specific values do you see in pupil self-evaluation by rating devices? In what ways might self-rating scales be useful in your classroom?
4. How would you develop a pupil self-rating scale to stimulate interest in neatness in written work?
5. Develop a rating device to assist in the evaluation of the products or procedures of pupil work in any one of the following areas: shop, English, art, science, handwriting.
6. (*a*) Select a subject area. Develop a definition and behavior description of study skills or work habits in that area. (*b*) Organize a rating instrument based on your definition and description of the trait. (*c*) Present reasons for your selection of a particular type of scale organization.

SUGGESTED ADDITIONAL READINGS

Cronbach, L. J.: *Essentials of Psychological Testing,* New York: Harper & Brothers, 1949.

Chapter 18 of this comprehensive text is a discussion of techniques of observing behavior in normal situations. The values and limitations of rating methods are considered.

Greene, E. B.: *Measurements of Human Behavior,* rev. ed., New York: The Odyssey Press, Inc., 1952.

Chapter 16, "Types of Estimates," includes a relatively comprehensive account of rating methods and devices.

Guilford, J. P.: *Psychometric Methods,* New York: McGraw-Hill Book Company, Inc., 1936.

Chapter 9 presents an excellent account of rating methods. Specific limitations and advantages of various types are indicated.

Jordan, A. M.: *Measurement in Education,* New York: McGraw-Hill Book Company, Inc., 1953.

Chapter 18, "Measurement of Personality Traits," includes a discussion of rating scales. Illustrative materials are included.

Micheels, W. J., and M. Ray Karnes: *Measuring Educational Achievement,* New York: McGraw-Hill Book Company, Inc., 1950.

Chapter 13 is concerned with observational techniques in relation to evaluation. Guiding principles are presented for using the results of observations.

Remmers, H. H., and N. L. Gage: *Educational Measurement and Evaluation,* rev. ed., New York: Harper & Brothers, 1955.

Chapter 12 includes a concise discussion of rating-scale methods. Suggestions for the development of graphic scales are presented.

Thomas, R. M.: *Judging Student Progress,* New York: Longmans, Green & Co., Inc., 1954.

Chapter 11 presents a relatively nontechnical account of rating scales and check lists. The discussion centers around school use of the instruments.

Thorndike, R. L., and E. Hagen: *Measurement and Evaluation in Psychology and Education,* New York: John Wiley & Sons, Inc., 1955.

Chapter 13 presents a relatively comprehensive account of rating methods. Suggestions for the improvement of ratings are included.

CHAPTER TWELVE

Constructing and Using Teacher-made Tests

Standardized tests produced by specialists have an important part to play in education when they are used with proper regard for their advantages and limitations. Some of these limitations can be avoided by using teacher-made tests. Tests prepared by the teacher compensate for some of the weaknesses inherent in standardized tests, but they are in turn subject to certain shortcomings. They are not a panacea for problems of evaluation, but they do serve important purposes. Careful test construction and interpretation can increase their usefulness.

THE NEED FOR TEACHER-MADE TESTS

As we have seen, standardized tests do not always fit local situations. For example, in one school a test of reading readiness is given to the entering first graders, and on the basis of the results certain pupils are started on the reading program. Gratifying success may be achieved by all these starters. However, when the same procedure is followed in another school, considerable difficulty may be encountered by several pupils for whom success was indicated by the test results. The difference may result from the fact that the reading materials used in the second school were more difficult than those used in the first.

Another example concerns achievement testing. In one school, pupils in the fourth and fifth grades show up year after year as substantially below the norm in arithmetic, though they do the work normal for their grade and age in other areas. Pupils who are above average in ability do above-average work in other subjects than arithmetic. In one such system the principal planned to bring in special help for the teachers because of their indicated need for guidance in teaching arithmetic. The explanation was discovered to be the fact that in this locality it had been previously decided that arithmetic instruction could profitably be delayed until the fourth grade rather than offered in the third. The disadvantage of the delay does not disappear until two or three years later.[1] By the time a group reaches the seventh grade, more of the pupils will be happy and successful in their work in arithmetic if they started studying it in the fourth grade than if they had started it in the third.

A third example of the influence of local norms was encountered in a school system where the formal study of American history was subordinated to the study of local problems as an approach to history. The pupils did not do well on standardized tests in which there was considerable emphasis on American history.

Different schools in the same community may find it desirable to interpret norms quite differently. A school which draws its pupils exclusively from a neighborhood composed

[1] W. A. Brownell and C. B. Chazel, "The Effects of Premature Drill on Third-grade Arithmetic," *Journal of Educational Research,* **29**:17–28, 1935.

of professional people and business owners may be unjustifiably proud of the record made by its pupils. Teachers in a school whose pupils come mainly from lower socioeconomic strata and less stimulating environments may be discouraged because of low standing on national norms when, in fact, they might well be proud of their record in "pupil adjustment."

Another shortcoming of standardized tests is that they are not designed to explore and analyze small units of subject matter. Thus, the teacher may wish to give a test covering a half semester's work or a unit on "Community Health Practices." Tests can be of assistance in the study of these smaller units, but the standardized test is not likely to help because of its comprehensive and general nature.

Local variations in curricular practices, the nature of the pupil population, and the division of work into smaller units may make it impractical to use standardized tests as the sole measuring device. In such situations the teacher-made test can make a valuable contribution to better pupil understanding.[2]

Uses of Teacher-made Tests

One of the values of teacher-made tests is that they compensate for the shortcomings of standardized tests. Thus, as we have seen, teacher-made tests can be better adapted to fit local pupil and curricular situations and are useful in exploring and analyzing small units of study. In addition, they can be made to serve as a means of motivation and diagnosis of weaknesses.

Teacher-made tests can be used to supplement and complement other kinds of motivation. It has previously been indicated that it is bad practice to consider a test result as an "end" of education. But the test which is used to indicate

[2] A. M. Jordan, *Measurement in Education,* New York: McGraw-Hill Book Company, Inc., 1953, pp. 40ff.

progress toward a goal and to challenge one's sense of achievement is a helpful educational instrument. Children can, and do in favorable circumstances, enjoy taking tests. When children fear tests, it is because of the emphasis placed on results.

Although much is heard these days about the desirability of making motivation intrinsic, or making the task interesting in itself, it is more exact to observe that interests grow, develop, and evolve. Interests are much more than discoveries of something innate; they often develop as the result of the student's originally being "forced" to engage in a given area of experience. Interests grow as the result of knowledge and the development of competence, of success, and familiarity. Hence, an examination or series of examinations may serve as the original motivation for the pupil to check his knowledge and progress and to gain success and familiarity. The teacher-made examination, given at shorter intervals than the standardized examination, can supplement other continuous experiences. It can easily be designed specifically as an additional source of motivation.

Teacher-made examinations can also serve as an approach to diagnosis; that is, the test can be so designed that the scores pupils make will reveal areas in which they are weak. Weaknesses in number combinations, for example, or in certain arithmetical processes can be detected from the results of a test which is so constructed that certain of the questions deal with specific skills or areas of knowledge.

Teacher-made examinations are probably customarily used to help evaluate pupil achievement. As we have seen, this is not an easy task. However, with study and care, it is possible to secure approximate and tentative data which will be of value in determining pupil progress. In order to obtain this information, the teacher-made test should be modeled after the standard examination by seeking to improve the degree of objectivity, reliability, and validity of the test.

APPLYING THE CRITERIA OF A "GOOD" TEST

The criteria which apply to standardized tests are to a large extent applicable to teacher-made tests. Objectivity is desirable; hence, it is recommended that tests be of the short-answer type in so far as possible. These would include true-false, multiple-choice, completion, and matching questions.

Examinations of the so-called essay type are too difficult to score objectively to warrant a great deal of consideration. The contention that essay examinations teach pupils to organize their thoughts can be disposed of with the argument that an examination, with its accompanying pressure, is not a situation that is particularly conducive to the stimulation of logical thinking. If organization of thought is the major objective, it might be better to offer this training in special papers or themes. The teacher's evaluation of the essay might be more accurate when it is a special paper than when it is part of an examination which must be given a grade.

One type of short-answer question is the completion item, which requires the pupil to fill in a word or group of words in a blank space in a sentence or paragraph; the part of the sentence which does appear gives the context into which the missing word or words will fit. Examples are: "Metals from which our common United States coins are made are pot metal, copper, ______ and ______." "Bobby's cafeteria lunch cost 25 cents. In addition he spent 5 cents on an ice-cream bar and 7 cents for pop. The total cost of his lunch was ______."

Completion questions are quite often difficult to formulate. All too frequently there is more than one word that is appropriate for a particular blank. After the teacher has made one or two exceptions to what he first thought the answer should be, it is difficult to determine how much deviation should be permitted. Completion questions have been criticized because they call for factual knowledge. Actually there should be no objection to the learning of facts—if they are meaningful to the pupil. This type of question is probably best for testing in such areas as arithmetic, knowledge of historical personages, geographical locations, and dates. It will be found to be inadequate for testing a knowledge of social trends, functions of the organs of the body, foods required in various diets, or commercial and agricultural products of nations or states.

The true-false, or right-wrong, type of test item seems easy to construct but is actually so difficult to design that it has relatively little usefulness. Experts in test making rarely use it. True-false questions tend to place a premium upon verbatim learnings; since few things are so clearly right or wrong, answers are often quite debatable, much to the chagrin of the teacher who made the test. Further, this type of question tends to penalize the brighter student, because it is he who most frequently thinks of the exception or conditional factors that can alter the meaning. Let us examine the item, "Coins of the United States are made of pot metal, copper, nickel, and silver." The statement is true in a sense, but gold might also have been included; thus it is false because it is not inclusive enough. If the statement were changed to "Coins of the United States are made only of pot metal, copper, nickel, and silver," the answer is still debatable. There are gold coins still in existence, but one could argue that they are not being made now. The limited number of possible alternatives increases the possibility of successful guessing and thus reduces the diagnostic value of the test.

Since test makers show a tendency to make more items true than false, the student may systematically mark all the items that he does not know as true and be gratified with the result. In order to avoid this, penalties are sometimes imposed for guessing—the total score being obtained by a "right-minus-wrong" formula. This practice can be criticized on the basis that complicating the scoring of an inadequate test does not make it more valid and reliable.

However, the true-false item is frequently used in the classroom, although it should not be relied upon to too great an extent. Measures can be taken to increase its usefulness, however.

1. All items should be brief and without conditional factors.
2. The use of such words as *always, never, entirely,* and *absolutely* should be avoided.
3. The true-false item is more useful in language studies and mathematics than it is in social studies and general science.
4. Statements should not be lifted from the textbook verbatim or with only minor revisions.
5. Items should not be arranged in a regular pattern, such as T, F, F, T, F, T, T, F, etc., or T, F, T, F, etc.

In general, it seems wise to recommend that true-false questions be cautiously used except for purposes of review and drill. Their use for evaluative or diagnostic purposes is highly questionable.

The matching question has been found to be quite practicable for classroom use. Two lists are set off or distinguished as pairs, as in the following example:

Place the letter of the item in the right-hand column in the space provided in the numbered (left-hand) column with which it is most closely associated:

_____1. heart	a. helps put oxygen into the blood
_____2. lungs	b. place where food is mechanically and chemically reduced
_____3. thyroid	c. carries blood to the heart
_____4. arteries	d. muscle which pushes blood
_____5. striated muscles	e. carries blood to the extremities
_____6. stomach	f. muscles used in digesting food
	g. controls oxygen metabolism
	h. muscles used in locomotion
	i. muscles used in breathing

Matching questions are time-consuming for the student, since he has to search for the relationships; and for the elementary pupil they may be confusing as well as time-consuming. Hence relatively few items should be grouped together. The columns should be of different lengths so that thinking will replace guessing at some of the more difficult items. Primary-grade teachers have found that it is easier for pupils to understand the directions if they are told to use a line to connect the two related statements. This makes scoring somewhat harder, but the advantage in pupil understanding may compensate. A combination matching-completion question can be made by providing a group of words or phrases from which the pupil can select to fill in the missing parts of a sentence or paragraph.

The user of standardized tests will note that the most frequently used type of test question is the multiple-choice item. This question is commonly found in the "test yourself" features in magazines and newspapers. It possesses several advantages: the number of alternate responses (3, 4, or 5) reduces the chances of guessing more than is the case with the true-false or matching type of question; the listing of plausible answers stimulates thinking; the limitation (as compared with the completion item) of possible answers eliminates ambiguity in scoring; and the technique of scoring is not complicated. Multiple-choice questions are good teaching devices because discussion of the alternatives and analysis of the student's errors after the examination provides the opportunity for careful explanation.

Some of the advantages of the multiple-choice item are counterbalanced by the difficulty of making the questions, however. It takes considerable time to construct fifty or a hundred items of this type—certainly much more time than it normally takes to construct ten essay questions. On the other hand, the time is compensated for by increased objectivity and ease of scoring.

It is recommended that the making of good multiple-choice items be a continuing project for teachers. This can be done —at a saving of time over a period of years—by making a set of 3-by-5 test cards for the various areas (social studies, health, science) with which the teacher deals. Each card will contain one multiple-choice item. A notation on the card indicates the phase of the subject with which it deals (history, "Pilgrims"). When it is time to make the test, the items that are most pertinent to the particular manner in which the unit was studied during the term are selected to be reproduced. After the test and the discussion of the items, an item analysis will reveal that some are of questionable value. A tally is kept on the effectiveness of each question. Some will be correctly answered by all; too many of these items will indicate that the test is too simple. If one item is missed by all, it is probably too difficult or is ambiguously stated. Poor questions are either revised or discarded. The next time the same area is to be covered by a test, a few new items are added to the revised set of cards to cover current emphases. By keeping separate the cards dealing with subdivisions of the total area, the teacher can easily make the test contribute to diagnostic purposes.

Although the questions are discussed after the test, the student does not keep his test. To permit him to do so might lead some of the more sophisticated pupils to get the exam and cram for the specific questions on it rather than to study widely. Just as important, however, is the fact that the teacher cannot afford the time to make a carefully constructed new set of multiple-choice questions every time the area is covered; besides, there would be a loss in terms of the experience gained. Economy of the teacher's time can also be achieved by providing a series of spaces on the left or right side of the paper in which to place the number or letter of the chosen response. After the test items have been checked through use, it may be advisable to have a separate answer sheet and ask the pupils to refrain from marking the question sheet. Defective items on the reused question sheet can be ruled out and a substitute item can be written on the board or mimeographed on a separate page to replace the deleted item.

The multiple-choice item satisfies to a large extent the criteria of a good test: it is objective, reliable, and economical of the teacher's time; it samples widely and can be so planned that it has a significant degree of validity. Techniques for securing this validity will be discussed in the following section.

TECHNIQUES OF TEST CONSTRUCTION

In constructing tests, it is important first of all to determine just exactly what should and will be tested; since the purpose of tests is to help determine the extent to which educational objectives are being achieved, the test should be devised in terms of the specific objectives of teaching a particular unit of study. The teacher who prepares lesson plans will have done this much earlier. For those who do not write lesson plans, it would still be desirable to state the objectives that will serve as a guide to the construction of the items that really test what one has been teaching. This is clearly a long step toward making a valid test—a test that actually measures what it purports to measure. Comparing each item with the final objective of the test will not assure validity, but it will probably increase it.

The goals or objectives of a unit must be specific in order to serve as a guide in making a valid examination. For example, such specificity is found in the following goals for each student in a unit in seventh-grade social studies:

1. Reads news of general (first-page) interest in the newspaper.
2. Listens to the radio for purposes of gaining information (weather, farm reports, news).
3. Can state the importance of some current news events.
4. Has some opinions on contemporary events.

5. Knows the names and positions of persons in the headlines.
6. Knows the geographical location of places in the news.
7. Knows what sections of the paper contain certain kinds of news.
8. Is acquainted with several features in the local newspaper.

Such a list of specific aims can readily be translated into test items. The teacher can determine the number of questions which should be allotted to each goal by analyzing its relative importance and reflecting on the amount of time spent on the particular topic in class. Robert M. W. Travers recommends that the teacher keep a "blueprint" of the class as a guide in making a valid examination.[3] To do this, the teacher lines off a sheet of paper in blocks and labels the horizontal blocks with the educational goals for the topical subdivisions of the course, represented by the vertical blocks. Thus, under the heading of the educational goal "ability to spend money wisely," reading across to the vertical column under the heading of "budget," the teacher writes descriptions of the activities by means of which one reaches the goal. When it is time to prepare a test, the entries in the boxes give clues to suitable items.

The following criteria will be helpful in making multiple-choice questions: The key proposition should be stated in the form of a problem; for example, "The first thing to do on learning of a case of scarlet fever in the community is to (1) . . . " This type of presentation is important even in testing for facts, because the ultimate goal is that pupils will use the facts to solve problems. The alternative responses should be as plausible as possible; unless they have some plausibility, the choice will be so easy that no problem is involved. In re-

[3] Robert M. W. Travers, *How to Make Achievement Tests,* New York: The Odyssey Press, Inc., 1950, pp. 25–29.

sponse to the problem stated above, each of the following has some plausibility: "(1) examine the water supply, (2) inoculate the citizens of the community, (3) examine the milk supply, (4) screen all windows, (5) spray all refuse piles and garbage cans with DDT."

The wording of the questions should be appropriate to the grade level concerned; if the items are too easy, the difficulty should not be increased by the introduction of more difficult words unless vocabulary development is the goal. No answer should depend upon knowledge of the answer to another question in the same examination. Conversely, the information given in stating an item should not provide a lead to answering another question. The statement and the alternatives should be as simple as possible—the correct answering of the question should not depend on the pupil's ability to interpret a difficult statement. The answer which is supposed to be correct should be unquestionably correct; that is, the various books available to pupils should agree on the point concerned. The teacher should never have to resort to saying, "In *our* book the answer is . . . " Alternative answers should cite commonly held erroneous views as a means of sharpening the pupil's perception of unjustified beliefs; for example, "A universal characteristic of adolescents is (1) they are physically awkward, (2) they resist school authority, etc." Whenever possible, test for knowledge of principles and generalizations as contrasted to isolated facts. Tests of memory show that facts are forgotten more quickly than principles and generalizations, which have greater significance than facts for solving problems later.

These observations may make the task of test making look formidable. Actually, practice and guided experience reduce the difficulty. Soon the teacher gives almost automatic heed to the suggestions cited above, and usable test items occur to him readily as the study of a unit progresses. A pair of teachers working together can be of great help to one another. But even though the task of making valid and objective tests is an arduous one, it will pay in the increased effectiveness of the teacher's testing program. Testing will serve the purpose for which it is designed: to facilitate the reaching of one's educational objectives.

Some Sample Setups

Careful attention to "setup" will help to make tests understandable and economical. For example, questions can be filed on 3-by-5 cards such as the one shown here.

health physiology

The use of beverage alcohol is condemned because

(1) it speeds up heart action
(2) it causes diseases of the liver
(3) it reduces physical and mental efficiency
(4) it slowly disintegrates the brain
(5) it hardens the arteries

Missed by ____ out of ____ taking the test.

Date used:

Pupil comments:

The notation in the upper left-hand corner indicates the broad area in which the question is used, and the note at the upper right gives the particular subdivision. The other notes can be reduced to 12/37, which means that the question was missed by 12 of 37 pupils; the date can be simply 11/12/57, and comments may be placed on the reverse side of the card.

After the cards have been prepared, those the teacher selects are placed on the test paper with appropriate headings:

HEALTH EDUCATION
11-12-57
PUPIL'S NAME ______________________

Place the number of the response which you select as correct in the space provided to the left of the number of the question. The first one is answered correctly.

__3__ 1. The use of beverage alcohol is condemned because
(1) it speeds up heart action
(2) it causes diseases of the liver
(3) it reduces physical and mental efficiency
(4) it slowly disintegrates the brain
(5) it hardens the arteries

_____ 2. Milk should be in the diet of most persons, adults and children, because
(1) it is the food Nature planned for us
(2) it contains so many ingredients that it rounds out the diet
(3) it is essential to growing sound teeth
(4) it is a clean, safe food
(5) it is inexpensive

It can readily be seen that a multiple-choice examination takes several pages of mimeographing; for this reason, and because pages must be turned for scoring, it is quite time-consuming. A separate answer sheet with a number of blanks on it helps to offset this disadvantage.

PUPIL'S NAME ______________________ DATE __________

SUBJECT ______________________________

Place all of your answers on this answer sheet. Do not write on the question sheets.

1. _____	26. _____	51. _____	76. _____
2. _____	27. _____	52. _____	77. _____
3. _____	28. _____	53. _____	78. _____
4. _____	29. _____	54. _____	79. _____
5. _____	30. _____	55. _____	80. _____

etc.

Such an answer sheet can be scored by writing the correct responses on strips of stiff paper or cardboard and laying the appropriate strip alongside the column of answers. This process involves the changing of strips or the shuffling of papers as each column is scored. However, scoring can be completed in one operation by cutting slots out of a piece of cardboard and writing beside each slot the answers for one of the columns, as in the accompanying sketch. The number of the

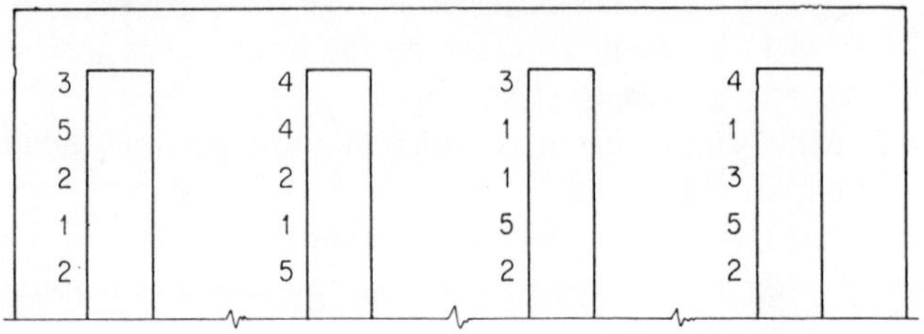

3	4	3	4
5	4	1	1
2	2	1	3
1	1	5	5
2	5	2	2

question is not indicated, since this would clutter the score card. Errors can be avoided by being careful to make the slots the exact length of the answer column.

Perhaps the most rapid hand-scoring method is to provide an answer sheet on which the student has to block out the correct response, as follows:

PUPIL'S NAME ____________________ DATE __________

SUBJECT ______________________________

Completely block out with soft lead pencil the number of the response which you select. Indicate only one answer for each item; double answers are scored as incorrect.

1. 1 2 3 4 5	26. 1 2 3 4 5	51. 1 2 3 4 5	76. 1 2 3 4 5
2. 1 2 3 4 5	27. 1 2 3 4 5	52. 1 2 3 4 5	77. 1 2 3 4 5
3. 1 2 3 4 5	28. 1 2 3 4 5	53. 1 2 3 4 5	78. 1 2 3 4 5
4. 1 2 3 4 5	29. 1 2 3 4 5	54. 1 2 3 4 5	79. 1 2 3 4 5
5. 1 2 3 4 5	30. 1 2 3 4 5	55. 1 2 3 4 5	80. 1 2 3 4 5

The scoring sheet for this type of answer sheet consists of a piece of stiff paper or cardboard with holes punched so that only the correct responses show.

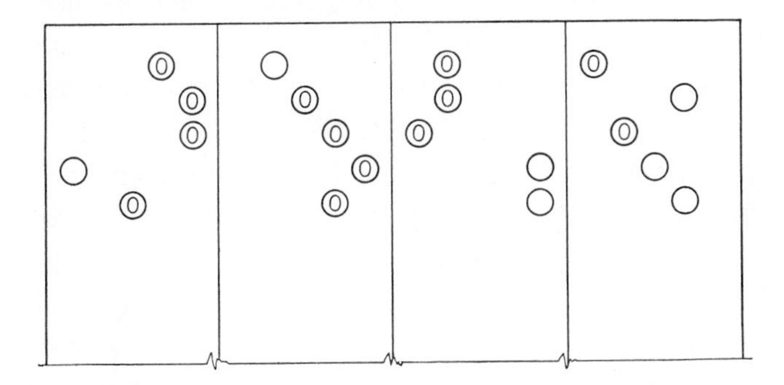

In using this kind of scoring device it is necessary first to scan the papers for double answers. (This is necessary also when papers are machine scored, so there is no relative disadvantage in this respect.) Each number that appears clear under the punch hole and thus has not been blocked out by the pupil is an incorrect answer; hence all one has to do is count these for the minus score. If an item analysis is to be made, it will be necessary to cross out the number with a colored pencil as one counts the incorrect scores.

The danger in this system is that, since the original setup is so time-consuming, the teacher will be tempted to use the same questions and the same answer sheets term after term. Actually this is not undesirable, providing the defective or outmoded items are constantly weeded out. This can be done simply by telling the pupils that question 23, for example, has been eliminated. "A substitute question 23 is written on the board [or on a mimeographed separate sheet]. Answer this question now—immediately—so that you will not forget and answer the question that is on the regular test sheets." It will be convenient if the question is so arranged that the response is the same as the one originally designated for the defective item; in this way the answer sheet or stencil will not have to be changed.

It is recommended that no scoring formulas be used, such as the right-minus-wrong (R — W) scoring of true-false answers to discourage guessing. Actually, differences in children are such that some will not be discouraged from guessing and others will not put down answers they are not sure of. Perhaps it is better to encourage intelligent, informed guessing than to discourage blind guessing. At any rate, the accuracy of the teacher-made instrument is not so great that its reliability will be significantly increased by scoring formulas. Further, it is not the score that is significant. Rather the object is to discover what areas need particular attention, what is causing a pupil's particular difficulty, and approximately what progress each pupil has made. Scoring formulas will not help to a significant degree in any of these purposes.

RELATIONSHIP OF TEACHER-MADE TO STANDARDIZED TESTS

Both teacher-made and standardized tests play important roles in the accomplishment of the ultimate purpose of all tests—to facilitate pupil growth. Standardized tests are probably more accurate than most teacher-made tests; they are more reliable, objective, and valid; but teacher-made tests have the advantage of being more readily adaptable to local conditions. They are relatively less expensive and can thus be used more frequently as checks on progress, as a means of motivation, and in some instances for aiding diagnosis. Since both kinds of test have a part to play in the understanding of pupils and in the stimulation of their growth, it is obvious that the teacher is not limited to the use of either one or the other exclusively; the two are supplementary to one another.

Most modern educators have no objection to drill and review providing it is motivated and the pupil understands the material. The inexpensive teacher-made test can provide some of this drill in a situation which is enjoyable for the pupil if the score is not overemphasized. The test can also provide a check on understanding, since the items are specifically designed to be discussed in class, whereas the discussion of items on a standardized test is specifically avoided because it would produce "practice effect" or coaching that would invalidate the test.

The teacher-made test is a useful factor in motivation. The knowledge gained in preparation for tests has led many pupils to develop new interests. It can accomplish this for more pupils when teachers stop making scores the basis for interpersonal comparisons and use the results to show each pupil what progress he is making and where he needs special work. The teacher should constantly bear in mind, however, that this transfer of interest from the test and its results to the subject under consideration is not automatic. It will be necessary for him to show how the interest should expand, how the knowledge can be used more effectively than it is in a pencil-and-paper test, and to indicate the personal value of increased knowledge.

Thus standardized tests are of greatest value in estimating achievement over a period of time—from the beginning to the end of the term—whereas teacher-made tests are of greatest aid in facilitating intermediate steps in this long-term growth.

SUMMARY

Standardized tests have inherent limitations. They often do not fit local situations from the viewpoint of the type of materials used, curricular emphases, and the ability and background of the pupil population. Teacher-made tests can be used to compensate for some of these limitations because they are readily adaptable to local emphases, they can be devised to fit small subdivisions of a subject area, and they can and do serve as sources of motivation. When carefully made and used with due caution, the teacher-made test is effective for diagnosis.

Teacher-made tests should meet the criteria of good standardized tests. Objectivity can be increased by using short-answer items broad enough in range to reveal ability and limited enough to be easily scored. Validity can be increased by clearly formulating the aims of the unit or area on which the test is based. Reliability can be increased by continuous study of the teacher-made test through periodic analysis of pupils' answers. Ease of scoring should be kept in mind in constructing the test, and special answer sheets and scoring stencils will increase economy. The authors feel that the over-all advantages of matching and multiple-choice answers are such as to warrant preferring them over completion and true-false items in short-answer tests and over the essay type of test.

Teacher-made tests are not intended as substitutes for standardized tests. Both types play valid roles in education, and both should be regarded as aids to instruction and as supplementary to each other, not as ends of education.

STUDY AND DISCUSSION EXERCISES

1. What advantages of teacher-made tests over standardized tests have you found, through your reading or experience, other than those listed in this chapter?
2. Under what conditions is it permissible for the teacher to use subjective data in the evaluation of his pupils?
3. Recall some of the experiences you had as a student taking true-false examinations. Would your experiences accord with the observations made in this chapter about the use of this type of question?

4. Make your own set of fifteen or twenty multiple-choice items to cover the content of a chapter or several chapters of this book and give it to others to take and then to criticize. Summarize what you learned about multiple-choice questions from this experiment.

5. Write out the objectives of a class you have taught or are preparing to teach and submit the list for criticism. Design the objectives in such a way that testing on them is feasible.

6. Examine the feature "It Pays to Increase Your Word Power" in any issue of the *Readers' Digest.* Point out the instances in which the author has attempted to mislead by presenting a "plausible" but incorrect response. How can you use this practice profitably in test construction?

7. Poll a group of persons who are interested in tests and summarize the techniques they suggest for improving such tests as the short test to stimulate interest, the pretest at the beginning of a unit of work, etc.

SUGGESTED ADDITIONAL READINGS

Greene, Harry A., Albert N. Jorgensen, and J. Raymond Gerberich: *Measurement and Evaluation in the Elementary School,* 2d ed., New York: Longmans, Green & Co., Inc., 1952, pp. 160–194.

This chapter deals with different types of objective questions (completion, multiple-choice, matching, etc.) and cites helpful suggestions for constructing them. The suggestions for each kind of test item are summarized.

Lee, J. Murray, and David Segel: *Testing Practices of High School Teachers,* U.S. Department of the Interior Bulletin 9, Office of Education, 1936, 42 pp.

This bulletin reports a survey of testing practices and evaluates their effectiveness as a basis for making suggestions for improvement. The bulletin is designed for administrators and forward-looking teachers.

Ross, C. C. (rev. by J. C. Stanley): *Measurement in Today's Schools,* 3d ed., Englewood Cliffs, N.J.: Prentice-Hall, Inc., 1954, pp. 139–206.

Part II, consisting of three chapters, deals with planning, preparing, and evaluating teacher-made tests. Different kinds of test items and the special problems each presents are dealt with, and suggestions are offered.

Torgerson, Theodore L., and Georgia Sachs Adams: *Measurement and Evaluation,* New York: The Dryden Press, Inc., 1954, pp. 220–243.

The uses and characteristics of good teacher-made tests are described. Suggestions are given for making essay, completion, true-false, multiple-choice, and matching questions. A check list is provided for evaluating teacher-made tests.

Travers, Robert M. W.: *How to Make Achievement Tests,* New York: The Odyssey Press, Inc., 1950, 180 pp.

This short book is full of practical suggestions for planning and constructing teacher-made tests. It covers all subjects, but science teachers will find the explanations and examples especially helpful.

CHAPTER THIRTEEN

Improving Appraisal Practices

Pupil development is a many-faceted phenomenon. Aspects of physical, mental, emotional, social, and academic growth are present in problems of measurement and evaluation. Many factors are at work to produce growth in any one of these areas or to produce interrelated (organismic) growth in all the areas. Among these factors the following are outstanding: hereditary potential, health, sensory equipment, home conditions, family relationships, community mores, political philosophy, curricular demands, educational philosophy, and the child's reactions to all these. Many techniques for measuring these varied facets of the *total personality* have been described in the foregoing chapters, and problems involved in measurement have been discussed. In view of the multifaceted nature of growth, it seems absurd to attempt to evaluate it with a single number, letter, or word. Yet the fact is that this attempt is made in what is called the "grading" or "marking" system.

The authors claim no originality in condemning the practice of attempting to summarize the many factors of growth with a simple number, letter, or word. Rather, our remarks reflect investigations by experts, critical examination of practice, and the reported experience of many teachers. Practices that hold a great deal of promise for the more effective stimulation of symmetrical pupil growth are already in operation. However, we should not be so sanguine as to believe that the answer to the question, "What are the best evaluation techniques?" has been given. As more teachers depart from traditional marking practices, better answers to this question will be given. Meanwhile, the departures that have been made will give teachers some idea of techniques which have been gratifying in bringing educational practice into closer accord with accepted child-growth theory.

SOME SHORTCOMINGS OF GRADES

The purpose of marks and appraisal is, theoretically, to foster pupil growth. They purport to tell something about the pupil that will make it easier for him and those who work with him to guide his future development. Although this is the theory behind grading, there are many practical reasons for doubting that it accomplishes this worthy aim.

1. Marks tend to become the end and aim of education. William H. Burton's statement represents a consensus of public school workers when he asserts that a misconception of education is that the symbols of education are equivalent to the outcomes of learning.[1] If you ask a first grader what he got out of school on a particular day, he will say, "I learned to read a story," "I learned to spell my name," or "I learned to print my name." If this same question is asked of a sixth grader he is likely to say, "I got an 80," or "I got a B." If the college student in general psychology is asked what he got from the course, he will probably indicate that he, too, con-

[1] William H. Burton, *The Guidance of Learning Activities,* New York: Appleton-Century-Crofts, Inc., 1944, pp. 52–59.

fuses the symbols of learning with the products of education. Learning is a sufficient reward for the first grader, but the symbol has become more important to the sophisticate.

2. Marks tend to emphasize subject matter. But among aims of elementary education are understanding and practice of cooperative social functioning; opportunity to exercise habits of reflective thinking; exercise of individual capacities; command of the fundamental processes of reading, writing, and arithmetic (communication); and gaining and keeping good physical and mental health. Marks tend to emphasize only the aim relating to academic accomplishment, which, admittedly, is very important; but this academic knowledge and skill is simply a tool for helping one to achieve the other aims on the list. Concern for marks sometimes results in an emphasis upon subject matter which may actually limit the possibility of the pupil's attaining the other goals.

3. Marks tend to discourage good teaching. At the risk of oversimplifying, we may define teaching as guiding or encouraging each child to come progressively closer to realizing his own potentialities in all aspects of growth. Thus teaching involves an intimate knowledge of the children one is teaching, the development of personal ambition, social orientation, originality (or, at least, uniqueness), and moral and ethical values. Teachers who use marks may keep these objectives in mind; but some teachers employ marks as a threat when their teaching methods fail. If the child does not see the value of assigned tasks or if he is worried about out-of-school situations, he can still be made to conform by the threat of a low mark or failure. Problems of getting to know pupils, encouraging growth, and promoting self-realization, need not necessarily be considered when one can use grades as a cudgel.

4. Marks tend to cause teachers to overlook differences. Every teacher is aware of the great individual differences be-

tween pupils; yet, all too frequently, the necessity for grading causes them to try to bring the slow growers academically "up to average." We know the futility of this attempt, yet it persists almost as a compulsion because of the pressure of grades. On the other hand, grades encourage mediocrity in brighter children because they can get satisfactory marks with the expenditure of little or no effort.

5. Marks create a situation that is "unlike life." It is frequently argued that grades are a lifelike phenomenon—that we are all graded in our commercial, industrial, and professional careers. We are, to some extent, graded in our vocational lives; but with definite differences. Few of us would freely continue to teach, to sell, to run a machine, or to build a home if a "big boss" looked over our shoulders each week and marked our cards with an A, B, C, or D. We do not need such prodding because each of us seeks the inner satisfaction of doing a job well. In fact, a great deal of the enjoyment we derive from work would be destroyed by a marking system patterned after school report cards. Another vast difference between school and life is that interpersonal comparisons in life are made between people *in the same occupation*. Typically, school marks are based upon the erroneous assumption that all children are the same—that they should run the same course and finish at the same time.

6. Grades tend to penalize those pupils most in need of help. It has been said, with some truth, that a child is most in need of love when he is most unlovable. We might say that when the child is most in need of encouragement (because a task is difficult for him) he is most likely to be discouraged by the awarding of a low grade. Frequently, it is the child who is working up to (sometimes apparently exceeding) his indicated capacity but who is below "grade level" who is further discouraged by a low mark.

7. Marks have little meaning in themselves. It is a delusion

to believe that they indicate to the pupil and his parents how the pupil is getting along. The truth is that, as parents, teachers, and pupils we have become accustomed to a symbol that has little meaning, as with men's wearing vests. Study after study has shown that the same paper will be graded by different teachers with a different value. Some teachers give a large proportion of A's, and others say, "No student can be perfect, and A means perfect." Some teachers have in mind academic accomplishments alone when they give a mark; others try to include such factors as industry, interest, sincerity, and originality. Many parents really have no idea how well their child is doing in relation to his ability or in relation to other children, but they are pacified by some meaningless jargon expressed as a grade. Parents who become accustomed to an improved form of evaluation assert that they do not see how they could have been satisfied with the old working system.

Contrasts between Marks and Appraisal

The seven items listed above are enough to indicate the reason for the present trend away from grades to more informative methods of evaluation. In fact, because of these characteristics of grades, we might even distinguish grading from genuine evaluation, as the following contrasts in concept indicate.

Both grades and evaluation are supposedly means of communication between teacher and pupil and between teacher and parents. But grades are likely to be communication *to*, whereas other forms of evaluation are often communication *with*.

Grades are ordinarily assigned on an absolute scale which places a high value on interpersonal competition and rivalry. True evaluation, on the other hand, stresses competition with oneself and places a premium upon the ability of the person to cooperate in work and play with others.

Subject-matter mastery is the primary emphasis of grades. Again, it must be admitted that such an emphasis is worthwhile, but not to the apparent exclusion of other values. Evaluation places subject-matter achievement in the context of pupil development.

Grades are typically given at the end of a period of work —at the conclusion of a unit of time, and as such have little value in diagnostic and remedial procedures. Evaluation is specifically designed to capitalize upon strengths and to remedy weaknesses. The purpose of grades is to judge the person and his work, whereas the purpose of evaluation is to guide the person and his work.

Grades often become the end and aim of learning activities, whereas evaluation points the way to more productive living and learning. Grades are, at least in part, a concomitant of the policy of blocking out subject matter in prescribed units, books, and courses. Evaluation is a personal matter, and its philosophy implies the use of subject matter to achieve the social ends which seem most appropriate to the individual.

These contrasts are, of necessity, generalizations that will not always hold true for specific cases. Some teachers may use grades in such a way as to approach the values indicated for evaluation; and the various means of evaluation may be used in such a way that they are no more meaningful than grades. This lack of sharp contrast or distinct differentiation between grades and evaluation leads us to recommend that systems of evaluation be introduced gradually in the school—by taking, for example, the first three grades for a "test run," by conferring with a few parents at the beginning, and by frankly admitting that the new system is experimental. But there should be no attempt to reconstruct, modify, or alter the traditional grading system because modifications can too easily return to the former inadequacies. The system should be abandoned because of the dangers which seem to be inevitably attached to it.[2]

PROMISING PRACTICES IN EVALUATION

The "promising practices" which follow are not listed in order of merit, for their applicability varies in relation to such factors as the community, the competence of the professional staff, and the intelligence and grade level of the pupils.

1. *Letters to parents.* In place of the report card with boxes containing marks after "reading," "arithmetic," "deportment," and the like, some teachers are writing letters to the parents to facilitate communication between home, school, and child. Sometimes these letters are completely informal, indicating only those factors that seem to be most distinctive concerning the particular child. Sometimes the letters are accompanied by an outline which includes such items as intellectual growth, emotional control, social development, unique weaknesses, and outstanding gifts and qualities. These letters need not be sent on definite dates. A guiding schedule may be worked out so that three or four letters are sent each week, but in the event of need a letter may be sent well ahead of schedule. In the course of a year, three letters or half-a-dozen letters may be sent regarding one child, whereas one or two will suffice for another. In fact, one of the specific merits of this plan is its flexibility.

2. *Home visits.* An excellent means of communication between teachers and parents is for the teacher to make calls at the child's home. There are, however, some hazards which must be evaluated if the plan is to succeed. Some persons who live in homes which they wish were considerably better feel embarrassed by the teacher's visit. Hence, home visits should be approved by the parent before the teacher calls. For ex-

[2] This is the author's opinion, but it is based on considerable study and reflection. It is our hope that discussion of the contention may lead to some fruitful conclusions.

ample, the teacher may offer to call at a specific time, but ". . . if it is inconvenient, we shall be glad to have you visit us at school on [a definite date]." Many parents are more at ease in their everyday surroundings than in the relatively strange atmosphere of the school.

A good deal of the objection to home visits comes from teachers who are somewhat reluctant to make calls. It may not be an easy thing for some teachers at first; but those who have become accustomed to it have frequently asserted that they could never return to another kind of reporting practice because of the new view of the child they got from the home visit. One teacher who has used the practice for years in the sixth grade remarked, "There are few things about which I am reluctant to talk to parents or which I hesitate to say. After all this time, I know the parents very well and have learned how to approach them. Pupil problems are so much easier to handle now." Another objection to home visits is the time required. School administrators are responsible for seeing that time is provided for this worthy enterprise. If the teacher does not have time to visit all the homes, he should attempt to visit selected homes. However, these should not be only the homes of the pupils who are having some kind of difficulty; even if only a few visits are possible, both the "good" and the "bad" should be included.

There are several ways of ensuring successful home visits. The teacher can prepare the parents by telling the child several times what the purpose of the visit is: "We are just going to have a talk. I hope to talk with the parents of all the children." A formal letter to all parents will supplement the explanation given to the child. A definite date and time should be set in advance. The visit should not be an inspection tour; any suggestion of evaluation of the home will spoil the accord which the visit is designed to establish. It is important to find something pleasant to say about the pupil; negative statements should be made only if it is absolutely necessary. The teacher should not attempt to solve problems on the first visit but rather to open the way to further cooperative study of the pupil.

3. *Teacher-parent conferences in the school.* Conferences at school have essentially the same purposes as home visits. The particular advantage of the school visit is that the parent can be shown some of the child's work and the objectives of school activities can be more clearly explained. Test data may be examined *and interpreted* with greater exactness when it is deemed advisable to reveal the information. Some parents may prefer visiting the school to having their living conditions or their immediate neighborhood revealed. School visits do not require so much of the teacher's time, but they should nevertheless be a scheduled activity and a responsibility of the administration as well as the teacher.

Many of the suggestions for making home visits successful apply also to teacher-parent conferences. Additional suggestions are as follows: Do as much listening as possible consistent with not permitting the time to drag. Maintain a facial expression of cheer and confidence; this may seem a superficial suggestion, but it is fundamental to the success of the conference. Avoid any indication of shock at outmoded concepts, rough language, or questions regarding morality. Keep the number of criticisms to a minimum. Give only one or two constructive suggestions at an interview; too much advice, even when it is good, is likely to overwhelm. If one of the parents is criticized by the other, do not take sides on the issue even if one is clearly wrong.

4. *Self-appraisal.* Self-appraisal is a difficult thing. Some of us are too critical of ourselves, and others are too lenient in self-evaluations. Nevertheless, the development of this skill is an exceedingly important educational objective, since it is a major factor in the individual's vocational success. Practice may be begun in the first grade. The naturalness of self-evalu-

ation is reflected in such statements by children as "This is good" or "This is no good" in referring to blocks they have piled up, pictures they have drawn, or games they are playing. Unfortunately, this tendency is curbed by grades and marks, which make the child dependent upon the teacher's evaluation to the extent that the one criterion of success becomes acceptability to the teacher. Teachers can help promote self-appraisal by commending effort and its products or by asking the pupil if the work could be improved. If the teacher feels that the youngster is wrong in his appraisal, he should not try to impose an evaluation. Skill in self-appraisal, like other human traits, is the result of growth and development.

Self-appraisal is not an ability that flourishes when exercised at six-week intervals; it requires daily practice. The teacher should record the pupil's oral efforts at evaluation and encourage the pupil to compare his present efforts with his past work. Group discussion, even in the primary grades, can help children achieve better self-evaluation. Classmates' praise or censure of the child's conduct and work stimulates him to make his own evaluation. As children progress through the grades, it is advisable that some of the evaluations be written. The child may write a letter to the teacher or parent regarding his evaluation of his performance in social and academic functions in the classroom.

Wherever possible children should evaluate their own work, judging accomplishment and progress by charts kept by each child. As children come to you with different capacities and training, the competitive system of marking most usually practiced becomes unfair competition and often leads to dishonest practice. It leads to pressure where it is least helpful and very often allows the bright child to maintain himself with no exertion.[3]

[3] Faith Pascal, "When the Child Makes His Own Report," *Records and Reports,* Bulletin 77, Washington: Association for Childhood Education International, 1942, p. 29.

Self-appraisal obviously cannot replace other forms of evaluation. As a supplementary device, however, it is worthy of careful trial because it contributes so much to the implementation of democratic theory.

5. *Teacher-pupil conferences.* Conferences between pupil and teacher are really an aspect of pupil self-evaluation, with a difference in emphasis. In pupil self-evaluation the teacher's role of adviser is held to a minimum and the relationship resembles client-centered counseling. Teacher-pupil evaluation is based on the belief that there is value in a give-and-take relationship. If the teacher has something critical to say, he will say it—always, of course, with the view in mind of promoting pupil growth. Teacher-pupil evaluation gives open recognition to the responsibility of the teacher for positive leadership.

In a way, this technique falls short of pupil self-appraisal, but it is a long step beyond the teacher's "giving" a grade. It brings the pupil more directly into the evaluation process, which is an integral part of the learning process, than do the traditional practices.

6. *Teacher-pupil-parent conferences.* Our discussions of parent conferences and pupil self-appraisal have anticipated consideration of this technique. The value of home-school contacts is widely recognized, but quite frequently this recognition seems to ignore the child, or at least to treat him as if he were a disinterested part of the entire procedure. There are probably times when it is advisable for the child to be kept uninformed about some matters bearing on his welfare. It is probable, however, that these situations occur less frequently than many anxious teachers and parents seem to believe. If reporting is a manner of communication, then it seems logical to admit that the pupil must be intimately involved.

The clear advantage of the three-way conference is that the likelihood of misunderstanding is reduced. Certainly, there is much room for misunderstanding when percentage grades and letter tags are used. It has been shown that there is relatively little consistency in the use of grades among teachers, and their meaning is likely to vary still more among those who deal with them less frequently. But if there is a lack of understanding between persons in a conference, questions will stimulate an answer that might lead to clarification.

The observations of both parents and teachers leave little doubt that the three-way conference increases understanding of the pupil. The parent knows his child better for seeing him in action in another part of his environment. The teacher knows the pupil better for seeing him in contact with the other adults who so greatly influence his life.

Some of the hazards and shortcomings of this method of appraisal are the following: The negative attitude of the teacher who feels that it is an imposition on his time to conduct these conferences is a very real obstacle to the success of this method. Also, holding conferences may cause teachers to neglect other means of evaluation, such as cumulative records and personnel cards, because no record is kept of the interview, although records are an important responsibility of the school. The technique will be increasingly difficult to use as the pupils progress through the grades, because departmentalization of instruction puts the pupil into contact with more and more teachers who know him less and less intimately. This defect is, however, no greater than the hazard of giving a child a grade on the basis of superficial knowledge about him. The teacher-pupil-parent conference is not a panacea for the problems of evaluation in education. It is another means of communication; but examinations, inventories, projective techniques, cumulative records, and staff conferences are also a part of the process of evaluation.

7. *Cumulative records.* The teacher's conviction that the child should be accepted for what he is should not blind him

to the fact that it is informative to know how the child achieved his present status. Quite frequently, considerable concern about the growth and status of a child would be allayed if the teacher could but picture clearly what the child was a few months earlier. When one sees a youngster every day, it is easy to overlook the minute increments of growth which add up to an encouraging total. The cumulative record can help teachers to see the child's progress more clearly.

It would seem desirable to have a nationwide standard cumulative-record card or folder, or at least a uniform card for use within each state. Such a card would facilitate the understanding of a pupil as he transfers from one school to another. Since we do not have standard cards, either nationally or within states, it is feasible for each school system to work out its own card, thus ensuring the recording of those data which are most important for the particular school system. The selection of the type of data to be recorded is not an easy task. One suggested guiding principle for making a cumulative record is to keep the information to a minimum, for a mass of data is discouraging to the teacher. System and regularity in keeping the record will make up for some deficiencies in the amount of information noted. With these observations as a starting point, it is recommended that the record include the following items:

Personal Data. Name, sex, birthplace, date of birth, father's name, nationality, occupation, mother's name, nationality, occupation, family status (married, divorced, etc.), siblings (sex and age), and language spoken in the home.

Chronology and Address. Several lines will be needed for changes of school and address: date entered, class and grade, name of school, home address, phone, and significant remarks about the home.

Conference Notes. Notes on the outcomes of conferences, with the date and grade status of the child at the time of the meeting, should be a part of the record. Care must be taken to avoid the temptation to record anything that is unnecessarily derogatory about the home, the child, or the parents; for example, "We have asked the Kiwanis to give Don a pair of shoes" is preferable to "Mr. B. has made no effort to see that Don is properly shod." Or, "Whenever possible, we should keep Don after school and let him work at the projects he likes so well" is better than "Don's choice of after-school companions is consistently bad."

Record of Attendance. This should include terms, dates, punctuality, and school progress.

Achievement-test Data. These must be complete to be meaningful. They might include date, grade, name of test, subject, form, and grade placement or other standard results such as percentile rank and standard score.

Intelligence-test Data. Date, grade, name of test, form, chronological age, MA, IQ, examiner (if an individual test), and other standard results should be included.

Significant Behavior or Personality Observations. Again, care must be taken to avoid unnecessarily derogatory remarks. The purpose of the whole field of measurement and evaluation is to help the child. It is doubtful if a recording of negative data that might prejudice the next observer will serve this purpose.

Anecdotal Reports. These might be subsumed under the previous heading, but since they may involve considerable space a separate heading might well be considered.

In some cumulative records considerable space is devoted to a description of the use of the various blanks. These explanations increase the usefulness of the record by providing a common basis for posting and interpreting. Holding a staff meeting at least once a year on the meaning and purpose of the record is a worthwhile practice.

Experimenting with Evaluation Techniques

It is all too evident that no single perfect method of evaluation has yet been devised. It is therefore recommended that each school have a committee to deal with evaluation problems, experimenting with techniques devised by members of the staff or adapting techniques in use elsewhere. Evaluation so intimately affects the entire operation of the school—curriculum, methods, promotion policy, philosophy—that it constitutes an effective focal point for critical examination of the entire school.

Many lists describing the effective teacher have been formulated, but one criterion is always present in some form: the good teacher is learning, growing, or progressing. Time spent on local problems of evaluation will be fruitful from the standpoint of teacher growth. Incidentally, it should be mentioned that the success of any of the techniques mentioned in the foregoing section (letters, conferences, cumulative records, student self-appraisal) will depend first of all upon the teacher's acceptance of the idea. Improvements in the techniques will also depend upon the teacher's acceptance and understanding. William L. Wrinkle, after a careful study of many practices in evaluation, concludes:[4]

> Perhaps no final bit of advice would be more appropriate . . . than . . . the following statement made by Franklin D. Roosevelt in his 1932 Baltimore address: "Do something; and when you have done something, if it works, do it some more; and if it doesn't work, do something else." There is one very happy aspect involved in attempting to bring about improvement in marking and reporting practices—whatever you may do has little likelihood of being more objectionable or less adequate than the practice it replaces.

[4] William L. Wrinkle, *Improving Marking and Reporting Practices*, New York: Rinehart & Company, Inc., 1947, p. 115.

If we reflect upon the purposes of the school and upon the purposes of evaluation, we immediately remember that education is a common enterprise involving the home, the community, the child, the teacher, and the administrator. In considering ways to improve evaluation procedures, it is heartily recommended that a committee or informal group be called together to discuss some of the problems. This group should consist of some parents who have evidenced interest in the school, some citizens who are willing to devote some of their time to the problem, a student or two who have the ability to speak with clarity (they need not necessarily be the brightest in the class), some teachers who can resist the temptation to dominate a discussion of educational problems, and an administrator. This group can consider the purposes, methods, and tools of evaluation. If changes in the system are warranted, it will be helpful to have a group of parents, citizens, and children who will serve as a vanguard in the job of interpreting the changes to the community.

The technique of involving parents, citizens, and pupils in a consideration of school problems has been tried in many localities, and the consensus of school workers who have evaluated such groups is that they are indispensable. Sometimes good practices have failed because of inadequate interpretation to the public. When a committee is called together, the urgency of this phase of forward movement is made so apparent that it cannot be overlooked.

ELEMENTS OF GOOD APPRAISAL PRACTICE

It has been shown that present methods of appraising pupil development and progress in the school are open to serious criticisms, and as yet, no universally acceptable substitute for the questionable practices has been devised. Marked improvements are possible, however, by means of techniques now being developed. The application of these techniques has led to the formulation of the following basic principles of evaluation:

1. Pupil evaluation is a means of communication between the school, the child, and the home. As such, it must be meaningful to all concerned.
2. The purpose of evaluation is to promote optimum growth. An indication of status is not enough.
3. Evaluation should indicate what steps should be taken next. A statement of desired behavior is an inherent responsibility of all the evaluators.
4. Appraisal should be in terms of individual accomplishment and not in terms of interpersonal comparisons.
5. Evaluation should be in terms of the stated objectives of education for the school level concerned. The demands of such groups as college professors, registrars, or employers should not shape the entire evaluation practice at any level.
6. Evaluation should be a continuing process. It is not an end in itself at any point in the pupil's growth.
7. Objective data are necessary, but these data are always relative to the living, dynamic person.
8. Alterations of evaluation procedures involve the entire philosophy of the school and must therefore be a matter for serious study. Change should take place only as rapidly as those concerned are convinced of its value.

SUMMARY

The object of appraisal practices is communication between teacher and pupil or between teacher and home. Because appraisal relates to all phases of a pupil's growth, it is difficult, if not impossible, to find a common denominator. But because appraisal is so intimately connected with pupil growth, the study of evaluation practices stimulates examination of education as a whole—its philosophy, methods, curricula, and materials.

Grades and marks are open to criticism because of such factors as the following: Marks tend to become the purpose of education for the pupil; he works for the grade. Marks tend to stress subject matter as a primary aim, whereas pupil development or pupil self-realization is the transcending aim of education. Marks tend to become a cudgel for the inept teacher, who uses them for incentive instead of establishing more persistent motives. Grades tend to force all youngsters to progress at the same speed and to conform to one mold. They are a threat to the maximum enjoyment of school, since slow pupils persistently tend to get low marks and particularly able pupils are likely to get good marks without learning the valuable habit of rigorous application. Actually, marks have little meaning because of the different values teachers assign to them and because those who look at the marks "read" them differently.

There are a number of contrasts between grading and other appraisal practices—contrasts that indicate the tendencies of the two practices. Some of these contrasts are communication *with* versus communication *to;* competition with self versus competition with others; subject-matter emphasis versus emphasis on pupil development; guidance versus judgment; and emphasis on the products of learning versus the symbols of learning.

A number of encouraging evaluation practices are now in operation. Although no one of these is perfect by itself, various combinations of the following methods will be improvements over "grades-and-marks" practices. Letters home, either informal or following a definite outline, make for increased clarity of communication. Home visits are valuable when both teachers and parents endorse this kind of contact. Teacher-parent conferences in the school have such inherent advantages as economy of the teacher's time, availability of cumulative data, and introduction of parents to the materials and methods with which the pupil and the teacher are familiar. Pupil self-appraisal should be an objective of all evaluation, and pupils must be given specific opportunity to practice self-appraisal. Teacher-parent-pupil conferences combine many of the advantages listed above and have the additional advantage of consciously bringing the pupil onto the scene. These various means of communication do not erase the need for cumulative records, which permit communication between various persons related to the pupil at successive periods of time.

No universally acceptable appraisal practice has yet been devised. Each local school system must plan its own most effective evaluation procedures. This is arduous work involving the coordinated efforts of teachers, pupils, parents, citizens, and administrators. The effort will be fruitful, however, not only because appraisal facilitates pupil growth but because the improved communication will result in better general educational practice.

STUDY AND DISCUSSION EXERCISES

1. Teachers often say, "We'd like to change, but the parents will not let us." Evaluate this statement by having a team of students who are studying this book interview ten teachers and ten parents. Contrast the degree of acceptance or repudiation of change for each group.
2. Do you agree with all the so-called shortcomings of grades that are listed in the chapter? Can you think of any other objections or advantages that have not been mentioned?
3. Has your own experience been one of satisfaction or dissatisfaction with grades?
4. Divide the class into groups and have each group draw up a list of ways of implementing each of the suggestions for improving appraisal practices. Bring the list to class for criticism and further suggestions.

5. Compare cumulative record cards or folders from several schools as to merits and shortcomings.

6. Consult some recent educational periodicals to see if there are any recent reports on the value of newer appraisal practices.

SUGGESTED ADDITIONAL READINGS

Association for Childhood Education International: *Records and Reports,* Bulletin 77, Washington: The Association, 1942, 32 pp.

Different phases of the problem of evaluation and reporting are discussed in this pamphlet by school workers with practical experience. Various views of pupils, parents, and teachers are represented.

Elsbree, Willard S.: *Pupil Progress in the Elementary School,* New York: Teachers College, Columbia University, Bureau of Publications, 1943, 86 pp.

The last two chapters in this booklet deal in scholarly detail with contemporary trends in the marking system and reporting to parents. The author's list of trends in reporting indicates some of the things one needs to include in his thinking about evaluation.

Smith, Eugene R., Ralph W. Tyler, et al.: *Appraising and Recording Student Progress,* New York: Harper & Brothers, 1942, 550 pp.

This is volume III of the series "Adventure in American Education," which deals with the widely known "Eight-year Study" or "Thirty-school Experiment." This book describes how evaluation was carried on in such areas as thinking, appreciation, personal and social adjustment, and interests.

Wrinkle, William L.: *Improving Marking and Reporting Practices in Elementary and Secondary Schools,* New York: Rinehart & Company, Inc., 1947, 120 pp.

This book is based on ten years of experimenting with better evaluation practices. The interdependence of appraisal, reporting, and educational practice and theory is recognized, and specific suggestions are made for tentative departures from traditional practice, but the author makes no pretense of having discovered a panacea.

CHAPTER FOURTEEN

Toward a Planned Program of Evaluation

Each chapter of this book has been devoted to a phase of the total testing program. The view presented in this book is that tests are samples of behavior which help the teacher to get a better view of the pupil in order to facilitate his future development. Both the uses and limitations of tests have been described in order that teachers may capitalize fully upon the values each test possesses. The specific problems involved in testing ability, estimating achievement, appraising personality, and evaluating classroom status have been discussed with a view to helping the teacher see how each device may be made to contribute to pupil development.

It has been necessary in this book to expand in later chapters concepts that were mentioned in earlier ones. By this procedure the concepts and skills needed in effectively utilizing tests have been presented by means of a spiral development. In this final chapter these concepts will be exemplified in a proposed testing program. This suggested program will provide a point of departure for those who would like specific advice regarding the development of their program.

This program is regarded as a minimum; without these basic tests effective instruction will be unnecessarily difficult. Although it is possible to do too much testing, it is advisable to use more tests than are included in this suggested program. Test results, as we have seen, are to be regarded as supplementary and corroborative data which are more likely to serve their purpose when they are correlated with information from other sources: teacher observation, cumulative records, and past school performance.

Determining the Objectives

In Chapter 3, "Choosing the Right Test," it was indicated that tests can be used for a variety of purposes. The superintendent or principal may wish to know more about the approximate level of ability of pupils in the school system and the extent to which pupils are capitalizing on that ability in terms of academic achievement. The supervisor may wish to use standardized tests to evaluate the effectiveness of instruction in the area of his jurisdiction. A one-session test will yield only a minimum of information; better results will be obtained when successive tests are used to give data regarding developmental trends. Thus it is clear that planning is necessary in even a simple situation.

We have seen that test data can be used to make instruction more effective. In order that these objectives be clearly stated and adequately understood, it is desirable that teachers participate in the meetings in which the objectives are determined. In larger school systems it may be impossible for all teachers to be active in the statement of objectives; in such situations bulletins and meetings can be devoted to interpretation and clarification.

Achievement of the objectives of the testing program will depend not only upon (1) the teachers' understanding the objectives, uses, and limitations of tests and (2) their conviction that some educational values will result, but upon the operation of the program. How well the program operates will depend upon (3) the choice of the most appropriate tests (see Chapter 3) and upon (4) a workable system for maintaining the results—a simple cumulative record. Unless the entire staff has participated in the formulation of objectives and plans for operating the program, it is desirable that (5) some training sessions be devoted to the administration, scoring, and interpretation of results.

Reading Readiness

The minimal testing program suggested here has as its objective helping the teacher understand the pupils rather than revealing to the administrator the status of the pupils or helping the supervisor evaluate instruction.

In the first grade, the information most vital to the teacher is whether or not the pupil is adequately prepared to begin his study of reading. The best test for this purpose is one designed to estimate readiness rather than to measure intelligence. There are several reasons for this. Group intelligence tests at best yield only approximations of intelligence, and when given in the lower grades are even less dependable. First-grade pupils are too small to grasp the importance of their task and too lively for prolonged periods of concentration, and successive scores on individual tests show that this type of intelligence test is more dependable for older pupils than for preschool and primary pupils. Hence it is probably wise to delay giving group intelligence tests until the pupil has become accustomed to his new environment and can give a more accurate account of himself. Further, it may do the youngster some harm, in view of the general failure to understand the meaning of test scores, to record in his cumulative record a score that might later cause some teachers to misjudge his ability.

Reading-readiness tests are subject to the same criticism of unreliability as group intelligence tests; but as applied to readiness tests the criticism is less serious. The results are for temporary use only and will not be considered important after the passage of a few months. In addition, the reading-readiness test has some value in diagnosis as well as in determination of status. That is, although it is informative to know that a child has a certain mental age—mental age is an important factor in readiness—it is possible that what appears to be adequate mentality may for a given child be composed of factors that are less directly related to reading ability than are the factors that result in the same mental age for another child. The readiness test, on the other hand, samples those abilities that are most directly related to the task at hand—learning to read. If the test is divided into parts, the relative standing of the child on the various parts may suggest the most suitable program for developing readiness in a particular child. For instance, the *Reading-aptitude Test* devised by Marion Monroe has sections devoted to the evaluation of visual, auditory, and motor functions as well as articulation, use, and comprehension of language. A low score on any one part suggests what may be done to promote the development of readiness.

Readiness tests should be given in the first grade, during the first three weeks of school. The teacher will then be able to offer those pupils who are ready for reading the experiences they are anticipating and to delay reading for those who, if started too early, would suffer the disappointment and frustration of failure.

Physical Examinations

The results of the readiness test may indicate the need for a physical examination to reveal remediable visual or auditory defects. The routine examination of tonsils, teeth, eyes, and ears is not enough. Physical status is as variable as intelligence-test results at this stage of development; hence, in addition to the periodic testing of children by audiometrists, physicians, ophthalmologists, and school nurses, the teacher must be persistently alert to the symptoms of visual difficulty, auditory difficulty, and acute and chronic infection. Representative of the telltale symptoms for visual difficulty are squinting, excessive blinking, twisting the head when looking at the chalk board, watering of the eyes, sties and granulated eyelids, attempts to brush material off the printed page, and bending abnormally close to a book. Common symptoms of auditory difficulty are turning the side of the head toward the source of sound, inattentiveness, boredom, cupping the hand behind the ear, ignoring simple requests and questions, complaints of buzzing in the ear or of earaches, speech defects and odd voice quality, and sometimes seclusiveness and poor schoolwork. Indications of acute or chronic infections may include many of the above symptoms, such as listlessness and inattentiveness, as well as frequent absences from school, drowsiness, lack of interest in play and schoolwork, and irritability.

These symptoms, like the scores on standardized tests, must be taken as informative data to be supplemented by corroborative evidence. The teacher does not diagnose on the basis of symptoms, but his awareness of them will make for earlier and more frequent referral of pupils who might profit from special medical attention.

Diagnostic Reading Tests

In the second and third grades, the major academic concern of the pupil and teacher is reading. Some children may not yet have accomplished the development that would indicate a general readiness for reading. Tests may show that others are psychologically ready, but actual performance may reveal achievement which falls short of their indicated ability. In order to save these pupils from the trauma of repeated and continued failure, it will be well to discover what their specific difficulties are. Early correction of remediable difficulties will prevent the development of the "reading block" so frequently referred to. Blocks against reading are, for the most part, dislike generated by chronic failure or a strong conviction that one just cannot learn to read.

Diagnostic tests will help the teacher to determine whether the pupil is having difficulty in one or more of the following areas of specific reading factors:[1] recognition of visual likenesses and differences in printed phrases, ability to analyze words, recognition and understanding of spoken words, adequacy of reading vocabulary, interpretation of the message contained in sentences and paragraphs, understanding of factual data, method for attacking new words, and skill in the use of tables of contents (a minor concern in the primary grades but of increasing importance at the upper grade levels).

The diagnostic reading test may be given during the first two or three weeks of school and used as a source of information for work with children as individuals and in groups. All pupils may profit from wise use of the results of the diagnostic test. The information may suggest ways to help the able student make even better progress and thus provide motivation for continued development.

Group Intelligence Tests

As the teacher diagnoses reading difficulty, he thinks immediately of the mental ability of the pupil. It is possible that mental testing should take precedence over diagnostic testing in the second and third grades. If both cannot be done, it will be up to the teacher or the testing committee to decide which will be of greater immediate value.

[1] Teachers selecting tests might keep these points in mind as they read the publishers' manuals, catalogues, and reviews of diagnostic reading tests.

Although the evaluation of general mental ability may not be the factor of prime importance in the primary grades, it becomes of greater interest in the intermediate grades. Hence it is recommended that the testing program include a series of group intelligence tests, beginning in the third grade. Some schools administer these tests in the third, fifth, and seventh grades. However, since group intelligence tests are of questionable accuracy and the rate of mental development is still variable in the elementary school years, it seems desirable to test in each grade if it is financially feasible.

The tests should be given during the fifth or sixth weeks of school rather than immediately. The pupils should be allowed time to settle down after the vigorous activities of their vacation, and new pupils should be given time to acquaint themselves with their new human and physical surroundings. (Pupils who enter during the school year should be given an intelligence test after they have had time to become acquainted.) The middle of the week will probably be the best time, but the test period should not coincide with a fall festival, school party, or athletic contest.

As we saw in Chapter 1, the teacher should respect his own skepticism if test results do not accord with his observation of the pupil. In the event that a score seems too low for a particular pupil, he should give an equivalent form of the test or, if a psychometrist is available, an individual test. Whether the score has surprised the teacher or not, it will be well to compare the pupil's present score with records from his previous school years.

General-achievement Tests

By the time the child has reached the fourth grade, he should be beginning to acquire the informational data he will need to live effectively. His interest should begin to shift from reading, writing, and computation to such subject-matter fields as geography, language, spelling, and social studies. In the intermediate grades, interest shifts from the acquiring of the tools of learning to practice in their use. However, this does not imply that all pupils have learned the skills so thoroughly that the "fundamental processes" can now be neglected. As we shall see in the next section, there should be continued emphasis on improvement of the skills throughout the elementary and secondary school years.

Effective use of achievement tests by teachers requires that data be available regarding pupils' ability. Intelligence tests give an indication of the pupils' present intellectual status, whereas achievement tests give evidence of how effectively the pupils are using their ability. However, as was indicated in Chapter 6, "Evaluating Pupil Achievement," high ability does not mean that the pupil should necessarily achieve at a high level; health, home factors, personality and social problems, past experiences, and the number of current out-of-school activities must be considered in interpreting the data.

In addition to indicating to the teacher whether the pupil's achievement corresponds to his indicated capacity, achievement tests help to evaluate the effectiveness of instruction. If the average ability of all pupils is near the national norm and achievement in language and reading is also close to the national norm while achievement in arithmetic and spelling is below average, it is possible that techniques of instruction in these two subjects should be examined. Individual teachers may find areas which they think, in terms of class averages, will need particular emphasis throughout the year. However, a class average above the norm in language does not necessarily indicate superiority of teaching; it may simply be a matter of the school's being in a superior neighborhood. Thus interpretation of data is essential.

If only one battery of achievement tests can be given per year, October or November is probably the best time. Pupils have had an opportunity to settle down and to be reminded of some of the things they may have forgotten during vacation, and there are few holidays to interfere with characteristic emotional stability. If the tests are given at this time, the teacher has had a chance to evaluate the pupils but still has enough of the school year remaining to benefit from the guidance of the test data. It would be highly desirable if an equivalent form of the test could be given in the spring to provide a basis for the student's evaluating his own progress and to give the teacher a chance to judge the effectiveness of his teaching.

Upper-grade Reading Tests

Most teachers appreciate the fallacy of the saying, "Practice makes perfect." It is much closer to the truth to say that one learns by doing. The quality of one's reading probably tends to improve if he does a great deal of reading. However, experimental investigation of reading also reveals that when one reads extensively he may simply fix more firmly the habits he has already developed. Maximum improvement will come with directed, correct, and purposeful practice. The importance of continued reading instruction in the intermediate and upper grades is emphasized by the fact that at the age of about twelve or thirteen, interest in reading reaches its highest point. Furthermore, it is at this age that interests shift from the juvenile to material which is of interest to adults. Data from educational psychology indicate that the better the skills are taught at this crucial period, the greater the likelihood that interest in reading will continue at a high level.

Time should be regularly scheduled for the development of silent-reading skills. A silent-reading test will indicate the areas that are in need of particular attention and provide a strong source of motivation for steady application, which is perhaps still more important. Some of the factors which a silent-reading test might evaluate are comprehension of paragraph meaning; appreciation of the organization of ideas—

key words and phrases, ability to locate information; skill in using indexes, tables of contents, references, etc.; and rate of reading. Many teachers have experimented with giving one form of a silent-reading test at the beginning of a six- to twelve-week period of special instruction and the equivalent form after the planned exercises have been completed. These experiments have been uniformly highly gratifying; students have shown gains as high as 50 to 100 per cent, often with average gains of 50 per cent in rate and comprehension of reading. (It should be noted, however, that unless there is some continuing emphasis on the elements of good reading, the pupil will tend to regress toward the level of his former reading habits.) Individual differences in ability and motivation will also influence the variation in achievement.

The importance of including silent-reading tests in the minimal testing program is indicated in the following passage:[2]

> One of the most important of the modern advances in teaching methods is the tendency to force elementary school and high school students to read widely in many fields. Instead of confining the students' reading to a few textbooks relating to a limited number of topics, the progressive school provides for and demands a wide range of reading activity. Furthermore, the solution of most classroom problems in the modern school requires the skillful use of books as sources of information. In this sense, reading comes to mean something more than merely rapid comprehension of printed symbols and the memory and organizations of materials read. It becomes also an ability to use books and libraries as efficient sources of information.

Evaluation of Personal and Social Adjustment

In our discussion of the uses and abuses of tests and inventories of personality in Chapter 8, "Appraising Person-

[2] H. A. Greene, A. N. Jorgensen, and V. H. Kelley, *Manual, Iowa Silent Reading Tests: Advanced Test,* Yonkers, N.Y.: World Book Company, 1931, p. 1.

ality," we saw that the defects of these instruments may sometimes outweigh their possible advantages. However, since personality and social factors are of major importance in the classroom, the cautious use of projective techniques and sociometry (see Chapter 9) may offer the teacher some help in handling personality problems.

Ink-blot, cloud, and picture-interpretation tests as means of evaluating personality should be used only by those who are specially trained to interpret them. Even in the hands of experts, these tests reveal both the strength and weakness of projective techniques; i.e., the subject puts himself into the test and the examiner projects himself into the interpretation of results. Some projective techniques can be of value if the teacher bears in mind this tendency of the person who administers and interprets the test to *make unique inferences.* Observation of children at play is recommended, not with the aim of policing but to see how the child orients himself to others, what his view of self is, and what his abilities are. The writing of themes, stories, and compositions is recommended; recurrent emphases or ideas, *when corroborated by other sources of information,* can give teachers *clues,* not data, on personal and social adjustment. Drawing, painting, and finger-painting also may afford some clues as to the child's emotional patterns. The teacher should remember, however, that special training is required for adequate interpretation, although he may gain a deeper understanding of the pupil through the cautious study of his creative products.

Something of the value of sociometry is revealed by the very common remark of teachers, "I was surprised by the difference between what I thought were the interpersonal likes and dislikes and what was indicated by the sociogram." These new insights can be of great help to teachers in developing seating and working arrangements for pupils in the classroom group. The teacher must remember that, as we saw in Chapter

9, the interpersonal constellations will shift with the passage of time and with changes in the situation. Therefore sociometric designs should be redrawn as the occasion demands.

Subject-matter Tests

Tests that possess some of the advantages suggested in the section dealing with silent-reading tests exist for other areas as well. There are arithmetic tests which give some indication of specific areas of strength or weakness, i.e., addition, subtraction, division, multiplication, or particular number combinations such as the misapprehension that six times seven is forty-four. English-usage tests are available which yield similar diagnostic information. By means of such tests, much time can be saved by avoiding repetitious general drill when a small amount of drill on a specific detail would suffice.

There are many tests in the social studies, and their composition varies with the purposes of the test constructors. Sometimes the emphasis is upon the mastery of information; since facts are the basis of sound thinking, this is a justifiable emphasis. Other test makers, however, place primary stress upon the use and interpretation of data and upon techniques for acquiring information. The individual or committee responsible for test selection will have to determine which kind of test will best fit the objectives that have been stated for the particular school concerned.

It is probably best to administer subject-matter tests near the beginning of the school year, though the time will depend upon the specific purposes of the test. In addition to a planned succession of tests on a schedule, it should be possible to test at irregular times transfer pupils and pupils who were absent at the time of regular testing. If data are not available on a child when needed, teachers may become discouraged about the testing program and abandon the advantages that could accrue from a dependable program.

A Check List for the Testing Program

A number of considerations are involved in obtaining the best results from a testing program. The following check list will provide guidance in determining responsibilities and duties and anticipating difficulties:[3]

	Check
1. Purposes of the program	
Clearly defined	____
Understood by parties involved	____
2. Choice of tests	
Valid	____
Reliable	____
Appropriate difficulty level	____
Adequate norms	____
Easy to administer and score	____
Best available for purpose	____
3. Administration and scoring	
Administrators well trained	____
All necessary information provided	____
Scorers adequately instructed	____
Scoring carefully checked	____
4. Physical conditions	
Sufficient space	____
Sufficient time	____
Conveniently scheduled	____
5. Utilization of test results	
Definite plans for use of results	____
Provision for giving teachers all necessary help in using scores	____
6. System of records	
Necessary for purpose	____
Sufficient for purpose	____
Convenient form for use	____

[3] Roger T. Lennon, "Planning a Testing Program," *Test Service Bulletin,* no. 55, Division of Test Research and Service, Yonkers, N.Y.: World Book Company, p. 3.

7. Personnel
   Adequately trained for the purpose ____
8. Affiliated research ____
   Full advantage taken of results ____
   Provision for special studies, analyses, etc. ____

It is likely that it will be possible to check more of the items in this list if planning for the program has been a co-operative affair. This group approach should include staff members' sitting in the meetings having to do with test selection, defining purposes, constructing the cumulative record, and planning the other details. This approach will do more than strengthen the testing program. It can be a means of welding the faculty into a stronger corps and a means of promoting individual teacher development.

Informal Evaluative Techniques

We have seen that formal and standardized tests constitute a substantial part of the program of evaluation but not the entire program. There are also informal techniques of evaluation, such as anecdotal records, rating scales, and observation, which provide valuable, though not statistically accurate, data. Creative writing, drawing, and painting are also useful in evaluation of pupil behavior.

Anecdotal records are valuable supplements to the evaluation program, but like standardized tests, they require the exercise of skill in use and caution in interpretation.[4] (1) The anecdotal record should be a systematically recorded description of the pupil's typical behavior, and (2) it should be used periodically so that time for growth is allowed between groups of three or four consecutive descriptions. (3) The temptation to record teachers' reactions to pupil behavior should be

[4] Helen Bieker in *Fostering Mental Health in Our Schools,* Association for Supervision and Curriculum Development, Washington, D.C.: National Educational Association, 1950, pp. 184–202.

avoided—for example, "Tommy sharpened his pencil five times today between 2:15 and 3:10, each time poking or brushing some other pupil on his way to the sharpener" rather than "Tommy's resistance to order and routine is revealed in his chronic tendency to irritate others." Teachers should avoid making immediate interpretations of behavior, since the value of the anecdotal record is in tying apparently discrete bits of behavior together into a pattern and affording perspective on the child's growth over a period of time. Of course, the record may also be used to study a particular child who is experiencing difficulty in adjustment; then the account may describe some particular behavior or situation which appears to be characteristic.

In the evaluation of the social effectiveness of a pupil, rating scales may prove to be significant. Since it is important to know what others think of an individual in order to point the way to personal and social improvement, the rating scale will provide clues to approaches. The more effective rating scales will deal with specific situations rather than intangible personality traits. The individuals doing the rating must know one another rather intimately. Since raters differ in the severity or leniency of their judgments, the final results are tentative in nature. Since relationships change with length of acquaintance, the results have temporary value only. Inasmuch as the sociometric design is closely related to the rating scale, these same precautions and reservations should be heeded in using sociograms.

Informal observations may prove to be a valuable supplement to the evaluation program—if the teacher can imagine himself in the role of a psychologist rather than that of a policeman. By doing more listening and less talking and by avoiding the show of shock, the teacher may obtain valuable clues to pupil behavior. Too frequently, though, teachers are full of good advice and the tendency to chide: "Tsk, tsk. You don't really mean that." Taking time for observation in the classroom, on the playground, in the gym, and in all school activities will result in insights that will go much further toward changing undesirable pupil responses than the show of disapproval or the autocratic blocking of wayward conduct.

Recording and Reporting

The testing program will lose a substantial part of its value unless careful records are kept. Too frequently tests lose much of their value because they are used to find status rather than to indicate pupil development and progress. It would be desirable to have a somewhat uniform cumulative record used in different schools so that when pupils transferred the data that accompanied them would be readily understood. No less desirable in the cumulative record is brevity. It should be short in order to avoid overwhelming the teacher with facts and figures and to prevent the teachers' spending hours on the clerical detail of recording. Spaces should be provided on the card or folder for personal data (name, sex, birth date, etc.), address, chronology of schools attended, achievement-test data, intelligence-test data and special test data (diagnostic, aptitude, etc.). In addition the folder may contain a few carefully selected conference notes, reports of observations, and anecdotal records. It should be kept in mind that the purpose of the cumulative record is to facilitate the adjustment of the child in his next school or to his next teacher.

The maximum benefit of a well-planned and well-executed program of evaluation cannot be realized if practices of reporting to parents remain on the traditional percentage basis, the A, B, C, D, F categorization, or even the C, S, N innovation. Letters home and home visits have proven helpful. But the more promising practice is teacher-pupil-parent conferences at the elementary level and teacher-pupil conferences at the high school level. An increasingly large number of schools are using conferences in place of report cards and are generally satisfied with the results. Two cities diagonally across the United States from one another may perhaps be considered representative—Arlington, Virginia,[5] and Vancouver, Washington.[6] Teachers and parents in these two cities answer in the following ways some of the questions that are most frequently asked in connection with this departure from the conventional report card: Yes, it takes time, but teachers find that their additional insights pay dividends in helping pupils. Yes, pupils work even harder when the threat of grades is removed. No, parents are not 100 per cent for the plan, but in Arlington, 92 per cent of them are. Yes, it takes a continuous parent-education program. Vancouver teachers report that parents must be reeducated each year. No, pupils do not lose in achievement. Pupils in both cities are, on the average, at or above the national norms for age-grade status. Yes, it is definitely worth trying, for pupils, teachers, and parents report increased understanding of one another and the result is better rapport.

SUMMARY

An effective testing program must fit the specific local needs. The minimal testing program suggested in this chapter must be considered only as a point of departure—a guide to planning.

Actually, minimum programs recommended by various scholars may vary from one test to as many as ten. If one test is used, it should be a mental-ability test; but in the primary grades, the reading-readiness test is a more accurate indicator of the ability required for school. Next in importance is either the general-achievement test or the diagnostic reading test—depending upon whether the pupils are in the upper grades or

[5] Raymond H. Rignall, "Are Report Cards Necessary?" *Family Circle,* **41** (3):104–111, September, 1952.

[6] Paul F. Gaiser, *A Guide to a Functional Program of Reporting Pupil Progress to Parents,* Vancouver, Wash., 1950, 56 pp. (mimeographed).

in the primary grades. Of perhaps equal importance with achievement tests are silent-reading tests, because reading skills so strongly condition the pupils' attitudes toward self and school. The evaluation of personality is often omitted from minimal programs. However, inasmuch as sociometric techniques and some projective techniques are inexpensive and informative and personality development is such an integral responsibility of the school, the authors recommend this approach to personal and social evaluation. The inclusion of subject-matter tests, which closely resemble diagnostic tests, would place the program which included them on the borderline between a strong minimal program and one that approached the ideal.

Planning an effective testing program is not easy, but neither is effective teaching a simple process. Just as good teaching is made up of many separate steps, so the effective use of tests involves attention to many small details. The rewards for taking these painstaking steps are great: teachers will get more satisfaction from their work because it is well done, and they will be fulfilling the fundamental human need for continued personal development. Pupils will be helped to develop more symmetrically while they are in school. But the greatest benefit is that another step will be taken toward developing the robust pupil who, when his school days are over, can steer his own course.

STUDY AND DISCUSSION EXERCISES

1. On the basis of what you can discover in a few hours, make a tentative list of the names of tests (and their publishers) which you would include in the minimum testing program described in this chapter.
2. Would you prefer to give a reading-readiness test or a group intelligence test in the first grade? State your reasons.
3. What tests would you use next if it were possible to add three more to the program outlined in the chapter?

4. Would you consider it more important to use equivalent forms of intelligence and achievement tests, or to give single tests in these areas and add others, such as mechanical- and musical-aptitude tests?

5. Draw up a tentative schedule for test administration for the entire year, giving the days of the week and the dates. Submit it to your colleagues for suggestions and improvement.

6. How would you suggest that the testing program in a ten-teacher eight-grade elementary school be launched? Give details.

7. Get the help of some of your colleagues in drawing up a cumulative record which would be adequate for what you regard as a good testing program.

SUGGESTED ADDITIONAL READINGS

Cole, Lawrence E., and William F. Bruce: *Educational Psychology,* Yonkers, N.Y.: World Book Company, 1950, pp. 625–671.

This survey of the origin, development, and use of tests provides a good background for wise selection of tests. The authors stress the need for keeping accurate records and for interpreting results.

Jordon, A. M.: *Measurement in Education,* New York: McGraw-Hill Book Company, Inc., 1953, pp. 67–94.

This chapter deals mainly with achievement testing, but the suggestions are detailed. Illustrative material is included.

Knapp, Robert H.: *Practical Guidance Methods,* New York: McGraw-Hill Book Company, Inc., 1953, pp. 1–54.

The author lists, from the pupil-guidance point of view, suggested tests in such areas as those mentioned in our chapter. He provides illustrations of cumulative records.

Mursell, James L.: *Psychology for Modern Education,* New York: W. W. Norton & Company, Inc., 1952, pp. 391–469.

Against a background of theory relating to intelligence and special abilities, the author describes and evaluates in these two chapters a number of intelligence and ability tests. The material provides a good basis for planning a testing program.

Tiegs, Ernest W.: *Educational Diagnosis,* Educational Bulletin no. 18, Los Angeles: California Test Bureau, 1948, 16 pp. (free).

This pamphlet is a description of the use of diagnostic tests in improving instruction. There are many sound and practical suggestions, although the endorsement of personality tests seems somewhat too hearty.

APPENDIX

Organizing Test Results for Interpretation

Developing effective ways to gather information about pupils is an essential teacher activity. An equally important activity is the task of organizing the data to permit analysis, comparisons, and interpretations.

The purpose of this appendix is to present some of the techniques which may assist the teacher to organize data in a meaningful way. Methods of ordering and recording scores and developing central reference points and certain relative measures are described, and an annotated list of references is presented to assist the teacher who is interested in developing an understanding of other, more rigorous statistical procedures. The content of this appendix has been selected on the basis of simplicity and possibility of use by classroom teachers rather than on the basis of a criterion of essential mathematical precision or adequacy.

Ranking Scores

Mr. Brown has just scored a science examination for his 30 eighth-grade pupils. The test contained thirty-five items, each valued at one score point. If Mr. Brown copied the scores from the answer sheets without a plan of organization, the results might appear like this:

24, 20, 26, 16, 23, 25, 30, 24,
19, 21, 24, 28, 20, 23, 32, 26,
21, 25, 21, 18, 32, 24, 23, 15,
25, 22, 29, 26, 23, 26. ($N = 30$)

Organized in rank order from high to low, the list of scores is more meaningful:

32, 32, 30, 29, 28, 26, 26, 26,
26, 25, 25, 25, 24, 24, 24, 24,
23, 23, 23, 23, 22, 21, 21, 21,
20, 20, 19, 18, 16, 15. ($N = 30$)

The Tally Sheet

Another means of giving meaningful organization to a set of scores is a *tally sheet,* or *frequency table,* such as that presented in Figure 20. Scores in this table are presented in units. In some instances the teacher might wish to group the scores in intervals of two, three, or five to provide a convenient summary table. Steps in preparing the tally sheet are presented with Figure 20.

The tally sheet has the following values for the teacher:

1. It presents test results organized in terms of size of score.
2. It represents a summary of the test results in a form easily scanned for information.
3. It presents scores in a form which permits checks and additional calculations if they are desired.
4. Properly documented as to date, type of test, grade, and teacher, the tally sheet constitutes a permanent record of the results of the test. The teacher may wish

Test score	Tally	Frequency	f (score)
35			
34			
33			
32	//	2	64
31			
30	/	1	30
29	/	1	29
28	/	1	28
27			
26	////	4	104
25	///	3	75
24	////	4	96
23	////	4	92
22	/	1	22
21	///	3	63
20	//	2	40
19	/	1	19
18	/	1	18
17			
16	/	1	16
15	/	1	15
N	30	30	711

FIG. 20. Tally sheet, or frequency table, of science-test scores of 30 eighth-grade pupils.

Tally:

1. List units for range of scores from highest to lowest (column 1).
2. Tally actual scores from pupil answer sheets; check tallies with number of test papers (column 2).
3. Sum tallies and record for each score (column 3).

Arithmetic mean (average):

1. In column 4 each score has been multiplied by the frequency of that score (e.g., $32 \times 2 = 64$).
2. At foot of column 4 is the sum of all the scores (the sum of column 4).
3. Divide the sum of all the scores by the number of scores or *N* at the foot of column 2 (e.g., $711 \div 30 = 23.7$).
4. The result of this calculation (23.7) is the arithmetic mean or average.

to use this record (*a*) in comparing two or more classes, (*b*) as an aid to the assignment of grades, (*c*) in comparing individuals with the group, and (*d*) in considering the status of individuals relative to the average or typical performance of the group.

REPRESENTATIVE MEASURES

The teacher may wish to establish a single score which best represents the performance of a group. For example, when asked, "How did your group perform on the test?" Mr. Brown might answer, "The average score was 23.7." In effect Mr. Brown has attempted to represent an entire set of scores by means of one quantity. Such measures are termed measures of central tendency. Three such measures, the *mid-measure,* the *arithmetic mean* (average), and the *median* are presented here.

The Arithmetic Mean. The *arithmetic mean,* or *average,* is a statistic with which most of us are familiar. It is one way of encompassing a variety of data in one quantitative statement. Thus we may describe a pupil as of average height or weight, of average intelligence, as an average fourth grader. Instead of the term *average* we might use *typical* or *representative.*

Aside from its value as a representative measure, the arithmetic mean can be utilized as a point of reference. For example, when we say that Judy is above or below average for her age or grade in any specified trait, we are using the average as a reference point. In educational evaluations, the reference point is seldom if ever an absolute quantity, like size of score; rather it is a point, usually somewhere in the center of a distribution of scores. The arithmetic mean is an example of this type of reference point to which a series of test scores can be related.

The arithmetic mean is calculated by summing all the scores and dividing by the number of pupils for whom scores have been recorded. Calculations may be developed from a tally sheet or frequency table in the manner outlined in Figure 20.

Some values and uses of the arithmetic mean are the following:

1. It is a relatively stable and accurate representative measure.
2. It may be used as a point of reference with which the performance of individual pupils within the group may be compared.
3. When the same test is used with two or more groups, the mean may form a basis for comparison of the groups.
4. The mean forms the basis for the calculation of other measures, such as the standard deviation and standard scores.

The Mid-measure. A second type of central reference point or expression of central tendency is the *mid-measure*. The mid-measure is the middle score of a series of scores. When the number of scores is even, the mid-measure is the average of the two scores nearest the middle of the distribution of scores. This measure is likely to be useful when the teacher needs only a quick and very approximate indication of central tendency. In the case of our distribution of science-test scores (Figure 20), the mid-measure (the average of the fifteenth and sixteenth scores) is 24.

The Median. The *median* is a point on a scale of scores which divides the distribution into two equal parts. That is, one half of the scores fall above the median and one half below this point. The median is computed from a frequency table or tally sheet such as that presented in Figure 21. For

Test scores	Continuous scale	Frequency	Cumulative frequency
32	31.5–32.5	2	30
31	30.5–31.5		
30	29.5–30.5	1	28
29	28.5–29.5	1	27
28	27.5–28.5	1	26
27	26.5–27.5		
26	25.5–26.5	4	25
25	24.5–25.5	3	21
*24	23.5–24.5	4	18
23	22.5–23.5	4	14
22	21.5–22.5	1	10
21	20.5–21.5	3	9
20	19.5–20.5	2	6
19	18.5–19.5	1	4
18	17.5–18.5	1	3
17	16.5–17.5		
16	15.5–16.5	1	2
15	14.5–15.5	1	1
		$N = 30$	

FIG. 21. Calculation of the median.

1. Find half the number of scores ($N/2 = 30/2 = 15$).

2. From column 4, find the cumulative frequency equal to or less than $N/2$ (i.e., 14). The median will lie in the score interval immediately above this.

3. Divide the size of the score interval by the number of scores in the interval which contains the middle score (i.e., $1 \div 4 = .25$).

4. Multiply this correction (.25) by the number of scores needed to reach the midpoint of the distribution, in this case 15 (midpoint) less 14 (cumulated below the interval which contains the fifteenth score) ($15 - 14 = 1$ and $1 \times .25 = .25$).

5. Add the result of calculations in step 4 (.25) to the lower limit (23.5) of the interval in which lies the midpoint of the distribution. The result is the *median.* The median is $23.5 + .25 = 23.75$

purposes of computation the scores are regarded as a continuous series. Each unit score—for example, a score of 25—is considered to represent a range of achievement from 24.5 to 25.5, much as an inch on a foot rule may be regarded as a distance on a continuous linear measure rather than as a point.

The method of computing the median is presented with Figure 21. This measure serves many of the same purposes as the arithmetic mean; it is a central reference point which may facilitate comparisons of individuals and groups. It is not ordinarily so stable as the mean, but it does have some advantages when the teacher wishes to avoid giving emphasis to extreme scores.

The median is essentially a counting or ranking measure which emphasizes relative position rather than actual size of score. For example, in the following series the arithmetic mean is affected markedly by alteration of one extreme score, whereas the median is unaffected by the change.

Series

A	90,	40,	38,	32,	30
B	45,	40,	38,	32,	30

Mean series $A = 220 \div 5 = 44$
Mean series $B = 185 \div 5 = 37$
Median series *A* and *B* $= 38$

STUDYING THE DISTRIBUTION OF SCORES

Although measures of central tendency such as the mean and median are useful as reference points for comparisons and interpretations, a single point in a distribution fails to tell the whole story. An important consideration may be the extent to which scores are distributed over the range of the test. For example, in Figure 22 the distributions of scores for

DISTRIBUTION OF SCORES

Score	Frequency, class A	Frequency, class B
32	2	
31		
30	1	
29	1	1
28	1	2
27		3
26	4	3
25	3	4
24	4	4
23	4	2
22	1	3
21	3	4
20	2	3
19	1	1
18	1	
17		
16	1	
15	1	
N	30	30
Sum of scores	711	715
Median	23.75	24.0
Mean	23.7	23.8
Range	17	10
Q_3	25.8	26.0
Q_1	21.0	21.4
Interquartile range	4.8	4.6
$Q = \frac{Q_3 - Q_1}{2}$	2.4	2.3

FIG. 22. Distribution of scores for class A and class B on an eighth-grade test in social studies.

class A and class B indicate that the two groups are not alike in performance on the test although the means and medians of the two groups are quite similar. The range of scores for class A is greater than that for class B.

The teacher may study the dispersion of scores by means of a tally sheet, and he may wish to record the range, which is the difference between the highest and lowest scores. In the case of class A (Figure 22) the *range* is 32 — 15, or 17. The range for class B is 29 — 19, or 10.

The range is a relatively unreliable measure, readily influenced by changes in individual scores at the extremes of the distribution. However, this measure provides (*a*) a simple method of describing the dispersion of a set of scores and (*b*) additional information beyond that represented by measures of central tendency.

Quartiles, Deciles, and Percentiles

A number of measures may be used to indicate various points in the distribution. Among such measures are *quartiles, deciles,* and *percentiles,* which divide the distribution into quarters, tenths, and hundredths. The first quartile (Q_1) is a point which sets off the lowest 25 per cent of the scores. The third quartile (Q_3) is a point below which fall 75 per cent of the scores. Quartile two (Q_2) is identical with the median in location and definition.

Deciles are points below which fall the indicated tenths of the scores (e.g., decile 7 marks off the lower seven-tenths of the distribution).

Percentiles mark off the indicated per cent of the distribution; for example, percentile 75 (P_{75}) is the point below which fall 75 per cent of the cases.

The calculation of all these measures is based on the assumption of a continuous distribution, and all are calculated in essentially the same manner as the median when the ap-

Percentile	Decile	Quartile	Median
95			
90	9		
85			
80	8		
75		3	
70	7		
65			
60	6		
55			
50	5	2	Median
45			
40	4		
35			
30	3		
25		1	
20	2		
15			
10	1		
5			

FIG. 23. Relationships between percentiles, deciles, quartiles, and the median.

propriate common or decimal fraction is substituted in the formula. Figure 23 illustrates the relation between these measures, and Figure 24 illustrates the method of calculation of percentiles. General procedures for the calculation of quartiles, deciles, and percentiles are as follows:

1. Multiply the total number of scores by the desired fraction (quartile, decile, or percentile).
2. Find the nearest cumulative total of frequencies *equal to* or *less than* the fraction of the distribution represented by the selected quartile, decile, or percentile point.

Test scores	Continuous scale	Frequency	Cumulative frequency
32	31.5–32.5	2	30
31	30.5–31.5		
30	29.5–30.5	1	28
29	28.5–29.5	1	27
28	27.5–28.5	1	26
27	26.5–27.5		
26	25.5–26.5	4	25
25	24.5–25.5	3	21
24	23.5–24.5	4	18
23	22.5–23.5	4	14
22	21.5–22.5	1	10
21	20.5–21.5	3	9
20	19.5–20.5	2	6
19	18.5–19.5	1	4
18	17.5–18.5	1	3
17	16.5–17.5		
16	15.5–16.5	1	2
15	14.5–15.5	1	1
	N	30	

FIG. 24. Calculation of percentiles: *How to find percentile 75.*

1. Find 75 per cent of 30, or 22.5. Locate in column 4 the cumulative frequency less than 22.5. This is 21.
2. Percentile 75 is located in the next interval above cumulative frequency 21 or in interval 25.5–26.5.
3. Find the difference between the computed P_{75} point (22.5) and the nearest cumulative total less than this $(22.5 - 21 = 1.5)$.
4. Since the size of the score interval is one unit and there are four scores in the interval in which P_{75} is located, each score has a value of $1 \div 4$, or .25.
5. Multiply $1.5 \times .25 = .375$. This is the correction which, added to the lower limit of the interval, brings us to percentile 75.
6. Add the correction (.375) to the value of the lower limit of the interval which contains percentile 75. $(25.5 + .375 = 25.875$, or, when rounded, 25.9.) Percentile 75 is 25.9.

3. Calculate the fractional "distance" into the next higher continuous score interval necessary to reach the desired point.
4. Multiply the fraction (step 3) by the size of the score interval.
5. Add this quantity to the lower limit of the score interval in which the desired quartile, decile, or percentile point is located. The result is the desired point in the distribution.

Measures such as quartiles, deciles, and percentiles indicate how an individual stands in relation to the group from which the measures were derived. Such information is likely to be more valuable than actual test scores (raw scores) for purposes of evaluation and for permanent records.

Interquartile and Semi-interquartile Ranges

The quartile points form the basis for a statistic which can be used to find the dispersion of scores around the median. The range is markedly affected by changes in scores at either extreme of the distribution. A more stable estimate of dispersion is provided by the interquartile range, or the difference between Q_3 and Q_1. This is the range of scores which includes approximately the middle 50 per cent of cases. For the score distributions of class A and class B in Figure 22, the values of Q_3 and Q_1 for each class have been indicated. The interquartile ranges have been calculated by the formula

$$Q_3 - Q_1 = \text{interquartile range}$$

It will be noted from Figure 22 that, although the range seems to indicate a marked difference in dispersion in the case of these two groups of scores, the interquartile ranges of 4.8 and 4.6 indicate that over the central area of the distributions the spread of scores is quite similar.

The *semi-interquartile range* (Q) is frequently used to describe the variability of scores around the median. Q is one-half the interquartile range. In the case of a set of scores which are distributed symmetrically around the median, the range of the middle 50 per cent of scores lies between the median plus Q and the median minus Q.

EXAMINING RELATIONSHIPS

For some purposes the teacher may wish to study the relationships between two or more sets of scores. For example, measures of ability and achievement are frequently compared.

To study the relationship between two sets of scores or characteristics which may be evaluated along a scale, the teacher may use a scattergram such as that illustrated in Figure 25. A scattergram such as that illustrated may help the teacher to locate pupils who (1) do not appear to be achieving at the level which might be expected of them, (2) are achieving at a level higher than might be expected, and (3) are working at a level of reasonable expectancy, although their achievement is low. The scattergram merely organizes the data so that relationships such as those above are more evident. Like the other techniques presented in this appendix, it is a method of organizing data to clarify certain characteristics and relationships of score distributions. These techniques do not tell the teacher how to *evaluate* these observations. For instance, from the scattergram illustrated in Figure 25, it appears that C. F. and D. R., although at the extremes of the class in both ability and achievement, are placed about where we might expect to find them. E. K., on the other hand, is commonly termed an *underachiever,* since relative ability is considerably in excess of relative achievement. N. T. might be termed an *overachiever,* since, with low-average ability as compared to the group, he is achieving a relatively high level.

Achievement

Ability	1	2	3	4
4				C.F.
3	E.K.			
2				N.T.
1	D.R.			

Rows (Ability): Q_3, Mdn, Q_1 — Columns (Achievement): Q_1, Mdn, Q_3

FIG. 25. A scattergram designed to indicate the relationship between ability and achievement for selected pupils. In this diagram, quartiles have been used to indicate relative standing within the group for each test. Results have been indicated by placing the pupil's initials in the appropriate cell as follows: (*a*) C. F. ranks in the highest quarter in ability (row 4) and also in achievement (column 4). Hence his initials appear in the cell representing the intersection of row 4 and column 4. (*b*) D. R. ranks in the lowest quarter of the group in each of the areas. Hence his initials appear in the cell representing the intersection of row 1 and column 1. (*c*) E. K. ranks in the third quarter in ability (row 3) and the first quarter in achievement (column 1). (*d*) N. T. ranks in the second quarter in ability (row 2) but in the fourth quarter in achievement (column 4).

Both E. K. and N. T. might be worth study on the part of the teacher to try to identify possible reasons for the discrepancy between achievement and ability.

SUGGESTED ADDITIONAL READINGS

Froelich, C. P., and J. G. Darley: *Studying Students,* Chicago: Science Research Associates, Inc., 1952.

Chapters 2 and 3 present an overview of methods of summarizing and analyzing test scores.

Remmers, H. H., and N. L. Gage: *Educational Measurement and Evaluation,* rev. ed., New York: Harper & Brothers, 1955.

Chapter 21 of this comprehensive text describes statistics related to the interpretation of test scores.

Ross, C. C., and J. C. Stanley: *Measurement in Today's Schools,* 3d ed., Englewood Cliffs, N.J.: Prentice-Hall, Inc., 1954.

Chapter 3 presents an account of statistical measures as an aid to the analysis of test results.

Thorndike, R. L., and E. Hagen: *Measurement and Evaluation in Psychology and Education,* New York: John Wiley & Sons, Inc., 1955.

Chapter 5 introduces statistical concepts related to the study and interpretation of test scores and distributions.

Wrightstone, J. W., J. Justman, and I. Robbins: *Evaluation in Modern Education,* New York: American Book Company, 1956.

An appendix, pp. 447–457, presents a concise discussion of fundamental statistical concepts.

Glossary

ability. Power to perform a specified act. Capacity for accomplishment as opposed to potential.

absolute measure. Units of measurement defined and interpreted in terms of a fixed standard or basis, e.g., units of linear measurement such as inches and feet.

achievement test. A test designed to measure the extent to which an individual has acquired certain knowledges or skills as a result of a program of instruction.

adequacy. Inclusion in a test of sufficient samples of behavior or performance to constitute a good indication of the total.

age norm. Average score obtained by pupils of a given age. The typical score or value representative of a certain age. (See *grade norm.*)

ambiguity. The capacity of a test item to be interpreted in more than one way; such items are subject to various meanings and thus undesirable as test items.

anecdotal record. A series of brief, written descriptions of typical behaviors of a pupil.

appraisal. An evaluation based on data from many sources or considering multiple facets of personality and achievement.

aptitude. The potential or combination of potentials indicative of one's probable capacity to learn in some particular area. (One may have an aptitude for music without possessing the ability to perform musically.)

attitude test. A set of questions or hypothetical situations designed to determine one's mental predispositions or leanings. A device for estimating how one will act or believe or what beliefs and actions one has readiness for.

average. See *mean.*

capacity. Potentiality for the development of a skill or knowledge. (One may have the capacity, or the potentiality for developing the ability, to play the piano.)

character test. A device used to evaluate that aspect of personality which relates to ethical, moral, and religious situations and concerns the right and wrong of conduct. Measures the inner, consistent trends of behavior.

check list. A device for gathering data by means of a list of predetermined items. The respondent has only to mark the items which are pertinent in his response.

coefficient of correlation (or validity, or reliability). A numerical expression of the extent of agreement between two measures or measuring instruments. It is expressed in decimal fractions ranging from a plus 1.00 (perfect positive agreement) through 0.0 (no relationship one way or another) to a minus 1.00 (perfect negative relationship—the more of one, the less of the other).

comparability. See *equivalent test.* The quality of tests that makes it possible to use them as substitutes for one another. Having the same number of items of the same degree of difficulty and covering the same scope or range of material.

completion test. A test made up of items consisting of a sentence or statement from which a word or words have been omitted. The student is expected to supply the missing word or words in giving his answer.

constant alternatives. A device used in rating techniques to provide a constant set of rating steps (e.g., excellent, good, fair, poor) which apply to a number of characteristics being rated.

criterion. A model, point, or standard for comparison which provides the basis for judging the merit of a test, behavior, or situation.

cumulative record. A card or folder, usually printed, which provides blanks or spaces for the periodic entry of significant data about the child's development. Birth date, family data, address, school record, results of ability and achievement tests, personality schedules, and anecdotal records are among the data commonly recorded.

deciles. Points in a distribution of scores which divide the distribution into ten equal parts in terms of frequency of scores.

derived score. A score which has been converted from the raw score, e.g., age scores, grade scores, standard scores, percentile scores. Derived scores give meaning to a given raw score.

descriptive rating scale. A rating scale providing a continuum that presents verbal descriptions and definitions of the degrees of possession of the trait being measured.

diagnosis. The interpreting of data in such a way as to determine what the specific causes of a pupil's difficulty are. Also, the verbalized statement of the interpretation of data.

diagnostic test. A test that indicates areas of specific difficulty, usually in skill subjects such as reading, spelling, or arithmetic. The actual diagnosis of the difficulty is made by the teacher or clinician who interprets the test results.

economy. The characteristic of a test relating to its cost, figured on the basis of how much the test does to facilitate instruction and how many pupils are serviced. Economy also relates to the saving of the teacher's time in test construction, scoring, and evaluation of results.

educational age. A derived score expressed in terms of the average score earned by pupils at a given age on batteries of subject-matter tests or on tests of specific subject areas. Often expressed as a grade equivalent.

equivalent score. An alternative way of expressing a score so as to give additional insight into its meaning. Thus a percentile score may be translated into "equivalent" grade-placement or mental-age scores.

equivalent test. A test designed to sample exactly the same area of behavior as another test, so that the scores do not vary significantly when the two tests are given under identical circumstances. An equivalent test should have the same number of items, sample the same areas, and contain items of equal degrees of difficulty.

essay examination. A series of questions which the pupil is to answer by writing compositions. The answer to the question is "discussed" in writing by the pupil.

evaluation. The process of determining the worth of a given individual's personality, performance, or merit. Usually depends upon data from many sources and of many varieties.

examination. See *test.*

fixed pattern. A relatively consistent rating tendency on the part of the rater, e.g., consistently rating most pupils high, low, or average, thus failing to disperse ratings over the length of the scale.

frequency distribution. A tabulation of scores (tally sheet) arranged in serial order (e.g., from high to low) showing the number of scores falling at each point in the distribution.

grade equivalent. See *grade norm.*

grade norm. A derived score expressed in years and months of location in the elementary and high school. A grade score of 8.4 means that the subject's score is about the same as that of the average child who has been in the eighth grade for four months. The grade norm may be based on either the median or the average of the distribution of the scores for the grade level.

grades. Numerical or alphabetical scores, assigned to a pupil in a given area of his school experience, which designate the value of his work and sometimes his conduct. The concept of grades and grading is open to criticism because it creates a tendency to ignore the nature and extent of individual differences and because it employs a single index to measure a number of complex growth phenomena.

group test. A pencil-and-paper test in which several subjects are tested simultaneously by one examiner. Most classroom tests are of the group variety.

"halo" effect. The result of influence of a rater's general impressions of the subject on his evaluation of the individual with respect to some particular quality or performance.

individual test. A test, either verbal or nonverbal, in which one examiner tests one subject at a time. The Stanford-Binet and Wechsler-Bellevue are examples of individual tests.

intelligence test. An evaluative device designed to express quantitatively the relative status of a subject with respect to mental maturity or level of mental functioning. May be designed to estimate general intellectual ability or to assess specified intellectual or mental factors or characteristics.

interest inventory. A means of measuring extent of attraction to certain specified types of activity. May be called *interest* or *preference tests* or *questionnaires* and may be designed to assess vocational, educational, social, or personal preference.

inventory. A term frequently used to replace the term *test* in measurement areas such as interest and personality.

I.Q. Abbreviation for intelligence quotient, an indication of present rate of mental growth determined by dividing mental age by chronological age and multiplying by 100. An index of relative brightness based on scores on a test of intelligence or mental ability. Typically derived as the ratio between mental and chronological ages.

isolate. A person who is not chosen by any of the members of his group on a sociometric test.

item analysis. A study of each question on a test for the purpose of comparing the number of subjects (out of the total number taking the test) who missed the item and the number who answered it correctly. Each question is then studied to detect ambiguity, validity, reliability, difficulty, and discriminating power.

marks. Letters or numerical symbols representing attempts to reduce the complexities of school achievement to a single index. See *grades.*

matching test. An examination consisting of two lists of words or phrases in columns in which the task of the subject is to pair off each item in one of the lists with a related item in the other list.

mean (arithmetic mean). The average obtained by dividing the sum of a group of scores by the number of individual scores in the group.

measurement. The application of a precise, quantitative unit of value to any property, quality, or outcome.

median. The midpoint of a set of scores arranged in order from high to low. The point that divides the distribution of scores into two equal parts so that half the scores fall above and half below the median.

nonverbal test. A test which does not require the individual to write or to read. Examples of nonverbal test items are piling blocks in a prescribed pattern, stringing beads, and assembling puzzles.

normal curve. A graphic representation of a distribution of scores or measures having a distinctively bell-shaped appearance. Scores are distributed symmetrically about the mean with a concentration of scores around the central point and decreasing frequencies toward the extremes. The normal curve has definite mathematical properties.

norms. Measures, based on test scores, which describe the performance of a specified group. Norms may describe average or typical performance or indicate the status of the individual or group with respect to the performance demonstrated by the specified group.

objective test. An examination which can be scored with a minimum of influence from the scorer's opinion or attitude as to whether it is right or wrong. Short answers and an established answer key provide a routine procedure for scoring of the test items.

objectivity. Absence or minimizing of the personal element in answering or in scoring a test or test item.

organismic. Denotes the intimate and inseparable nature of all the many facets of growth and behavior in the functioning individual. For example, organismic age refers to the average of chronological, mental, emotional, carpal, physical, physiological, etc., ages.

pencil-and-paper tests. Tests which require the subject to write his responses. Used in contrast to performance tests in which the examiner must record the responses or behaviors.

percentile. A point in a distribution of scores below which a stated percentage of the cases falls. For example, percentile 30 is a point in a distribution below which 30 per cent of the cases fall.

percentile rank. The percentile at which a given score falls. For example, a percentile rank of 20 implies that 20 per cent of the subjects attained scores equal to or below the specified score.

performance test. See *nonverbal test.* A test in which the subject is requested to do some motor act in a prescribed manner. A test dependent on a work sample.

personality test. A test or inventory designed to reveal those personal characteristics of the individual which are considered to be related to his personality. These instruments also may be designated as *adjustment, personality,* or *personal inventories.*

potentiality. An undeveloped aptitude or capacity. Sometimes thought to be an inherited characteristic but probably *also* dependent upon environmental factors for its nourishment.

practice effect. The influence of practice or previous experience with a test upon current test results.

prognostic. Partaking of the nature of prediction. A prognostic test is intended to predict behavior or performance in a particular area.

projective technique. A method of studying personality or attitudes through reactions to pictures, meaningless forms, or material to be assembled. It is assumed that the individual "projects" his personality, interests, or attitudes in developing an interpretation of the materials presented to him.

Q. The semi-interquartile range—that is, one-half the range of the middle 50 per cent of scores in a frequency distribution.

quartiles. Points in a serially arranged distribution of scores which divide the distribution into four equal parts.

questionnaire. A device designed to provide a rapid means of gathering data about an individual. Typically presents a list of statements or questions calling for a response. Frequently applied to personality and interest inventories.

rapport. In the area of tests and testing, the development of favorable attitudes on the part of the subject toward the test materials and testing procedures.

rating scale. A set of criterion answers or models by means of which values can be assigned to the samples being judged, i.e., a handwriting scale. See also *graphic rating scale* and *descriptive rating scale.*

raw scores. The result obtained from scoring the responses to test items. Usually the number of correct answers, but may involve required weighting of responses or application of a formula to correct for guessing. (See *scoring formula.*)

readiness test. A test designed to help determine whether a child has the degree of maturation, physical and mental, and the fund of background experience which will enable him profitably to begin the study of the area to which the readiness test applies.

recall item. A test question which requires the student to remember the word or answer which is most appropriate. Examples of the recall question are completion and essay questions.

recognition item. A test item that requires the subject to identify an answer. Examples are multiple-choice, true-false, and matching questions.

relative measures. Measures based on comparisons or relationships rather than on fixed or constant units. Test norms, for example, are relative measures in that their derivation and meaning are based on relationships to a series of scores rather than on any absolute or fixed value.

reliability. The extent to which a test is consistent in measuring what it purports to measure. Usually indicated by a coefficient of reliability or by an indication of the error of measurement.

sampling. See *wide sampling.*

scale. A calibrated instrument for measurement. Subdivisions of a trait or behavior are "laid off" at intervals along a continuous line. As one progresses along the scale the items vary in nature, degree, or difficulty.

scaled test. A test in which the items become progressively more difficult.

schedule (personality). An inventory or list of personality characteristics.

scoring formula. A method of systematically deriving a score from test data. Formulas may refer to weighting of items or corrections for guessing.

sociogram. A graphic representation of the social preferences of a specific group. A mapping of personal preferences.

sociometric test. An instrument designed to provide a basis for evaluating the interpersonal relationships prevailing among the members of a group.

sociometry. The study of the attractions and rejections among various members of a group.

special aptitude. An indication of an individual's ability to acquire a specified skill or knowledge. (See *aptitude.*)

standard. A mark or goal to be achieved. Should be distinguished from a norm, which is the average or typical score rather than the desirable score.

standard deviation. A measure of variability or dispersion of scores around the mean of the distribution.

standardized test. A test which represents a sample of performances taken under controlled conditions (of administration and scoring) and providing a basis for interpretation in the form of norms or comparable information. A test for which norms have been established.

standard score. Refers to a score based on the variability of a distribution of scores around the mean of the distribution. The basic unit of such scales is the standard deviation.

stencil. As used in this book, not simply a mat for reproducing a test but a piece of stiff paper in which holes are punched to reveal correct responses on an answer sheet.

subjectivity. As used in the area of evaluation or measurement, this term typically refers to the fact that the judgment of the person scoring responses to test items may be a deciding factor in evaluation of the responses.

test. An instrument designed to measure any quality, ability, skill, or knowledge. Usually a sampling, comprised of test items, of the area it is designed to measure.

test manual. A pamphlet or booklet that accompanies most standardized tests. Explains the purpose of the test, sometimes relates its historical development, cites statistical data obtained during standardization of the test, presents and interprets norms, cites limitations, and gives careful directions for administrating and scoring.

trait. One limited aspect of personality or character, e.g., honesty, sincerity, intelligence, determination, initiative, etc.

true–false test. A series of statements which the testee is to indicate are either correct or incorrect. Sometimes an alternative is provided so that the item can be marked "doubtful" or "questionable."

validity. The characteristic of a test of really sampling what it is designed to sample. A valid test of reading really indicates skill in reading rather than knowledge of a given area or skill in vocabulary.

verbal test. A test which requires the use of verbal or language skills. Many group intelligence tests consist largely of verbal items.

Name Index

Subject Index